TACKLING MEN'S VIOLENCE IN FAMILIES

Nordic issues and dilemmas

Edited by Maria Eriksson, Marianne Hester,
Suvi Keskinen and Keith Pringle

P̃P

First published in Great Britain in June 2005 by

The Policy Press
University of Bristol
Fourth Floor
Beacon House
Queen's Road
Bristol BS8 1QU
UK

Tel +44 (0)117 331 4054
Fax +44 (0)117 331 4093
e-mail tpp-info@bristol.ac.uk
www.policypress.org.uk

British Library Cataloguing in Publication Data
A catalogue record for this book is available from the British Library.

Library of Congress Cataloging-in-Publication Data
A catalog record for this book has been requested.

ISBN 1 86134 602 6 paperback

A hardcover version of this book is also available

Maria Eriksson is Researcher at the Department of Gender Studies at
Göteborg University, Sweden. **Marianne Hester** is Professor at the School
for Policy Studies, University of Bristol, UK. **Suvi Keskinen** is Researcher
at the Institute of Women's Studies at Åbo Akademi University, Finland.
Keith Pringle is Professor at the Department for Social Studies and
Organization at Aalborg University, Denmark.

Cover design by Qube Design, Bristol.
Front cover: Photograph kindly supplied by Stephen W. Ellis.
Printed and bound in Great Britain by MPG Books, Bodmin.

Contents

List of tables and figures   iv

Acknowledgements   v

Notes on contributors   vi

one   Introduction: Nordic issues and dilemmas   1
           Maria Eriksson and Keith Pringle

two   Children, abuse and parental contact in Denmark   13
           Marianne Hester

three   Commitments and contradictions: linking violence,   31
           parenthood and professionalism
           Suvi Keskinen

four   "Talking feels like you wouldn't love Dad anymore":   49
           children's emotions, close relations and domestic violence
           Hannele Forsberg

five   Bypassing the relationship between fatherhood and   67
           violence in Finnish policy and research
           Teija Hautanen

six   Marching on the spot? Dealing with violence against   83
           women in Norway
           Wenche Jonassen

seven   Children's peace? The possibility of protecting   101
           children by means of criminal law and family law
           Gudrun Nordborg

eight   A visible or invisible child? Professionals' approaches 119
           to children whose father is violent towards their mother
           Maria Eriksson

nine   "Take my father away from home": children growing up   137
           in the proximity of violence
           Katarina Weinehall

ten   Neglected issues in Swedish child protection policy   155
           and practice: age, ethnicity and gender
           Keith Pringle

eleven   Tackling men's violence in families: lessons for the UK 173
           Marianne Hester

References   183

Index   207

List of tables and figures

Tables

7.1 Important but ignored differences between criminal cases 117
and cases of custody, contact or residence

9.1 The perpetrators, the assaults, and the alcohol/drug use/ 139
abuse children were exposed to at home

Figures

2.1 Process for negotiating parental authority and contact 17
in Denmark

8.1 A mother-centred family model 131

8.2 A symmetrical family model 133

9.1 The increasing emotions and accumulating bad life 152
conditions the lonely child gets no help to cope with

Acknowledgements

The contributors want to thank the Nordic Council of Ministers' Gender and Violence – a Nordic research programme 2000-2004 – which provided a grant to the Nordic Network on Violences, Agency Practices and Social Change and thereby made this book possible. The contributors also want to thank the coordinator of the network, Suvi Ronkainen, for her support.

Notes on contributors

Maria Eriksson, PhD, is a researcher at the Department of Gender Studies at Göteborg University, Sweden, and programme coordinator of the Nordic Council of Ministers' Gender and Violence – a Nordic research programme 2000-2004. Her current research concerns violent fathers' everyday life after separation or divorce; and abused children as social actors in legal processes regarding contact, custody or residence. She is also one of the lead researchers in a Coordination Action on Human Rights Violations (CAHRV), funded by the EU 6th framework programme.

Hannele Forsberg, PhD, is Assistant Professor of Social Work at the University of Tampere, Finland. She has written extensively about families, children and emotions in social work practices. She is currently working on an exploration of the position of children in supervised meetings with their non-residential parent(s). She is a member of the board of the Childhood and Family Research Unit at the University of Tampere and the nationwide Graduate School of Family Studies in Finland coordinated by the University of Jyväskylä.

Teija Hautanen, MSocSc, is a PhD student and works in the Department of Women's Studies, University of Tampere, Finland. She is writing her doctoral thesis in the fields of social policy and women's studies about the ways in which the institutions of the Finnish welfare state perceive the fact that, while being fathers, some men at the same time are violent within their family. The study focuses on divorce and separation, and the data consist of court records of civil action cases including the assessments given by municipal social welfare boards.

Marianne Hester is Professor of Gender, Violence and International Policy at the School for Policy Studies, University of Bristol, and part of the Violence Against Women Study Group. She has carried out research into many aspects of violence against women since 1980. Her recent work includes studies on domestic violence and child contact in Denmark, domestic violence and abuse of children in China, attrition of domestic violence cases entering the criminal justice system, and evaluations and overviews on domestic violence and on street prostitution for the Home Office Crime Reduction Programme.

Wenche Jonassen is a sociologist who works as a researcher at the Norwegian Centre for Studies on Violence and Traumatic Stress in Oslo, Norway. She was an activist in the shelter movement and has completed several studies on the organisation and running of Norwegian shelters since 1986. She has written a report about battered women's experiences with support agencies (with Frøydis Eidheim) and has also evaluated a training programme for professionals working with domestic violence. She is currently undertaking a study on residents of battered women's shelters in Norway in 2003.

Suvi Keskinen, PhD, has recently concluded her doctoral thesis on the discursive practices of professional work with men's violence in families. She has also conducted research on the life stories of abused women. She is currently working as a researcher at the Institute of Women's Studies at Åbo Akademi University, Finland, in the EU-funded research project 'Changing Knowledge and Disciplinary Boundaries Through Integrative Research Methods in the Social Sciences and Humanities'.

Gudrun Nordborg, LLM, works as information manager at the Swedish Crime Victim Compensation and Support Authority. Previously, she was a Senior Lecturer at the Department of Law, Umeå University. She has published a number of articles and edited scientific journals and books on women's law, for example *13 kvinnoperspektiv på rätten* [*13 women's perspectives on law*] (Iustus förlag, 1995); on feminist knowledge, for example *Makt & kön. Tretton bidrag till feministisk kunskap* [*Power and gender. Thirteen contributions to feminist knowledge*] (Symposion, 1997); and on victimology, for example *Våldets offer. Vårt ansvar* [*Victims of violence. Our responsibility*] (Brottsoffermyndigheten, 2003).

Keith Pringle is Professor of Social Work at Aalborg University, Denmark, and holds visiting professorships at both Mälardalen University College, Sweden, and Warwick University. His main research fields are comparative welfare analysis and power relations – especially regarding gender, ethnicity and age. He has authored or co-authored three books and edited two more on these topics. He is currently co-editing two books arising from a recently completed European-funded transnational project on men which he coordinated, as well as the Routledge *International encyclopaedia on men and masculinities*.

Katarina Weinehall, PhD, is a Senior Lecturer at the Department of Law at Umeå University, Sweden. Her previous research has mainly concerned young people's experiences of violence, both in their families and in other contexts, and she is the author of the first major piece of work in Sweden on children growing up in the proximity of violence. Currently, she is working on a research project on the position of crime victims within the legal system, which is funded by, among others, the Swedish Crime Victim Compensation and Support Authority.

ONE

Introduction: Nordic issues and dilemmas

Maria Eriksson and Keith Pringle

The Nordic countries[1] are characterised by, and internationally famous for, strongly pronounced ideologies of gender equality and child-centredness anchored in legislation and other sources of public norms[2]. They are welfare states where women especially have a relatively strong position in the public sphere. The consensus-oriented Nordic research on gender equality and gender politics has led to substantial improvements within many sectors of these societies. This positive development is, however, not as evident in the area of gender and violence, for example regarding violence and rape against women and girls in intimate relationships. It is clear that a context with strong ideologies of gender equality and child-centredness does not wipe out men's violence against women and children. This fact makes Nordic research especially, and internationally, interesting (Gender and Violence, 2000).

The most recent national surveys on men's violence against women in the Nordic countries indicate that the social problem of men's violence is no less serious in these countries than in other parts of the Western world (Heiskanen and Piispa, 1998; Lundgren et al, 2001). According to the Finnish study, 22% of all married and cohabiting women have at some point been victims of physical or sexual violence or threats of violence by their present partner (9% in the course of the past year) (Heiskanen and Piispa, 1998). In the Swedish study, the comparable figure is 11% (Lundgren et al, 2001). Furthermore, according to the latter study, 35% of separated or divorced women have been exposed to physical or sexual violence or threats of violence by a previous partner (in Finland the comparable figure is 50%).

Today, there is increasing public recognition in all of the Nordic countries of men's violence against women as a social problem. The long-standing political work of voluntary organisations supporting women and children, such as women's helplines, refuges and shelters, has without doubt been central to this development. However, as will be shown in this book, the Nordic countries are different. For example, the development in Finland has followed a different trajectory compared to Norway and Sweden. From the beginning, the explicit aim of the Finnish shelters was to work with the whole family, not only women and children. Child protection and a family-centred orientation became the cornerstones of their work. In this context, international conventions seem to have been of special importance for the growing awareness of the problem (see Chapter Three).

This increasing political and professional awareness should also be seen as at least partly linked to a growing body of research on men's violence against women. In an international context, Nordic research on this issue has previously been rather limited. A recently completed European research project on the social problem and societal problematisation of men and masculinities shows that far less research on men's violence has been carried out in the participating Nordic countries (Finland and Norway) than is the case, for example, in the UK. Furthermore, the study shows that even though there is a substantial body of Nordic research on men, the specific issue of men's violence has not been a central research topic (see Hearn et al, 2002). However, there are exceptions to this general picture. For example, two Norwegian research programmes in the 1980s, funded by the Norwegian Research Council, were very important in establishing feminist perspectives as key perspectives in this field of research in the Nordic countries (Gender and Violence, 2000). Since then, two other major research programmes have aimed at elaborating these critical perspectives further: the *Gender, power, and violence* programme funded by the Academy of Finland (2001-03), and *Gender and Violence – a Nordic research programme 2000-2004* (www.nordforsk.org), funded by the Nordic Council of Ministers (see Eriksson et al, 2002).

This book has resulted from the latter programme and from cooperation among a group of researchers concerned with the ways in which men's violence against women and children are tackled by Nordic welfare agencies. The aim of the book is to make the state of knowledge and some of the ongoing Nordic debates in research available to an English-speaking audience. Furthermore, the contributors want to move the general state of knowledge forward in relation to a number of specific issues. First, most of the contributions discuss either the links between men's violence to women and the welfare of children; and/or the post-separation/divorce safety of women and children; and/or parenthood and parenting in the post-separation context. So far, these issues have not been sufficiently explored in research on men's violence (either inside or outside the Nordic countries), and yet they are all key issues in interventions targeting men's violence to known women and children. Second, the authors wish to contribute to a discussion about the conceptual frameworks for researching men's violence and welfare practices, especially as regards intersecting, or mutually constituting, relations of power. Such an analysis has important implications well beyond the confines of the Nordic region, not least for the welfare terrain of the UK.

Image and self-image as welfare systems

The image that Nordic countries project to the rest of the world – and in many cases to themselves – is one of societies that are among the most enlightened in terms of issues of class, gender, ethnicity, age, disability and sexuality. In many ways, such an image does reflect material reality. Nordic welfare benefits tend still to be among the most generous in the world (Kvist, 1999), even if there has been some erosion over the past two decades. Daycare provision for children and paid parental leave for both women and men remain relatively impressive in most of the Nordic countries, even if other European countries (such as Belgium and France) can outstrip them in some respects (Hantrais and Letablier, 1996). The Nordic countries did clearly lead the way in the banning of corporal punishment of children and evidence suggests that these policies have been largely successful, even if a degree of serious physical child abuse still exists[3]. Institutions for the explicit promotion of children's rights tend to exist to a greater extent in the Nordic countries than in the rest of the world. Internationally, the Swedish law on the regulation of prostitution – which criminalises the act of buying but not the act of selling sex – is seen by many feminist and pro-feminist commentators as being the most progressive in the world (Månsson, 2001), even if there is less enthusiasm for its clear focus on the users of prostitution in some other Nordic countries, especially Denmark. Moreover, the Swedish social concept of, and law concerning, 'women's peace' (*kvinnofrid*; see Chapter Seven in this volume) is for many feminist and pro-feminist commentators in other countries a source of envy and inspiration.

So, there are some good reasons why the Nordic countries have earned their positive international reputation – and indeed their positive self-image. However, in recent years, a critique has begun to develop questioning whether this enlightened reputation can be justified in such a general way as has been the case in the past. In other words, some commentators have begun to recognise that on some social issues, at some times, certain Nordic countries have been far less enlightened than has been assumed previously. In particular, there is growing recognition that previous (Esping-Andersen, 1990, 1996) – and indeed many current (Arts and Gelissen, 2002) – mainstream welfare analyses have focused too narrowly on the extent to which the Nordic welfare systems have performed well on the dimension of class and poverty – and have neglected to assess welfare enlightenment (or, rather, lack of it) along other dimensions of, for example, gender, age, kinship, ethnicity, sexuality and disability. It is beginning to become clearer that such a broad welfare analysis along a whole range of dimensions of social disadvantage produces a com-parative picture of the Nordic countries that is far less flattering than a narrow focus on class and poverty alleviation would suggest (Pringle, 1998, 2002; Pease and Pringle, 2001).

One of the earliest of these critiques focused on how far the Nordic welfare systems were 'woman-friendly' in terms of work in the home and in the labour market, which in turn led to a clearer recognition of the heterogeneity of the Nordic systems in this respect (Lewis, 1993; Sainsbury, 1999). While recognising that many of the Nordic systems are relatively supportive to women and the labour market compared with most other European countries, these (largely feminist-inspired) critiques have demonstrated that the picture is less clear-cut and more qualified than previous studies had assumed. A related critique has developed about the extent to which, especially in Sweden, the massive social policy interventions designed to increase men's active parenting have had an impact (Bekkengen, 2002; Bergman and Hobson, 2002; Björnberg, 2002). Once again, there is recognition that more progress has been made in this respect than in many other countries and also that the extent of this progress has often been overestimated in many previous analyses – and that the limitations on progress are linked to ongoing relations of patriarchal power in Sweden (see Chapters Seven, Eight and Ten).

In more recent years, ethnicity has become another focus for academic critique with a recognition that discrimination on the grounds of ethnicity and 'race' in fields as broad as employment, housing, criminal justice and health is widespread. Once again, this critique has become especially strong in Sweden (Kamali, 1997; Molina, 1997; Andersson, 1998; Pred, 2000; Pringle, 2002). Indeed, much evidence for this discrimination is now being provided by government institutions such as the Swedish Migration Board. However, one must be careful not to confuse the extent of research on discrimination with the patterns of discrimination in the Nordic region. It would be all too easy to regard Sweden as having a particularly poor record on ethnic discrimination, compared with its Nordic neighbours, because of the relative abundance of research evidence there. However, by simply looking at government policies, there are good reasons to believe that ethnic discrimination and day-to-day racism is no less evident in many of Sweden's neighbours. The fact that more research has been carried out on these issues both by academic and government institutions in Sweden than elsewhere in the Nordic region may well be a sign that the problem is closer to being openly addressed in Sweden than in, say, Denmark or Finland.

Thus, there is a developing and welcome tradition of critique beginning to enter into debates about Nordic welfare. However, as we have already seen, this recent tradition has developed to a greater extent in some Nordic countries than in others. Moreover, apart from this geographical and cultural limitation, there are other major limits to the critique as it has developed so far. There are at least three such limitations. First, the critique has been largely restricted to aspects of gender and, to an even lesser extent, ethnicity. Critical analyses of the Nordic welfare systems along dimensions of disadvantage associated with age, sexuality, kinship and disability are rare. Second, in so far as gender has been an important critical comparative focus, it has been almost exclusively focused on those aspects of gendered power relationships associated with labour in the home and the marketplace. There has been very little critical comparative analysis on other aspects of gender, for instance on how far Nordic welfare systems address issues of men's violence to women and children in a transnational perspective[4] – and how far the patterns of comparative welfare performance that emerge from such an analysis would match the patterns that emerge from a labour-centred gender analysis. The third and final limitation on previous critical analyses of the Nordic welfare systems is that they have largely ignored more sophisticated models for understanding how various forms of disadvantage interconnect with one another in societal relations and in the day-to-day existence of individual human beings: models that adopt the concepts of 'intersecting' (Crenshaw, 1991; Brah, 2001) and 'mutually constituting' relations of power (cf West and Fenstermaker, 1995; Acker, 2000; Eriksson, 2003).

Bearing this in mind, the current volume, with contributions from authors who are either Nordic by origin or who are based in Nordic countries, seeks to broaden and extend the process of critique in several important ways. First, it places a primary focus on the dimensions of gendered violence and age – as well as giving consideration to other dimensions such as kinship, ethnicity and, indeed, class. Second, several contributions seek to make such analysis using the concepts of 'intersecting' or 'mutually constituting' relations of power.

The link between men's violence to women and violence to children

Since the 1980s, research from a range of countries and evidence from women's refuges, both within and outside the Nordic countries, have shown that men's violence against women is an issue of direct concern for children (Eriksson and Hester, 2001). It is well documented that almost all children in these families are subjected to the emotional cruelty of witnessing or being aware of violence against their mother. Furthermore, many of the children are themselves subjected to physical violence and/or sexual abuse by the father/man (see, for example, Roy, 1988; Christensen, 1990; Jaffe et al, 1990; Weinehall, 1997; Hester et al, 2000; Peled, 2000). These findings suggest, among other things, that the behaviour a father/man develops through violence to his partner also has implications for his relationships with children, as well as for his practices as parent (for an elaboration on this point, see Eriksson, 2002, 2003). As indicated above, it is also known from research that the violence does not necessarily stop at separation or divorce: the man/father can both continue to be violent and in some cases (initially) increase his violence post-separation (see Christensen and Koch Nielsen, 1992; Hester and Radford, 1996; Mirrlees-Black, 1999; Fleury et al, 2000; Walby and Allen, 2004). When a man has a history of being violent to his partner, it cannot be taken for granted that the violence and threats to the mother end with separation; nor that the father–child relationship develops in a way that is in the best interests of the child post-separation or divorce.

At least since the first half of the 1990s, the special problems that women who are mothers face when leaving violent men, as well as the problems in protecting children from violent fathers post-separation, have been clearly documented through research in England and Denmark (Hester and Radford, 1996). Later Nordic studies point in the same direction (Mellberg, 2002; Eriksson, 2003; Skjørten, 2004). For example, according to the Swedish national survey, one in four abused women with children has experienced threats in the context of the children's contact with the violent father/ex-partner (Lundgren et al, 2001, p 33ff).

Nordic family policies and the violence of fathers

The findings quoted above represent important knowledge, not least in the Nordic context where shared parenting, joint custody and contact between children and non-residential parents is increasingly emphasised in social policy. In that sense, there are clear parallels between the Nordic countries and, for example, England[5] (see Eriksson and Hester, 2001; Chapter Eleven in this volume). The development has not been identical in the different countries, but the overall picture is very similar: Nordic family policies today presuppose shared parenting and a high degree of parental cooperation post-separation/divorce (see Kurki-Suonio, 1995; Eriksson and Hester, 2001; Chapters Two, Five, Seven and Eight in this volume).

The policy is based primarily upon the notion of the child's right to close contact with both parents. Face-to-face contact between children and non-residential parents is generally presumed to be in the best interests of the child. However, the rationale for the emphasis placed upon shared parenting is not just 'the best interests of the child'. The policies are also intended to facilitate increased gender equality. They follow the aim of many other Nordic welfare reforms, which is to enable both parents to take part in the everyday care of children (for an overview, see Højgaard, 1997). Furthermore, the policies are also supposed to contribute to the development of the 'new father' (Hearn, 2001; Bekkengen, 2002; Bergman and Hobson, 2002; Klinth, 2002; Chapters Two and Five in this volume).

The question is what these policies mean for the post-separation/divorce safety and wellbeing of mothers and children. So far, the issue of men's violence has to only a very limited extent been discussed in relation to (continued) parental cooperation and the wellbeing of children post-divorce/separation (see Eriksson and Hester, 2001; Chapters Two, Five, Seven and Eight in this volume). In spite of the growing recognition of the gendered features of violence in heterosexual relationships, Nordic social and family policies seem to a large extent to construct fathers as essentially non-violent (cf Eriksson and Hester, 2001). This lack of critical public discourse regarding fathers' violence has specific consequences for welfare professionals that are explored in more detail in some of the chapters in this volume (Chapters Two, Three, Eight and Nine).

The world outside

Analysis of the Nordic welfare systems, especially critical analysis, is not simply of 'academic' interest to those who live beyond the region. There are a number of reasons for this, but the most important has already been hinted at above. For the largely positive reputation of the Nordic welfare systems[6] has made them – and still is making them – a role model for other countries and supranational bodies on a broad range of policies. A case in point, as regards supranational bodies, is a recent UNICEF-commissioned report that uses a wide range of quantitative measures and once again holds up the Nordic countries, especially Sweden, as a model of good practice for child welfare (Micklewright and Stewart, 2000).

In relation to the impact of the image of Nordic policies on other welfare systems, one needs look no further than the United Kingdom. At the most general level, Esping-Andersen (2003) has recently characterised the 'third way' embodied in Blairite/Brownite social policy as nothing more than a rehash of rather old Nordic policies – and, one might add, Nordic policies minus the intensity of funding support that characterised them in their original Nordic form. One might consider the advocacy of both Conservative and Labour governments in the UK since the early 1990s on changing the balance of child welfare services away from child protection to family support (Parton, 1997). Several commentators have seen this shift as inspired by French and/or Nordic social policies (Pringle, 1998; Ruxton, 1997; Pringle and Harder, 1999). What partly characterises the shift – as well as its 'continental' and Nordic inspirations – is precisely the kind of denial of gendered power relations within families and within broader society this volume seeks to uncover and to challenge across the Nordic countries.

Thus, one underlying objective of this book is to say to readers in countries outside the Nordic region that they should exercise extreme caution when they meet blanket assertions about the overall welfare primacy of the Nordic countries. Moreover, they should be similarly careful when considering the value of translating Nordic policies to other contexts for two reasons. Partly, this is because those contexts may be very different. Partly, it is because some Nordic policies, even in their own contexts, are highly oppressive – for instance, to women and/or to children and/or to people from within minority ethnic groups. The focus of established ideologies in the Nordic countries on consensus and gender neutrality creates difficulty in making visible age- and gender-based power asymmetries within families. Of course, there is still much to admire — and to learn — from various Nordic societies, especially if one comes from Britain where many people (though perhaps not enough) dearly wish for the full banning of corporal punishment of children. However — and this is the central point of this book — there are also many aspects of Nordic policies and practices that we would suggest other countries should strenuously avoid, in particular some of the policies and practices in relation to men's violence towards women and children. What characterises these policies and practices, which are surveyed in this book, is the absence of a power analysis that recognises how social locations constituted by, for example, age, gender, ethnicity, sexuality, kinship, class and disability are central to understanding social problems and how to address them.

The structure of the book

To enable a more comprehensive understanding of both continuities and discontinuities between the Nordic countries, the chapters that are concerned with the same country are grouped together. Especially as regards Finland and Sweden — discussed in three and four separate chapters, respectively — the contributions provide different points of entry into the analysis of how men's violence is dealt with in specific local policy and welfare contexts.

In Chapter Two, Marianne Hester examines the changing policy discourses and practices in Denmark during the past decade. This contribution gives an in-depth survey of recent developments in policy regarding custody, contact and fathers' violence. The chapter indicates that the features of professionals' practices identified as especially positive for mothers and children facing violence from ex-partners/fathers in a previous study on Denmark and England have now largely disappeared in practice. It is argued that this change is — paradoxically as it might seem — partly linked to current attempts to support gender equality and 'equalise' the position of fathers and mothers within families.

Hester's chapter introduces several of the themes that are explored further in other parts of the book. One such theme — how gendered notions of parenthood contribute to the lack of focus on violent men as parents — is discussed in the following chapter (Three). Here, Suvi Keskinen analyses how violence and parenthood are discussed and worked with in Finnish family counselling agencies. This chapter also points out a specific trait of refuges for abused women in Finland, more specifically, the lack of a feminist refuge/shelter movement in this local context. As indicated above, child protection and a family-centred orientation have been the cornerstones of Finnish shelter work and the organisation of shelters has been very similar to that of other social services. This situation seems to have had some impact on the development of professional responses to men's violence. Keskinen shows, among other things, how the historically close connection between the ideologies of social and healthcare bureaucracies and voluntary interventions to combat men's violence against women shape the ways in which both trauma theory and feminist perspectives are currently negotiated and incorporated into professional responses to men's violence in families.

The 'child- and family-centredness' of the Finnish shelters is possibly one of the explanations for another interesting specificity of the Finnish shelters, seen in a comparative Nordic perspective: the work with children that has been developing in recent years, first through the Child's Time project and later as a permanent part of the shelter activities. Drawing on a study of such treatment encounters with children in Finnish shelters, Hannele Forsberg (Chapter Four) attempts to capture the way children exposed to violence in their own home construct emotions related to familial relationships, especially emotions connected to the violent father.

The section on Finland concludes with Chapter Five, where Teija Hautanen explores the question as to why fatherhood and violence are so rarely treated simultaneously in the same research or policy context, using Finland as the case in point. This chapter also exemplifies how cultural patterns found more broadly (such as the gendering of parenthood) take on locally specific forms. In this case, the gendering of parental responsibilities is shaped by, among other things, the culturally well-established notion of the strong, proud, hard-working and independent Finnish mother.

Moving into the next section of the book, Wenche Jonassen describes developments in the field of violence against women in Norway during the past 20 years. Unlike the situation in Finland, a feminist movement has for a long time been quite vocal in the Norwegian public debate on violence against women. However, Jonassen's chapter shows that, despite a 'mainstreaming' of feminist perspectives into social policy, change in practice has been slow. There are some striking similarities between Finland and Norway, for example, as regards the central role played by voluntary organisations. The chapter highlights, among other things, the continued key role of the voluntary women's refuges/shelters in the welfare system for women subjected to violence in Norway.

The following chapters move into the context of Sweden. First, in Chapter Seven, Gudrun Nordborg discusses the legal position of women and children within Swedish criminal law and family law. This chapter shows, for instance, that on the one hand the new gender-specific law on violence in close relationships – the law on 'women's peace' – that is unique to Sweden opens up possibilities to protect children. On the other hand, Nordborg demonstrates that the relationship between the law and everyday life is all but straightforward.

This point is explored further in the next chapter. Here, Maria Eriksson gives a detailed account of professionals' practices, discussing the position of abused children in investigations concerning custody, contact and residence, using the practices of Swedish social workers as the example. This analysis clearly demonstrates unintended and problematic consequences of current Swedish policy as well as problems in professionals' responses in cases where fathers are violent to the mothers/co-parents and/or their children. For example, it highlights the double standard for the parenthood of fathers that renders the notion of 'bad parent but good dad' culturally intelligible and provides violent fathers with a vast space for action.

The relationship between law, policy and professional practice is also a theme in Chapter Nine, albeit discussed with children's perspectives as the point of departure. Here, Katarina Weinehall focuses on young people's narratives of growing up in the proximity of violence, including their views on strategies to survive and attempts to seek help and support. These narratives give a disturbing picture of the 'child-friendly' welfare system in Sweden. As experienced from the position of a victimised child, the professional actors involved collaborate to make the problem of the father's violence invisible, to keep the crimes hidden, and to allow the child to be forgotten.

The last chapter on Sweden adds further to the critical review of the child welfare system. Here, Keith Pringle explores how oppressive power relations associated with age, ethnicity and gender interact and shape responses to men's violence in families. This chapter brings together many of the themes addressed in the previous chapters, places them within a broader welfare perspective, and links the contributions in this book to current international discussions on welfare regimes and power relations.

The book concludes with a chapter linking the themes from the previous chapters to current issues in the UK. Here, Marianne Hester reviews recent policy developments and discusses the lessons that can be learnt in the UK context from the Nordic experiences and dilemmas.

Notes

[1] The 'Nordic countries' connotes the five countries Denmark, Finland, Iceland, Norway and Sweden, as well as the self-ruling areas – the Faeroe Islands (Denmark), Greenland (Denmark) and Åland (Finland).

[2] For recent examples of portrayals of the Nordic countries – and especially Sweden – as gender equal and/or child-friendly, see Micklewright and Stewart (2000) and James and James (2004).

[3] The evidence for both these observations is particularly clear in Sweden, thanks to the work of the parliamentary Committee against Child Abuse there (2001).

[4] There are, of course, exceptions to this, including Hester and Radford (1996); Pringle (1998, 2002); Eriksson and Hester (2001); Hearn (2001) Hearn et al (2002).

[5] Since the legislation is different in the different parts of the UK, the authors in this book sometimes refer to a specific country or part of the UK, sometimes to the UK as a whole.

[6] However, we should remember that not everyone has regarded the allegedly enlightened policies of the Nordic welfare systems as positive. Most (in)famously, Margaret Thatcher explicitly condemned Sweden as the kind of 'nanny state' she was actively seeking to avoid in the UK.

TWO

Children, abuse and parental contact in Denmark[1]

Marianne Hester

Since the 1980s, there has been a growing emphasis on the involvement of both biological parents in the care of their children post-separation and divorce in Europe, North America, Australia and New Zealand (see also Chapters Three, Five, Seven and Eight in this volume). This reflects article 9 of the UN Convention on the Rights of the Child, concerning children's right to know their two parents. The emphasis on involvement of both biological parents has involved shifts in family law to include a variety of joint parenting arrangements, for instance in the form of joint custody[2] (in Denmark – 1985 *Myndighedslov* [Custody law] and 1995 *Lov om Forældremyndighed og Samvær* [law on Custody and Contact]), or shared parental responsibility (in England and Wales, the 1989 Children Act). It has also meant increasing emphasis on contact by non-residential parents with their children post-separation, as exemplified by the existence of a contact presumption.

The contact presumption has, however, been challenged in recent years as research has increasingly indicated that contact or access does not always or necessarily equate with the welfare or best interests of children. For instance, where there is a history of domestic violence, children may also have suffered harm, and both women and children may face ongoing violence and abuse from the abuser post-separation. In such circumstances, children may face continuing detriment and possible long-term harm if there is contact or access with the violent parent. These issues are beginning to be taken into account in judicial discourses and practice in the UK, New Zealand and elsewhere (Kaganas, 2000; Eriksson and Hester, 2001; Jaffe et al, 2003).

In Denmark, recognition of links between domestic violence and possible harm of children were implicit in professional practice and discourses related to custody and contact during the earlier part of the 1990s, and led to a safety-oriented 'pragmatic' approach with regard to child contact arrangements (Hester and Radford, 1992, 1996). The latter part of the 1990s, however, has seen a shift away from such a safety-oriented approach towards a much stronger emphasis on contact. Arguments favouring 'equality' between parents and recourse to outdated and misleading evidence concerning 'father deprivation' has underpinned an ideological or rights-based change in legislation and policy[3]. Abusive child contact cases are increasingly coming to the attention of children's organisations in Denmark – such as *Børns Vilkår* [Children's Circumstances] and *Red Barnet* [Save the Children Denmark] – and has led these organisations to actively question the intransigence of decisions made against children's welfare (Boserup and Rabøl Hansen, 2003).

This chapter examines the changing policy discourse and practice in Denmark related to custody and contact during the past decade. It is argued that the shift away from pragmatism towards a more ideological or rights-based approach has had a negative impact on children's welfare and quality of contact as well as mothers' safety. In Denmark, children's contact with non-residential parents is being emphasised to the detriment of children's safety and welfare.

The chapter draws on research co-directed by the author between 1990 and 1996 in England and Denmark examining arrangements for children's contact with parents after the latter's separation or divorce, in circumstances of domestic violence (Hester and Radford, 1992, 1996), and a smaller follow-up study. The chapter examines in particular some of the shifts and changes apparent since the mid-1990s with regard to custody and contact in Denmark. To understand these shifts, it is important to consider changes in legislation as well as the apparent impacts on professional practice in recent years. It should be noted that in Denmark the law is considered a vehicle of social reform and social engineering to an extent that is not usual in the UK, where legal change usually reflects rather than pre-empts change in social practices.

The context and research

The earlier study, co-directed by the author and carried out between 1990 and 1996[4], involved an in-depth examination in England and Denmark of the processes and outcomes concerning arrangements for children's contact with parents after the latter's separation or divorce, specifically in circumstances of domestic violence (Hester and Radford, 1992, 1996). The study looked at the effect of contact negotiations and outcomes on the safety and wellbeing of women and children, via:

• multiple interviews with 53 mothers in England and 26 mothers in Denmark over the period of the research;

- interviews with 77 relevant professionals and advisers in England and 22 similar professionals in Denmark concerning their practice and perceptions;
- observation of contact or access negotiations and arrangements; and
- analysis of documentation related to the contact/access cases.

In the Danish part of the research, the 26 mothers were interviewed in depth, four were interviewed a number of times over a period of up to 10 months, others kept in contact by telephone during the research period, and most were re-contacted by telephone towards the end of the fieldwork period to enable updating of their circumstances. Between them, the 26 women had a total of 65 children. Of these children, 51 were the subject of custody and/or contact negotiations and arrangements examined by the study. The 22 professionals included county authority registrars [*statsamt jurister*], county advice counsellors, solicitors, social workers and psychologists from *Mødrehjælpen* [Mother's Help – a parent support organisation] and other relevant voluntary sector organisations and staff from refuges.

The earlier study was carried out in the context of the Danish 1985 legislation on custody and contact, the Law on Custody (1985 *Myndighedslov*)[5]. Towards the end of the fieldwork period, in 1995, a new law concerning custody and contact was enacted in Denmark, coming into force as the study ended in 1996 (1995 *Lov om Forældremyndighed og Samvær* [law on Parental Custody and Contact]).

The follow-up study compared post-1996 legal approaches, professional practice and outcomes for mothers and children with regard to custody and contact arrangements in circumstances of domestic violence with those pre-1996. The study involved analysis of legal, policy and related documentation, interviews with similar professionals and advisers to those interviewed in the earlier study, and, as before, interviews with mothers involved in ongoing negotiations concerning contact. This chapter is based primarily on analysis of the policy, legal and other documentation, supplemented by interviews with eight professionals and advisers (solicitors, psychologists and social workers, including staff from two of the main Danish children's organisations, the parent support organisation *Mødrehjælpen* and a refuge) and four mothers, as well as informal discussions with a range of professionals in children's organisations and legal services.

The negotiation of custody and contact in Denmark

In Denmark, childcare law is set out in three main pieces of legislation: the Social Services Law [1998 *Servicelov*], the Parental Custody and Contact Law [1995 *Lov om Forældremyndighed og Samvær*], the Child Support Law [1960 *Børne Forsørgelses Lov*][6] and the new Children's Law [2001 *Børnelov*]. Decisions about childcare post-separation or divorce are covered by the Parental Custody and Contact Law. The Social Services Law is concerned with issues of child protection, as well as social benefits for adults and children generally. The Child Support Law outlines financial obligations for parents. The new Children's Law deals with paternity as well as paternity/maternity in situations of artificial insemination.

In Denmark, the formal processes regarding divorce, separation and the related arrangements for children are primarily administrative, taking place outside the courts. The county authorities [*statsamter*] are charged with the responsibility of making final decisions about custody and contact. Only where parties do not agree about outcomes for the children, or in circumstances of appeal against earlier decisions, might these be considered by the courts. Even so, the county authority is still responsible for decisions concerning contact. The process for negotiating parental authority and contact is outlined briefly in Figure 2.1 (see also Hester and Radford, 1996).

The Danish findings

In the earlier Danish study (Hester and Radford, 1992, 1996), we found an increasing presumption among professionals and in legal discourses that contact between children and non-resident parents should be paramount. Nonetheless, professionals interviewed in the study – that is, refuge workers and most of the voluntary sector parent support staff [*Mødrehjælpens medarbedere*], as well as some of the county authority advice counsellors [*rådgivere*] and registrars [*statsamt jurister*] – placed a greater emphasis on children's safety than on the paramountcy of contact. The Danish professionals were prepared to restrict contact with violent fathers if they felt this would be detrimental to the welfare of the child. We concluded that this Danish 'pragmatic' approach to contact was more positive with regard to women and children's safety and wellbeing than the more 'ideological' or rights-based contact-oriented approach being applied at that time in England and Wales.

Of key importance to the pragmatism of the Danish approach was

Figure 2.1: Process for negotiating parental authority and contact in Denmark

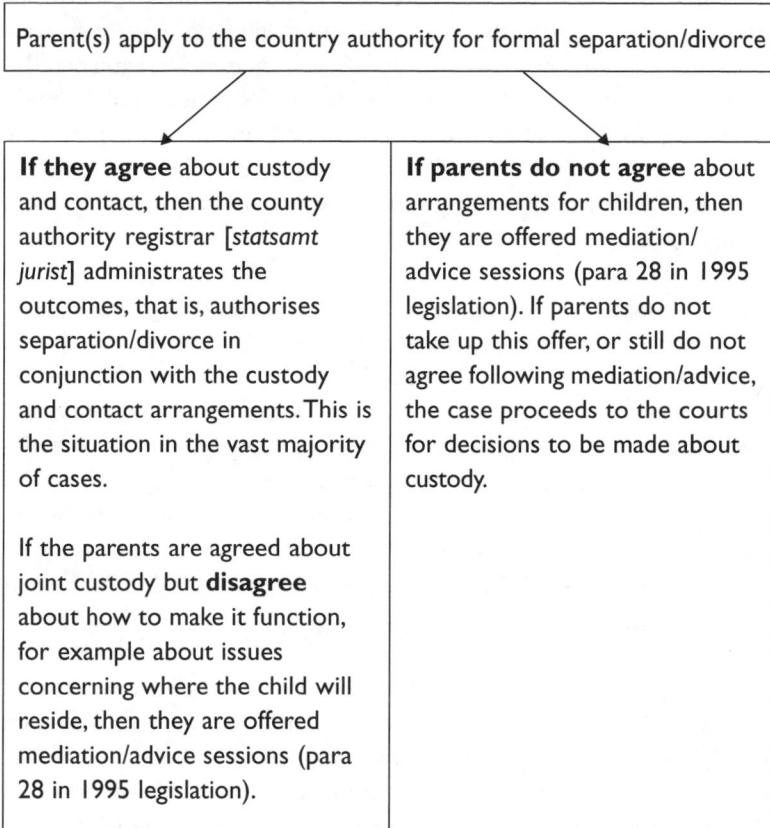

Parent(s) apply to the country authority for formal separation/divorce

| If they agree about custody and contact, then the county authority registrar [*statsamt jurist*] administrates the outcomes, that is, authorises separation/divorce in conjunction with the custody and contact arrangements. This is the situation in the vast majority of cases.

If the parents are agreed about joint custody but **disagree** about how to make it function, for example about issues concerning where the child will reside, then they are offered mediation/advice sessions (para 28 in 1995 legislation). | If parents do not agree about arrangements for children, then they are offered mediation/ advice sessions (para 28 in 1995 legislation). If parents do not take up this offer, or still do not agree following mediation/advice, the case proceeds to the courts for decisions to be made about custody. |

the guiding principle of *agreement between parents* underpinning the Danish legislation (*enighedsprincip*; see Danielsen, 1997). This notion of agreement between parents, unique to Denmark and not even replicated in the other Nordic countries, entailed an emphasis on parents' actual ability to work together effectively to ensure children's welfare. This focus on ensuring that the parents *can* work effectively together to ensure children's welfare was the preferred outcome regarding custody and contact, and such agreement was seen as crucial for joint custody to work. The principle of agreement also formed the basis for the non-intervention in the private sphere of families preferred by the Danish authorities (Danielsen, 1997, pp 137-43). Moreover, it provided recognition that actual agreement between parents may not always be possible or even desirable. Where parents were unable to agree about outcomes for their children, Danish lawmakers and related professionals surmised that there needed to be well-defined arrangements concerning the children. In the practice of the professionals we interviewed in the earlier study, this had the following implications: where mothers disagreed with their ex-partners about contact due to concerns about safety, these concerns were likely to be taken into account by the Danish professionals concerned. A child-centred approach resulted, where lack of agreement between parents would be seen as indicative of problems for any future arrangements for the children and hence of the need to define carefully such arrangements.

The retention of sole custody in the 1985 legislation was an important consequence of the Danish principle of agreement and also contributed to the pragmatism of the Danish approach. Where parents were unable to agree about outcomes for the children, or where contact arrangements did not work because of violence, the residential parent would retain or be able to apply for sole custody. We found that in practice this created a much better 'safety net' for the women with sole custody, as in these instances there was more active intervention by the authorities, which were reluctant to intervene if parents held joint custody. Indeed, interviews with mothers indicated a lack of interference by professionals when parents had agreed to joint custody, even when the professional concerned was uneasy about the outcome. Sole custody also allowed the authorities to define the involvement of the other parent, and in particular to define contact arrangements. It was especially striking that, by the end of the fieldwork in 1995, only one married woman in our Danish sample still retained joint custody with the father. Previously, 22 of the women (nine unmarried and 13 married) had had joint custody with the fathers. Eighteen women had thus obtained sole custody of their children. A further four women were seeking sole custody but final outcomes were not known. By the end of the fieldwork period, 11 of the fathers had contact. However, 10 of the mothers had children who had no contact with the fathers. The authorities had formally ordered all of these 10 instances of no contact due to concerns about the children's safety and welfare (Hester and Radford, 1996).

Our findings in the earlier study – both in England and in Denmark – indicated overwhelmingly that children's welfare might not be best served by contact with a father who is violent to the mother and/or in other ways abusive to the child. The women interviewed in Denmark had extreme and persistent experiences of violence from their male partners. Fifteen of the women mentioned that the violence had gone on for up to nine years. In what has been shown to be a typical pattern, the violence against the women was particularly extreme and likely to flare up when women leave and in relation to child contact and handover (McMahon and Pence, 1995; Jaffe et al, 2003). With regard to the impact of domestic violence on the children, most of the women (20 out of the 26) talked about the detrimental effects on their children of living with violent fathers or mothers' violent male partners (see for example McGee, 2000; Mullender et al, 2002). Nineteen women reported that their children had experienced a range and combination of physically, sexually and psychologically abusive behaviour from the men, including children being hit when they tried to protect their mother, being hit while held in the arms of the woman who was also being hit, or being attacked directly as part of the abuse against the mother. The children were described as having experienced many psychologically abusive acts, such as threats from the father that he would kill them, violence to pets, shutting a four-year-old out of the house at night and abusive 'tricks', such as a father pretending to be dead so that the child got the mother (who had left) to return. Three of the 26 fathers were formally investigated for sexual abuse of their children. In all, 12 of the women described direct effects on the children's mental and physical health and wellbeing from experiencing the abuse of their mothers by their fathers. Children of six mothers were given counselling as a result.

Cases where the contact with violent and abusive parents 'worked' in the long run were very limited. In only two cases in Denmark was contact eventually set up so that there was no further abuse and harassment of the mother or the children. Even with direct support from the authorities and despite provision of resources such as housing and education for women leaving violent men, in Denmark contact 'worked' no better in situations of domestic violence than in England, where such support and resources tended to be much less available. In the final analysis, the overriding problem was the men's continuing abusive behaviour to their ex-partners and/or their children. In Denmark, however, the 'pragmatic' approach meant that children's welfare was more likely to be taken into account by the professionals concerned, with sole custody for the non-abusive parent and no resulting contact with the abusive parent.

The 1995 legislation

In the earlier study, we had identified a developing tension among professionals in Denmark between an (increasingly) ideological or rights-based approach and (the former) pragmatic approach to child contact: on the one hand, that contact with both parents should be paramount, and, on the other hand, that agreement is fundamental to good parenting. We found an increasing emphasis on the former, and a wide variation in professionals' practice linked to these differing approaches. The women we interviewed experienced the more pragmatic 'agreement' approach, rather than the 'contact paramount' approach, as more likely to take their own and children's safety needs into account.

Since then, the shift towards a much stronger contact presumption has been codified in the new Danish legislation [1995 *Lov om Forældremyndighed og Samvær* (law on Parental Custody and Contact)]. Flendt explains a main feature of this shift as follows:

> While the concern in 1986 was to strengthen collaboration between parents and the use of divorce counselling/ mediation to facilitate this, 10 years later the theme was instead to provide equal rights between parents in relation to their children as well as to establish the principle about having two biological parents. (Flendt, 1999, p 10; translation by author)

She suggests that the reason behind the shift was entirely 'political' or ideological, rather than being based on the increasing evidence from research concerning child welfare – which suggests that the main issue concerning the welfare of children is that of *quality* childcare, not merely or necessarily biological parenting (Amato, 1993; Hester and Pearson, 1997; Richards, 1997).

In the lead-up to the new Danish legislation, the Ministry of Justice established a consultative committee with members drawn from the judiciary, county authorities and legal profession. The committee reported in 1994, and provided an initial draft law for consideration by the government (Justitsministeriets Forældremyndighedsudvalg, 1994). The basis for the proposals were threefold:

- to ensure greater contact between children and both parents post-separation;
- to remove any mechanisms that may hinder parents from taking full parental responsibility; and
- to ensure a more equal division in allocation of custody between parents (Justitsministeriets Forældremyndighedsudvalg, 1994, p 30).

The final version of the legislation adopted in 1995 differed only in matters of degree from that proposed by the consultative committee.

Joint custody and increased rights for fathers

As with the 1985 law, so the 1995 law automatically grants married parents joint custody [*fælles forældremyndighed*] of their children. In the 1985 legislation, mothers not married to the child's father automatically had sole custody, and thus overall control and responsibility for the child. This emphasis on maternal preference for unmarried parents was reconsidered with regard to the 1995 legislation and in the light of equalising men's and women's involvement with children. The 1995 legislation emphasises more explicitly that unmarried parents may make an agreement to have joint custody, and this is the preferred outcome. Failing such an agreement, unmarried mothers retain sole custody (1995 *Lov om Forældremyndighed og Samvær* [law on Parental Custody and Contact]), para 5 – referred to as 1995 LFS from now on).

The focus is now on increasing the rights of unmarried fathers, and maternal preference is therefore no longer automatic as in the 1985 legislation. Now, where unmarried parents have lived together 'for a longer period' (1995 LFS, para 12), and if the father wants custody at the point of separation, the courts will decide with respect to 'what is best for the child' which of the parents should be awarded sole custody. This is outlined in para 12, and entitled 'Transfer to the father by judicial ruling'. This is a more obviously father-oriented (and gendered) approach than that in the 1985 law, where the equivalent section was merely entitled 'Transfer of custody by judicial ruling' (1985 *Myndighedslov* [Custody law], para 14).

Moreover, when transfer of custody from the mother to the father is considered, particular stress is placed on taking into account whether the custodial parent has 'without justifiable reason' [*uden rimelig grund*] hindered contact with the other parent – in other words, whether what the government's guidance to the law presents as 'contact sabotage' [*samværssabotage*] has taken place (Civilretsdirektoratet, 1999a). In particular, the concern is to stop what is seen as 'sabotaging' mothers impeding contact by fathers (1995 LFS, para 12, clause 2). It should be noted that in this respect the legislation goes further than originally envisaged by the consultative committee. The possibility of contact sabotage as a possible hindrance to fathers' increased involvement in childcare was a concern discussed by the consultative committee. However, it did not include a specific clause regarding this in the draft legislation (Justitsministeriets Forældremyndighedsudvalg, 1994).

The codifying of 'contact sabotage' is a worrying addition to the 1995 legislation, not least because it appears to have resulted primarily from pressure by fathers' groups rather than any research-based evidence (Flendt, 1999; interviews with Danish professionals). No research has been carried out in Denmark concerning so-called contact sabotage. There is a general lack of evidence (beyond the anecdotal) that contact sabotage is a problem in the manner suggested. The research evidence from elsewhere indicates that the reason women may attempt to stop or hinder contact is a real fear of abuse against the children and/or themselves (Hester and Radford, 1996; Radford et al, 1999; Brown et al, 2001). It should also be noted that the use of evidence in the Danish courts in relation to custody cases is often limited. Rasmussen (2000) points out that Denmark is somewhat unique within the international context in the extent to which parents' own testimonies are relied on by the courts. Parents' statements are the sole evidence in virtually all cases considered by the town courts (*byretterne*) and in almost half the cases heard in the national courts (*Landsretterne*), although reports from child professionals are also increasingly being requested (Rasmussen, 2000, pp 195-6). Moreover, the government's guidance for county authorities indicates that ensuring contact should be the overriding consideration in contact disputes (Civilretsdirektoratet, 1999a, p 9). Information about either party cannot be given without the consent of the party concerned (Civilretsdirektoratet, 1999a, p 8), which again makes it difficult to present evidence concerning actual harm to a child[7].

According to the children's organisations in Denmark, the difficulties associated with consideration by the county authorities of evidence of harm to children, combined with the overriding presumption that contact should take place, has led to abusive fathers being awarded custody. There have been a number of instances where mothers, in the attempt to protect their children from sexual abuse from fathers, have denied these fathers contact. Consequently, the fathers have sought and been awarded sole custody. The inclusion of 'sabotage' in the law drew on a similar notion already used in legal practice in Sweden (see Chapter Seven in this volume). In Sweden, abusive fathers have also ended up with sole custody as a result (Nordenfors, 1996; Eriksson and Hester, 2001).

Transfer of custody has also been made easier since the 1995 legislation. It can be carried out if *specific [særlige]* circumstances indicate in favour, where previously decisions about transfer had to take into account both the best interests of the child and *substantially* altered circumstances. Rasmussen (2000), in his overview of Danish family law, explains that the reason for this change has been to create the greatest possible 'peace and quiet' regarding the child's upbringing, and at the same time "the rules have been slackened so as not to be experienced as difficult or unfair by fathers" (Rasmussen, 2000, pp 60-1; translation by author). Again, the law stipulates that the possibility of contact sabotage by the custodial parent should be taken into account when deciding about transfer of custody (1995 LFS, para 13).

Principle of agreement and contact presumption

During the period leading up to the 1995 legislation, the government consultative committee, legal academics and politicians debated whether the uniquely Danish principle of agreement should be retained (Justitsministeriets Forældremyndighedsudvalg, 1994). It was decided to retain the notion of agreement, at least for the time being. Alongside this, sole custody was also retained as an outcome where parents are unable to agree and where there may be problems with contact. However, the emphasis on contact for all non-residential parents, as outlined in paragraph 16 of the 1995 legislation, indicates that Denmark is in practice moving away from the earlier notion of *actual* agreement towards a greater focus on *ensuring* agreement, and thus increasingly towards 'coerced' agreements – as has been the case in the UK and other countries (see also section on mediation/advice sessions below; Dingwall, 1988; Hester and Radford, 1996; Eriksson and Hester, 2001).

Parents who have joint custody of a child are deemed to share in decision making and general care and control issues, including where the child resides. Prior to 1995, and in accordance with the principle of agreement, contact arrangements for parents with joint custody were not defined by the authorities. Since 1995, the greater emphasis on contact with both parents and the possibility that even with joint custody parents may not be able to agree, there has been a shift to allow contact arrangements with *any* non-residential parent to be defined by the county authorities (whether the parents have joint custody or not). In the 1995 legislation, this is expressed as the *right of the non-residential parent to contact* – not the right of the child to have contact with the parent (1995 LFS, para 16)[8]. In practice, fathers are more likely to be non-residential parents than are mothers, and this widening of formal arrangements again reflects the wish to 'equalise' fathers' involvement with their children. An unmarried father can now be given contact with his biological child even if he has never lived with the child's mother or the child, or had any close contact with the child. Moreover, contact may be established even if the father has not seen the child for five years (Flendt, 1999).

Given the strong presumption of contact, coupled with notions of 'contact sabotage', it is perhaps not surprising that abusive child contact cases are increasingly coming to the attention of children's organisations in Denmark, such as *Børns Vilkår* [Children's Circumstances] and *Red Barnet* [Save the Children Denmark]. Cases have in particular come to the fore since the late 1990s via parents, other relatives and children themselves (Boserup and Rabøl Hansen, 2003). The severity and magnitude of the cases has led children's organisations to believe that they have to act, and to question the intransigence of decisions made against children's welfare. In interviews with staff from the main children's organisations and a parenting support organisation, it was made clear that the organisations have found over and over again not only that the presumption of contact overrides the welfare of children, but also that it is virtually impossible to stop contact once it has been imposed. While individual professionals interviewed disagreed as to whether the legislation as such has codified this change, it was felt that the government's intention concerning the law has negated children's welfare in favour of contact. Directives from the Ministry of Justice since 1996 were felt to have imposed an ever-stronger presumption of contact and increasingly stringent tests for constraining or stopping contact. This is borne out by the Ministry's own annual reports. The May 2000 report from the Civilretsdirektoratet [Ministry of Justice], for instance, states that:

> ... there has been a marked increase in the extent of contact since the new legislation came into force on 1 January 1996. This development ... is in step with the intentions of the law.... (Civilretsdirektoratet, 2000, foreword, translation by author)

There has been a parallel reduction in the denial of contact since the implementation of the 1995 legislation (Civilretsdirektoratet, 1999b, Table 4.2; and see Civilretsdirektoratet, 2003)[9].

The head of the Danish children's organisation *Børns Vilkår* expressed his concerns as follows:

> We have recently experienced a large increase in referrals concerning highly problematic contact situations. We have used much time and many resources to advise parents, and have found that it has been impossible to challenge decisions

which, where we are concerned, have been made without due consideration to children's welfare and instead have been based on the non-residential parent's right to contact. (Aasted Halse, 2000, p 1; translation by author)

Aasted Halse identifies the emphasis on 'equality between parents' behind the new legislation as especially problematic. He argues that the new approach, while attempting to provide children with contact to both parents, has in reality created an imbalance where children's welfare takes second place to the non-residential parent's right to contact:

> However, the good intentions concerning children's right to contact with both parents, and thereby the equalising of parents, must never predominate in favour of ensuring children's welfare. (Aasted Halse, 2000, p 1; translation by author)

A conference about contact and harm to children was held in Copenhagen in April 2000 where numerous examples of difficult and abusive contact cases were outlined (Børns Vilkår, 2000; Boserup and Rabøl Hansen, 2003). Delegates, including county authority registrars [*statsamt jurister*], lawyers and others working with child contact cases talked about the retrogressive nature of the 1995 Danish legislation. They commented that, since the changes in the Danish legislation, the positive ability of Danish professionals working in the field of divorce and separation to emphasise children's welfare had become much more difficult. It was noted that the 1995 legislation is also, in its emphasis on parents' and especially fathers' rights, in contradiction to the new Danish Social Service Law [1998 *Servicelov*], which places greater emphasis on children's rights to protection from harm, while the custody/contact legislation offers scant protection to children who may be neglected or abused by a parent while on a contact visit (Højlund, 2000, pp 29-34).

Contact presumption – the (lack of an) evidence base

In the Danish family law discourse, there is clear emphasis on the notion of gender equality. Similar arguments have also been evident in other countries, linked to greater involvement of fathers in childcare, and to the argument that greater involvement of fathers in custody or residence and contact will 'equalise' men's and women's position in the family (see Chapters Three, Five and Eight in this volume). Feminists have also demanded that men should become more involved with childcare (Hester and Harne, 1999). It has to be questioned, however, whether a policy of ensuring contact between children and non-residential parents is necessarily in the children's best interests. It may be argued that violent and abusive fathers in particular do not in practice want to be equal *carers* with mothers in the sense of *caring for* their children. Instead, claims about fatherhood and involvement in childcare may be seen in the context of men's wider concerns about threats to their position vis-à-vis women and ownership of children, and their attempts to forge new identities in this context (Hester and Harne, 1999). Demands for equal parenting are in this sense concerned to a greater extent with control and power over women's and children's lives post-divorce and separation than with the best interests of children. As Lewis and O'Brien suggest:

> Recent accounts of fatherhood should be replaced by an understanding of paternal involvement in the context of the continuing domination of women by men in the public sphere, and in certain respects within the family itself. (Lewis and O'Brien, 1987, p 2)

In order to ensure children's safety and wellbeing, any custody and contact policy must include specific safeguards with regard to violence and abuse of either the mother and/or child. In New Zealand, for instance, the law requires the court to consider domestic violence allegations in relation to custody and contact applications and to make a detailed risk assessment (Busch, 1998; Jaffe et al, 2003). Guidelines in England and Wales and legislation in Northern Ireland also indicate the need for courts to consider domestic violence as a potential risk of harm for children in contact cases (Children Act Sub-Committee, 2000; Hester et al, 2000; Kaganas, 2000).

In Denmark, there is no requirement to consider domestic violence in relation to outcomes for children. While arrangements for the mother's safety are recognised, for instance recognition that her address may need to be kept secret (Rasmussen, 2000, p 75), violence to mothers is not seen as indicating a potential risk of harm to the children concerned. This apparent lack of knowledge about the links between domestic violence and abuse of children is especially surprising, given that the earliest research in the European context to indicate the abusive effects of domestic violence on children was carried out by a Danish researcher using Danish samples (Christensen, 1988, 1990).

Also related to the 'equal parenting' discourse is the idea of 'father deprivation' – that the presence of fathers is crucial to the wellbeing of children whose parents separate or divorce. In both the European and North American contexts, the 'father deprivation' discourse has been central to an increasing emphasis on contact with absent parents (in particular fathers), which has appeared alongside the development of joint custody or shared parental responsibility policies. The idea is largely derived from studies carried out from the late 1970s to the mid-1980s that looked at children and divorce (in particular Wallerstein and Kelly, 1980; see also Hester and Harne, 1999). This research suggested that, for children, divorce of their parents equates to problems in later life, and especially for boys. Boys from divorcing families were deemed to have more difficulties than girls where there was an absence or loss of contact with the father (McKee and O'Brien, 1982; Richards and Dyson, 1982). Such 'father deprivation' was thought to lead to delinquency. Since then, more research has been carried out that has been more complex, and has included longitudinal work. This has shown that the real problem is neither divorce nor father deprivation, not even for boys (Amato and Keith, 1991; Mott, 1993; Hooper, 1994; Marsiglio, 1995; Richards, 1997; Rodgers and Pryor, 1998). Mott and Hooper, for example, have both stressed that it is not the presence of fathers per se in families that enhances children's emotional and cognitive development, but the quality of children's contact with caring individuals.

The main conclusion that can be drawn from research since the mid-1980s to the present day, where children's welfare post-separation is concerned, is that the quality of parenting, and the lack of conflict between parents, are crucial. In relation to children's contact with their non-residential parent, absence of violence or conflict and quality childcare are particularly important to positive outcomes for children in the longer term (Rodgers and Pryor, 1998). In other words, mere father presence does not automatically lead to positive outcomes for children, and indeed the opposite is likely where fathers are violent and abusive. This research evidence appears to have been ignored or deemed largely irrelevant in relation to the Danish legislation on custody and contact (Justitsministeriets Forældremyndighedsudvalg, 1994; Civilretsdirektoratet, 1999a).

Mediation/advice sessions

The 1985 Custody Law in Denmark introduced for the first time the use of a form of mediated agreement for parents unable to agree on outcomes for children (1985 *Myndighedslov* [Custody law], para 27a). The sessions are funded by the state and offered on a voluntary basis to parents, and to a lesser degree also to the children. The mediators/ advisers are drawn mainly from child-related professions, such as child psychology, child psychiatry and child social work. We found in the earlier study that this professional base allowed the mediators/advisers to take a relatively child-centred approach with respect to contact negotiations, which included ongoing meetings and discussions with the children (Hester and Radford, 1996). In instances of domestic violence, the more discussions the professionals had with the children concerned, the more likely they were to recommend that no contact take place with the violent or abusive parent.

Prior to 1995, the use of mediation/advice sessions relied on a lack of agreement between parents and a willingness of both parents to attend (see Figure 2.1). The 1995 legislation extended the offer of mediation/advice to those parents who do agree but would still welcome discussion of outcomes. In what is considered a shift of principle, the sessions are also available if only one of the parents is willing to attend (Westh, 1995, p 2203). It should be noted that the party who does not attend might be considered in a negative light in any following court case related to custody. As Westh points out:

> ... the possibility cannot be excluded that a party's passivity or direct unwillingness to take part in the offer of a mediation/advice session will not be damaging in any consequent court case regarding custody. (Westh, 1995, p 2204; translation by author)

Both the earlier study and a national survey of mediators and court welfare staff in the UK indicated that such a potentially punitive approach is likely to adversely affect women who have experienced domestic violence (Hester and Radford, 1996; Hester et al, 1997). Women who have experienced such violence may be unwilling to attend or be involved in any direct negotiations with their abusive ex-partners due to fear of further violence or abuse during negotiations and eventual outcomes. If women are unable to talk freely about abuse because their abuser is in the same room, his power and control will extend to the mediation process and indeed be furthered by it (Roberts, 1988; Hart, 1990; Grillo, 1991; Hester and Pearson, 1993; Hester et al, 1997). Without specific consideration and screening in relation to domestic violence, it is the violent party that may end up being viewed more positively in custody and contact negotiations (Hester et al, 1994,

1997; Hester and Pearson, 1997). As recognised by mediation services in other countries, such as National Family Mediation in the UK, mediation tends not to be appropriate in cases involving domestic violence and needs to be considered carefully (Hester et al, 1997, appendix D; Humphreys et al, 2000). These are lessons still to be debated more fully in the Danish context.

In the earlier research in Denmark, we found a willingness by some county authorities to run separate mediation/advice sessions for parties where there were problems such as domestic violence. In addition, the need for attendance by both parties meant that the sessions would be less likely to take place in circumstances involving domestic violence. Since 1996, the greater emphasis on mediated outcomes and on showing willingness to attend may be placing greater pressure on women to take part in mediation sessions with or alongside their abusers. That this is the case was evident from interviews with Danish refuge staff.

Conclusion

The issue of children's custody and contact visits with parents who have separated or divorced is an issue that engenders much emotion and heated debate. It is also a very important issue. Children's custody and contact in circumstances of domestic violence is an issue where, if we get it right, we will vastly improve the circumstances and the human rights of both women and children. If we get it wrong, then we continue to allow violent and abusive parents (fathers in particular) to use the pretext of parenting to continue their detrimental and destructive behaviour in relation to women and children. The Danish features identified as especially positive for women and children facing violence from ex-partners/fathers in our earlier study have now largely disappeared in practice. The presumption that the right to contact by non-residential parents equals the best interests of the child is compromising children's safety and welfare in Denmark.

As this chapter is being written, there are positive signs that the Danish government has begun to respond to the problems engendered by the 1995 legislation on custody and contact, and a working party has been established to develop proposals. Thus far, however, the issue of men's violence in families, which underlies the problems relating to custody and contact discussed in this chapter, has not been tackled by the working party.

Notes

[1] An earlier version of this chapter was published as Hester (2002).

[2] In Denmark, it was decided to retain the notion of 'custody' or parental authority, rather than adopt the notion of parental responsibility with residence and contact, as has been the case in the UK.

[3] Bailey-Harris et al (1999), for instance, discuss the contact presumption in England and Wales as a rights-based approach.

[4] Assisted by Maja Føgh, Julie Humphries, Anne Mette Kruse, Chris Pearson, Khalida Quaiser and Kandy-Sue Woodfield. Funded by grants from the Joseph Rowntree and Nuffield Foundations, the Danish Academy of Research and the British Council.

[5] Direct translation is Law of Authority.

[6] Entitled the Children's Rights Law [Børns Retsstilling] until July 2002.

[7] In a recent case involving sexual abuse of a child (investigated and documented by child protection professionals), a mother was found guilty of libel because she had presented the information about child abuse in a dispute about contact without the (abusive) father giving his consent for this information to be divulged (interviews with children's organisation social worker and with mother concerned).

[8] It is interesting to note that the government consultative committee intended there to be less emphasis on the parent's *right* to contact, and recommended a general change in terminology from 'contact right' to 'contact' (Justitsministeriets Foraeldremyndihedsudvalg, 1994). Despite this change being implemented, the right of the non-residential parent has in reality been strengthened (cf Chapter Seven in this volume).

[9] The main basis for the decisions, in nearly half the cases (49%), was the views of the children concerned that they did not want contact to proceed. Violence, incest and other abusive behaviour constituted the basis in 8% of cases where access was stopped or not established by the authorities (Civilretsdirektoratet, 2000, Table 2.4). These proportions have continued to be reflected in cases where contact has been denied, with children's views becoming slightly more prominent (Civilretsdirektoratet, 2003).

THREE

Commitments and contradictions: linking violence, parenthood and professionalism

Suvi Keskinen

Whereas in most Western and North European countries the discussion of wife abuse was brought to the public agenda by the feminist movement, the Finnish history of dealing with this question has been different. The feminist movement has been relatively weak in Finland, and the issue discursively constructed in gender-neutral and family-centred terms. A social service-like approach has been characteristic of the Finnish shelters. During the past decade, a view of wife abuse as a gendered phenomenon has received growing attention. The discursive shift has many connections with social and healthcare bureaucracy and professional services. This background has led to a mixture of professional and feminist influences in the discussion on violence and family relations.

This chapter analyses how violence and parenthood are discussed and worked with in Finnish family counselling agencies. It traces the different discursive resources that are drawn upon when these issues are handled and examines their common points and discrepancies. The combination of professional and feminist influences is essential in the analysis of the agency practices. The chapter is based on an ethnographic study that focused on family counselling professionals' work with violence.

From family violence to violence against women

The first shelter in Finland was established in 1979 by the Federation of Mother and Child Homes (later the Federation of Mother and Child Homes and Shelters), an organisation providing housing and social services for single mothers with babies. From the beginning, the explicit aim of the shelters was to work with the whole family, not only women and children. In the late 1970s, a few efforts were made to open a discussion from a feminist point of view. The League of Finnish Feminists collected women's stories of their experiences of violence and one shelter was established with a feminist orientation. The feminist movement was, however, not strong enough to make its voice heard in the public discussion and these views were marginalised for more than a decade.

The issue of wife abuse was formulated as the discourse of 'family violence'. This is based on gender-neutral rhetoric in which all types of violence within the family context are equated (Ronkainen, 1998, pp 12-13; see also Dobash and Dobash, 1992). Violence is regarded as an interactional problem between two equally situated parties (see also Chapter Five in this volume). In the course of the 1990s, a discursive change took place and the issue started to be discussed as 'violence against women'. Pressures from international conventions that Finland had ratified paved the way for a more active government grasp of the issue. In 1998, a five-year government programme for preventing violence against women was launched. Within the programme, municipal and other local service providers have been educated in violence issues and the programme has initiated forms of collaboration and development for local services.

Professional influences and feminist commitments

The Finnish version of the 'violence against women' discourse is influenced by its close connection to the social and healthcare bureaucracy and professional services. Gender and power are considered to be relevant in understanding violence, but they are viewed as traits of a violent relationship. Power is what violent men use and women who have experienced violence are regarded as victims. However, an analysis of gender and power as part of the gender order in society as a whole, which is essential for most feminist refuge movements (Jeffner, 1994; Lupton, 1994, p 55), has not been the focus of attention in the Finnish discussion.

One implication of this is that professional theories have become interwoven with views that emphasise gender and power. In particular, trauma theory is a very influential professional resource that is drawn on (see, for example, Oranen, 2001a; Rautava and Perttu, 2002). The gender-neutral and professional character of trauma theory has made its adoption into existing practices easy; but at the same time it means that its relationship to feminist ideas of gender and power needs to be continuously negotiated within agency practices.

The 'violence against women' approach has caused changes in the practices of social and healthcare agencies and the police. Increasingly, the preferable way to tackle wife abuse in shelters and therapeutic settings is by working with women and men separately, whereas earlier the aim was to work with the couple and look for ways to keep them together (Nyqvist, 2001, p 235).

The feminist critique that has been directed towards tendencies of professionalisation within anti-violence work has focused on the problems of individualisation and medicalisation (for example, Foley, 1994; Lupton, 1994). This critique has pointed out that professional theories, such as trauma theory, turn the attention to the victims' responses to violence, their physical reactions and the categorisation of these (for instance in different trauma types). The focus is often on the victim's personal history and earlier experiences of traumatisation. Thus, the violence question is formulated as an individual, psychosocial problem that requires individual intervention (Profitt, 2000, p 29). Feminists have also criticised the importance given to neutrality and distance within the professional orientation, as well as the emphasis on expert knowledge (Foley, 1994, p 40). These starting points differ in many ways from the principles upon which feminist shelter movements base their work[1]. These are identified by Maud Eduards (2002, p 98) as believing in what the women coming to the shelter tell, solidarity between women working in and seeking help from the shelter and anonymity.

This chapter now looks at how the tensions highlighted above are encountered and negotiated at the local level of Finnish family counselling agencies. How are professionalism and feminist views of violence combined and negotiated in local practices? In particular, I will look at situations when parenthood is discussed, because this context shows the tensions in a very visible form. Parenthood is one of the key areas of family counselling and dealing with it involves a vast array of professional discourses, definitions and practical suggestions. What happens when these institutionalised and firmly grounded discourses and practices are confronted with the newer discourses and practices of 'violence against women'?

Research on local practices

This chapter is based on an ethnographic study that was conducted in three family counselling agencies during 2000-01. I attended meetings between clients and family professionals, as well as some meetings between professionals and other authorities (for example, child protection). The length of fieldwork varied from three to 18 months, but its intensity differed depending on the agency. The material consists of recorded encounters between clients and professionals (33 encounters), field notes from encounters (an additional 32 encounters), interviews with the professionals (11 interviews) and some textual material related to the agencies' work (project reports, newspaper articles, and so on). The extracts used in this chapter are taken from the recorded and transcribed material. In the analysis I have combined an ethnographic approach with discourse analysis (see, for example, Wilkinson and Kitzinger, 1995).

In two of the agencies, the professionals emphasised the gendered aspects of wife abuse and talked about violence as use of power. They also said that the preferable way to work was to meet with the woman and the man separately. Thus they were rather committed to working along the lines of the 'violence against women' discourse. On the whole, their work with violence was done with women and children. The third agency differed from the two other agencies. There, the understanding of violence was to a higher degree related to the discourse of 'family violence'. The professionals worked mainly with couples and focused on the relationship between the woman and the man. In this agency, they also encountered many young couples without children. Because of this, the issue of violence and parenthood did not receive much space during the meetings; nor was the tension between professionalism and feminist ideas visible there. In what follows, I will discuss the violence work carried out in the two first-mentioned agencies.

Supporting women and making men responsible in a professional context

Following to a large extent the recommended work principles presented in discussions and conferences on 'violence against women' (for example, Keeler, 2001), the professionals in the researched agencies discussed three kinds of general aims for their violence work. First, they thought it was important to believe and support women who had experienced violence. Second, they emphasised the need to place responsibility on men who had used violence. The third aim was to take into account the children in these families. All of these aims are parallel with those raised by feminist researchers and activists who hope to influence policy and practice (for example, Itzin, 2000b). The means of achieving those aims may, however, be somewhat different.

When the professionals in the researched agencies emphasised the need to listen to abused women and believe them, they used arguments that were based both on feminist ideas of violence as a gendered issue and on professional theories, especially trauma theory. These discursive resources were combined and used together. The professionals talked of the importance of meeting abused women on their own and hearing their story before any arrangements were made to meet the men who had used violence. The main part of the work was dedicated to listening and giving support to women and children. The professionals explained to me that the initiative to support the woman client in building her story of the abuse and her previous life came from trauma theory. Constructing the story was understood to be a dialogical act in which the therapist was engaged through questions, acknowledgement and validation. The professionals said that when women came to therapy they might not have a name for their experiences of violence, and even if they did name them as violence, most women needed a supportive listener to be able to construct the story of how things had happened and what their life had been about.

Trauma theory has brought a major breakthrough in the understanding of women's experiences of violence in Finland. Within the 'family violence' discourse, violently treated women were regarded as equal parties engaged in a 'row' or a 'fight'. There was not much space for recognising power asymmetry, fear or other victimising effects of violence (Ronkainen, 2001b). In the agencies I researched, trauma theory was used to motivate the need to deal with the effects of violence on abused women and their children. Discussing emotions such as fear, powerlessness and shame were regarded as an elementary part of the work. Moreover, the many physical effects of experiencing violence, including sleeplessness, nightmares and shaking hands, were also taken into consideration and women were offered help in dealing with these issues. Going through experiences of violence and the emotions connected to them in therapy was seen as a way of opening up possibilities for a better future.

When working with abused women, their safety and the different means of achieving this were also regarded by the researched agencies as basic issues. Safety plans were drafted during the meetings at the agencies and the alternatives about how to act in dangerous situations were often discussed. Making these kinds of preparations was seen to improve the women's capacity to find solutions in risky situations and help them to confront feelings of powerlessness. In these discussions, the professionals mainly drew on ideas that had been formulated within feminist discourse. There was also much resemblance to feminist views in the way the professionals pointed out that help for individual women and children is not always sufficient where violence is concerned. The professionals stressed the importance of peer support and the commonalities in women's (and children's) experiences of violence. The number of groups for supporting abused women and their children has been growing in Finland and even in the researched agencies the professionals were very positive towards organising groups of this type.

The way the professionals in the researched agencies emphasised making violent men responsible points to another major change that has occurred in the Finnish discussion and practices. While men who have used violence were previously seen as victims in need of help, the focus has now turned on the need to clearly place the responsibility on them (for example, Perttu and Söderholm, 1998; Rautava and Perttu, 2001). In the agencies I researched, it is interesting to note that this commitment is mainly manifested when professionals talk to abused women about violence and the events that led to it. In these encounters, the professionals often point out to women that they are not responsible for the violent events and that they need not blame themselves. The professionals also state that violence is a crime and encourage abused women to contact the police in threatening situations. Undoubtedly, this is helpful for women who have experienced violence. However, men who use violence are seldom confronted directly at the agencies and thus responsibility is not an issue discussed with them (with few exceptions). The professionals comment on their own readiness to do this, but men who have used violence are not often clients of the agencies, and when they are, they usually only come in a few times. It is also common practice that men are referred to specialised services for violent men. This is seen to be a solution that both provides proper services for men and – in a situation of scarce resources – enables the family counselling agencies to concentrate their work on women and children.

When men who have used violence come to the family counselling agencies, this causes some tensions. These tensions are connected to the agencies' role as part of a service sector in which professionals are expected to be neutral and impartial towards all clients. Although the professionals are committed to believing abused women and supporting them, in these situations they need to balance the different stories they hear from men and women. It is then difficult for the professionals to ally themselves with the women. Instead, they often become mediators who try to suggest compromises, for example, in child contact arrangements, and aim to give as much significance to claims from both parties. In addition, attempts to discuss responsibility for previous violent acts with the perpetrator may cause tensions. For example, in one of the cases I followed during the research a (male) social worker who cooperated with the (female) family counsellors criticised them for being too offensive towards a man who had used violence. The social worker regarded the family counsellors' efforts to place responsibility on the abusive man as aggressive and causing the man to take a defensive position. It seems that the ideal of professional neutrality and not taking a stand appears to be rather demanding, despite the family counsellors' commitment to make men responsible for their violent acts.

Taking children into account and supporting them is the third central element in the violence work carried out by the researched agencies. In family counselling agencies, issues relating to parenthood and the development of children form basic elements of the work, but children's experiences of violence did not receive any special attention until the 1990s (see also Chapter Four in this volume). Recent changes in practices in Finland have included new means to work with children and adopting a view about the traumatising effects of violence on children. In the researched agencies, children are encouraged to talk about the violence they have witnessed or experienced. The professionals discuss with the children emotions related to violence and possibilities for agency support in threatening situations. The implications of violence for parenthood are, however, a more controversial issue. When parenthood and violence are discussed in the agencies, the contradictions between feminist views of violence and professional discourses become very visible. Professional discourses on parenthood are usually regarded as authoritative and 'truthful' knowledge, which means that they are seldom questioned or reflected upon within professional work.

Motherhood weakened by traumatisation

The centrality of trauma theory when dealing with domestic violence could even be seen in the way motherhood was discussed in the researched agencies. The most common way to talk about this was to stress the impact of traumatisation on the quality of motherhood. The mother was regarded as so traumatised by violence that her capacity to ensure the safety and take care of the children was severely weakened. Neither was she thought to be able to recognise the needs of the children. In these discussions, the motherhood of an abused woman was seen to lack essential elements and create a risk for the child's normal development:

> ... the mother can't give security to her children, you know
> ... she can't guarantee that her children feel safe and secure.
> And she doesn't necessarily see very clearly what the
> children's needs are. She has her own trauma and she lives
> in fear and it results in her having no chance of noticing
> what her children really and actually need ... and what
> they're feeling and how they are. I mean it's pretty rare that
> a woman in that kind of situation can see and think clearly.

In the professionals' talk, these weaknesses continue to be part of
motherhood even after the violence towards the mother has ended,
for example, even if she has left the man who used violence towards
her. Traumatisation is a mental and physical state that can only be dealt
with through therapeutic means. Trying to end the threat of violence
by changing physical living conditions is not regarded as sufficient.
The only 'real' help is therapy. A traumatised mother is not seen as
being able to interact with her child in the expected way and this
pattern defines their relationship several years later. Following these
lines of reasoning, the professionals focus on the traumatisation of the
mother and the effects of this on her relationship with the child, even
in cases where violence has ended four or five years earlier. The attention
and work in the family counselling agency thus turns to the relationship
between the mother and the child who 'shows symptoms'. Other
changes in living conditions, for example, a new stepfather and younger
siblings, are ignored. When asked whether things are the same even in
situations where women are divorced, one of the professionals replied:

> I don't think things necessarily change until the woman is
> able to process her own experiences, you know – her own
> trauma. Somehow ... the divorce as such is not so crucial....
> If she doesn't do anything about dealing with her own
> trauma, I don't think she'll be able to see the children's
> situation either. I mean that ... it's of course an advantage
> to have divorced in the sense that you get rid of the abusive
> man and it sort of seems to ... or it helps the situation, but
> if she doesn't deal with it [the trauma], it isn't necessarily
> beneficial in the end.

Within these words, the motherhood of an abused woman is described
in rather static terms. Attention is focused on the victimising effects of
violence that are seen to determine the quality of the woman's
motherhood. She becomes fixed into the position of a victim and her

motherhood is reduced to weaknesses. Aspects of survival and gaining strength seem gradually to vanish from the image, as well as the positive elements of motherhood. As the feminist critique suggested, there is a tendency among professionals to focus on women's reactions to violence and turn the violence question into their individual problem. Solutions offered are framed as therapeutic services with an emphasis on the psychological. Thus, actions such as trying to end the violence by means of divorce become second-class issues when compared with therapeutic treatment.

This individualisation of the violence question does not, as one might assume, mean sensitivity to differences within experiences. On the contrary, it seems that adopting trauma theory brings with it universalising trends. All women who have experienced violence, and the motherhood of these women, are understood to be affected in the same way. It seems to be difficult to distinguish differences within motherhood when traumatisation becomes the main defining feature.

The use of trauma theory and its impact on practices can thus vary. Although it can be used to make women's experiences of violence intelligible and give means of support to women, my research points to the conclusion that the emphasis on motherhood and the responsibility culturally connected to it brings out very different notions. Within professional thought, there is a long tradition of linking responsibility for children to motherhood. Motherhood was regarded as the most important factor in child development for decades, and even though fatherhood has lately received growing attention, mothers are still placed at the centre of childcare and rearing (Vuori, 2001). Within professional discourses and practices, motherhood has been filled with detailed norms, measured and evaluated. Feminist analyses have shown that, following this logic, many professionals and authorities turn their attention to the mother's behaviour and its presumed weaknesses in cases of wife abuse or child sexual abuse (Hooper, 1997; Hester, 2000, p 97; Mellberg, 2002; Eriksson, 2003). Paradoxically, it is the mother who becomes defined as the problem, instead of the father who has used violence. The talk of traumatised mothers follows the same line of reasoning and bears much resemblance to these constructions.

Dyad of mother and child

Another common way of talking about the motherhood of an abused woman in the family counselling agencies was to emphasise the tie that binds the mother and the child together. Both mothers and children were seen to be affected by violence and therefore the agencies wanted to help them together. The wellbeing of the child was seen to be closely related to the wellbeing of the mother. In order to help the child, it was necessary to work with the mother and support her. In this kind of talk, the mother–child connection is regarded as a resource and described in positive terms, in contrast to the talk focusing on traumatisation and weaknesses. This way of speaking is illustrated by the following professional who said in the interview:

> An important part of motherhood is to secure the safety of the children, but being a good mother also means looking after one's own safety. The safety of the mother is also seen to form the basis of a safe environment for the children.

This talk on motherhood has close connections with feminist interpretations of the situation of abused women and their children. Feminist researchers and refuge workers have paid attention to the connections between men's violence towards women on the one hand and children on the other, pointing out that children are both witnesses to violence directed towards other people, as well as being abused themselves (for example, Hester and Radford, 1996, p 26). Within the feminist refuge movement, this work has been oriented towards women and children, although, in the early phase, the work with children tended to be given a lower status than the work with women (Hague et al, 2000, p 114). The feminist strands in the talk of shared interests between mothers and children sometimes make it difficult for professionals to draw upon this rhetoric. In particular, the principle of neutrality is often regarded as contradictory to the idea of workers allying themselves with mothers and children.

However, in a professional context such as the family counselling agencies, this feminist discourse is not the only discursive resource being drawn on. It is combined and negotiated with many professional discourses, especially those concerning motherhood. Within professional thought and public discussion, mothers have been defined as the primary caretakers of children and the ones who bear the main responsibility for them. Looking at mothers and children as a unity has been a common way of understanding this relationship historically (Nätkin, 1997, pp 150-60).

In the talk of the 'dyad of mother and child' used in the family counselling agencies, the starting point is clearly the interconnectedness and shared interests of the mother and the child. They are not regarded as two separate individuals whose interests differ. This became evident, for example, in one situation where social workers had decided to take some children into care because of the threat of violence posed by the father. This decision and the social workers' definition of the situation implied that the mother was incapable of providing safety and proper living conditions for the children. Yet, as I discuss more thoroughly elsewhere (Keskinen, 2002), the family counsellors using the rhetoric of 'dyad of mother and child' were able to focus attention on the interconnectedness and shared interests of the mother and children even in a situation such as this.

Despite several differences between the two discussed constructions of motherhood concerning abused women ('traumatised mothers' and 'dyad of mother and child'), there are also commonalities. In both ways of talking, there is a tendency to focus on the responsibilities of motherhood and regard mothers as the protectors of children. Unless there exist notable forms of support actions and concrete ways to ensure the children's (and mothers') safety in threatening situations, this emphasis on mothers' responsibilities can turn into unreasonable demands and mother blaming. There are some examples in my material of professionals heavily criticising abused women for not taking care of their children's safety and standing up to the threatening man. This shows one of the contradictions in the researched professional practices. The counsellors talked about the need to support abused women and note the effects of violence. Yet, their discussions on motherhood and children could result in bypassing the women's fear and the threats to their safety.

Problematic fatherhood

Dealing with the fatherhood of a man who had used violence also included many contradictory elements in the researched agencies. The problematic aspects of this kind of fatherhood were acknowledged, yet there also seemed to be a lot of hopes pinned on fatherhood. On the whole, the question of what the use of violence means in combination with fatherhood was not as easy for the professionals to answer as was the question of the connection between violence and motherhood (cf Chapter Eight in this volume). Their answers often contained hesitation and concern for not making too 'gross' a generalisation about this kind of father-hood. The professionals also stated that there were differences in the fatherhood of men who had used violence. There is an interesting contrast: differences were not mentioned when the same professionals talked about motherhood. The links between fatherhood and violence are not discursively very strong. Violence towards the mother and fatherhood are often regarded as two separate issues (Eriksson and Hester, 2001). There is no straight-forward discursive resource to draw on in this respect.

The problematic aspects of fatherhood received attention during the client–counsellor encounters at the agencies. In particular, problems with child contact and custody arrangements were frequently taken up by women clients. The threat of violence towards the mother and the uncertainties that children have to put up with in contact situations were topics discussed between the professionals and abused women. The professionals often linked this to the control that the violent man tries to continue exercising towards the mother in child contact situations:

> We thought a lot about ... what she could do about these contact situations. I mean that the children were constantly living in a kind of uncertainty about which weekend it would be when they'd meet with dad. Because the father would never tell about it until the last minute. And I'm sure he did it solely for the purpose of hindering Laura [mother] from making any plans or enjoying her free time. And when the mother was out on a trip, the man could call her the moment the train arrived and say 'you have to come and get the kids *right this minute*'. He had, in other words, a need to control things.

In the interviews I made with the professionals they pointed out that often the problem in the relationship between the father and the children was that the father was not interested in the children, but was instead more preoccupied with the heterosexual relationship. The professionals described the fatherhood of these men as very 'weak' and at times nearly non-existent. The children's previous experiences of witnessing violence and their fear of the father were also taken up in the interviews:

> ... even after the divorce, it's the woman who's still more important ... the children's mother ... than the children. And especially ... or I'd think that if the violence has been going on for very long, what happens is that the children don't want to have any contact with their dad either. Don't dare to, and don't want to. They haven't

necessarily even established any kind of proper relationship with their father.

A rather common topic of the discussions between abused women and the professionals was how to find a means to resist men's control efforts in child contact situations. The advice given by the professionals focused on what women and children could do in these situations and how they could try to minimise the threat of violence. Directly addressing the fathers who had used violence was not very common. There were a few situations mentioned where professionals had met the father at the family counselling agency and presented the children's experiences to the father. The professionals told me that their aim had been to address the man expressly as a father and make him see the situation from the children's point of view. As to why that kind of talk and those practices were rare, I interpret this as being partly related to the weak discursive connection between violence and fatherhood. In addition, the absence of violent men from the encounters at the agencies gave few opportunities to the professionals to take up these issues. However, these examples show what kinds of practices professionals can engage in when they focus on the connections between violence and fatherhood.

Thus, sometimes links between fatherhood and violence were made in the professionals' speech. Referring to children's reluctance and fear, the professionals at times even wanted to question the need for arranging contact with the father. However, they had to bear in mind the existing legislation and practices around child contact (see Chapter Five in this volume). Therefore, what the professionals ended up with, at most, was demanding more supervised contact. The emphasis was placed on finding a means to regulate the conditions of the contact in order to make it safe. Addressing violent men and making them accountable did not seem to be an available option in this kind of discursive context.

Fatherhood of possibilities

Although on the face of it, there seems little to be positive about in barely existing or problematic forms of fatherhood, there lie hidden possibilities even in the fatherhood of a man who has used violence. The present discourse on fatherhood is mainly positive and encouraging in tone (Huttunen, 2001; Vuori, 2001, pp 356-8). Many hopes are attached to the engagement of fathers in childcare and upbringing. Hannele Forsberg (1995, pp 137-8), in her research on Finnish social workers, has noted that the active 'new' fatherhood is a construction that is usually spoken about in the conditional. It appears in professional speech and practices as aims or wishes of what fathers should be like, whereas the concrete everyday caring is left to mothers. When these kind of discursive resources are drawn on in connection with men who have used violence, I have called it a 'fatherhood of possibilities'.

This construction is most apparent in the rather self-evident and unquestioned view that fathers are important for children's development and that contact between children and fathers needs to be organised in some way after divorce. The use of violence may call for some special arrangements to take heed of safety issues, but does not require that the importance of fatherhood be profoundly questioned. Professionals were the ones to be active and take up possibilities for contact arrangements. Time after time they turned the discussion to these possibilities and pondered on the practicalities of organising contact. This happened even in situations where the father had not been active in arranging contact (or had said that he did not want contact arrangements), the mother did not want to arrange contact (at that specific moment) and the child had confessed to fear of the father (because of previously witnessed violence). The belief in the importance of the father relation is very strong and contacts are assumed to be in the best interests of the child:

> Professional: What about this contact issue of Maria and her father? (Client: Mmm.) Maria has said that 'perhaps' [she is willing] (Client: Perhaps.) and will contact him or …?
>
> Client: No. She hasn't contacted.
>
> Professional: I see. Has she said anything about whether she's given any *thought* to the matter, or…? […]
>
> Professional: So, could this sister of the father's possibly act as a mediator? […]
>
> Professional: Have you spoken about this with his sister, I mean would she be willing?
>
> Client: No, I haven't yet, it's still so … I've only been thinking about it at this point, so …
>
> Professional: I see. It's of course the *child's* right to meet, so that, um … (Client: Right.) it's worthwhile to give some thought to it and keep it in mind. […]

Professional: Yes, it's probably worth keeping in mind in the sense that Maria ... so that she wouldn't *be left* with the feeling (Client: Mmm.) that it's absolutely ... that her dad is absolutely horrific. [...] It's *her* relationship with dad.

Client: Right, that's why I have ...

Professional: [says something simultaneously]

Client: ... that's why I *am thinking* about the matter. But I've thought that I'll need to figure out what the options are ... (Professional: Mmm.) the ways to make it work. So that I could then lay them out for him. (Professional: Mmm.)

In this extract, we can see how the professional repeatedly takes up the need to organise contact between the child and her father. The professional points out that it is the *child's* relationship with the father and her right to maintain the contact that is important. By this emphasis, a clear line is drawn between the child's relationship and the mother's relationship with the father. There is also a moral undertone in this argument. A good mother does not want to be a hindrance to something that is good for the child. This makes it difficult to resist the demand without being positioned as a bad and selfish mother. The use of such arguments places the mother in a defensive position, although the conflict stays on a latent level. The child's right and her relationship with the father are here treated as abstract categories used in a rhetorical way to convince the mother. The professional is not referring to the specific relationship between the child and the father, which would make it obvious that the child has been hesitating and talking about her fear. The professional's focus is on a positive image set in the (near) future. The extract also shows how the mother becomes the one who has to take responsibility for the safe arrangement of the contacts. She has to reflect on the different choices and present them to the father.

In the professional discourses drawn on in the researched agencies, the father is seen to be important to the child's development in his special way. His importance is even stronger if the child is a boy. Developmental psychology in Finland has been strongly influenced by psychoanalysis (Vuori, 2001, p 34). The Freudian rhetoric can be heard in the family professionals' concern about what impact the absence of fathers or discontinued contacts may have on children. The professionals explain the importance of fathers by concluding that fathers help children become independent of the mother. This is seen to be essential for the development of an autonomous individual. The separation-individualisation process is built on assumptions of a gendered division of parenting: the mother's role is to ensure a close primary relationship and the father's role is to disengage the child from this (Vuori, 2001, p 222). If this process does not succeed, there will be problems in the child's development. According to psycho-analysis, the separation-individualisation process also forms the basis of gender identities and sexual identities, which makes its successful implementation even more important (Vuori, 2001, pp 224-5). Although not explicitly mentioned in the researched agencies, according to this psychoanalytic talk, a successful separation-individualisation process is the precondition of forming 'normal' heterosexual identities and relationships:

> Professional: When it comes to Alex, there's quite a risk [laughs briefly] I mean that *now that he'd need a father* (Client 2: Yes.) ... these are pretty important, these coming years ... in the sense that, um ... it would be really important that Markku [father] and Alex could find something interesting (Client 2: Right.) to do together. (Client 2: Right.) Because, well, there's a ... it may otherwise happen that Alex is ... will depend on you a lot (Client 2: Right.) and that will then affect *his* development, you know ... from now on ... so that.... It's the fathers who are in a way kicking the kids out (Client 2: Right.) away from their mother's apron strings. *Helping* them to get out ... I don't mean kicking but, you know ... helping them to get ... (Client 2: Right.) a bit further away. To become independent and to grow up. (Client 2: Right.) And I think Alex needs his father for that.

At the same time as the father becomes a positive figure who guarantees the normal development of the small boy, the mother becomes an obstacle. Her apron strings bind the small boy to dependency and infancy, from which only the father can help the child out. Thus, the setting turns upside down. Motherhood and a close connection to the mother become a threat, whereas the threat posed by the man who has used violence disappears and his fatherhood becomes highly valued.

What is also remarkable is that becoming an important figure, whose fatherhood is valued, requires no acts or proof on the part of the father in question. He does not have to show interest in his child, nor prove that he is a safe contact person. The talk of a 'fatherhood of possibilities' follows the encouraging and positive rhetoric of fatherhood that has been highlighted in several recent studies on parenthood. In this rhetoric, fatherhood is something men should be persuaded and talked into – by mothers and professionals. Instead of being confronted with demands of responsibility or criticism, men should be supported and helped in their fatherhood according to this rhetoric (Kuronen, 1995, p 128; Vuori, 2001, p 359). It also means that very little space is left for presenting criteria for 'good' fatherhood or rhetoric that would demand safety considerations on the part of fathers.

Conclusion

One conclusion suggested by the research is that, within local practices, there is a continuing process of negotiation going on between feminist interpretations and professional interpretations. Gender and power are used as a means to make sense of violence and its effects on the life of those involved, but so are many other discursive resources. When the aspects of power and gender become lost, the interpretations may for instance turn into scrutiny of the mother and her capabilities. The tendency of professional theories to individualise and at times even 'pathologise' the violence question can have serious consequences for abused women, if the focus turns solely on their weaknesses and failings. It seems that parenthood is an especially tense area, where professional constructions rely on wider discourses of motherhood and fatherhood. This makes elements such as responsibilities of motherhood and possibilities of fatherhood play an important role in the constructions related to violence and parenthood. The discrepancies between the different discourses make it understandable that professionals can on one occasion take women's stories of experienced violence seriously and support them, whereas on another occasion they can pressure mothers to arrange contact between the threatening father and the children. The weak discursive link between fatherhood and violence is one crucial factor enabling this.

Mothers are most often present at the agencies and discussions on motherhood include negotiations between the idealised image of a 'good' mother and concrete everyday motherhood, whereas the fatherhood of men who have used violence is often presented as a positive future vision and remains largely on an idealised level. As abusive fathers are most often absent from the agencies, this also enables professionals to attach hopes to their fatherhood and ignore an analysis of its concrete implementation. It should be time to pay attention to the concrete fatherhood of men who have used violence and to regard violence as something they are accountable for.

The research also shows that it may be possible to combine professionalism and feminist ideas to a higher degree than has been suggested in some feminist analyses (for example, Foley, 1994; Lupton, 1994). However, it also shows the difficulties and limits of the professional context in promoting feminist ideas. Professionals who regard domestic violence as an issue related to gender and power can give a great deal of support and practical advice to abused women and their children. However, the contradictions posed by their professional position and the multiplicity of discursive resources lead to constant negotiation and varying practices, some of which are not in the least supportive to women and children.

In addition, the research shows a peculiarity in the Finnish system. The family counselling agencies, targeted (in principle) at the whole family, actually mainly work with abused women and their children. Thus, there is within their practices space for making alliances with these women and for applying feminist ideas to some degree within professional work.

Note

[1] There are links between trauma theory and the feminist discourse and these are most visible within feminist therapy. These connections will not, however, be dealt with here. I regard trauma theory as a professional theory based on a medical model that can be problematic for feminism. It is therefore useful to analyse these two discursive resources separately. With reference to the use of medical and bodily metaphors, diagnostic categories and causal explanations in trauma theory, Jeanne Marecek (1999) has also argued that the trauma model is a variant of the medical model.

FOUR

"Talking feels like you wouldn't love Dad anymore": children's emotions, close relations and domestic violence

Hannele Forsberg

Children's emotions – as described by children themselves – have not been very widely portrayed in social scientific research on family and close relationships in general, or in literature on violence in familial relationships or child abuse in particular. This chapter attempts to capture the way children exposed to violence in their own homes construct emotions related to familial relationships, especially the emotions connected to the violent father. I am interested in how and with what words children speak of their emotions during the process of recovering from violence, in situations where children's workers at shelters, specialised in helping children exposed to violence, make space for these children's 'emotion work' (Hochschild, 1983). My examination is theoretically and methodologically anchored in the interest within childhood sociology in highlighting the world from the children's perspective, through the children's own way of assigning meanings.

The data are derived from treatment encounters with children in Finnish shelters of the Federation of Mother and Child Homes and Shelters[1], and from interviews conducted with the children approx- imately a year after the close of the helping period. In examining the data, I concentrate on the 'emotion talk' of children who have experienced severe violence against themselves and their mothers, but who are nevertheless attached to their violent father. I place the children's emotions in a dialogue with the recent sociological debate on 'the new family' and close relationships and, more particularly, with research on children exposed to violence at home/child abuse. Through the non-encounters and gaps between these two discourses, I explore a question closely linked to emotions, the question of morals and power and their links to the social order.

Children's emotions as a challenge to social scientific research

Children's emotions have received little attention in social scientific literature in general (Mason and Falloon, 2001). There is very little research, for example, on children's emotions towards people with whom they share a close relationship (Hughes and Dunn, 2002). Even though the thesis on the increased significance of emotions has attracted plenty of attention in recent sociological debate on family and close relationships in general, children have been neglected in the argumentation or, at most, have been seen as the objects of adults' emotions. One could make the parallel claim that in narrower examinations of violence in familial relationships or child abuse, children's emotions have been overshadowed by adult-centred viewpoints. In these examinations, children's emotions have a significant role, but they are typically named from the viewpoint of the adult professional, with a preponderance of diagnostic psycho-vocabulary, such as 'post-traumatic stress' or 'attachment disorder'. Even though these concepts are valuable in describing children's experiences at a general level, they do not capture the children's own activity, their own particular constructions of emotion as such.

In recent years, many social scientists have underlined the importance of emotions as factors that shape – construct or 'do' – family relationships in Western societies. Among others, Anthony Giddens (1992, 1999, pp 59-66) and Ulrich Beck together with Elisabeth Beck-Gernsheim (1995) have brought emotions and the negotiations connected with them into the focus of current debate on the new family and close relationships. In Finland, the family sociologist Riitta Jallinoja (2000) has followed the same direction in her book *Perheen aika* [*Family time*]. The basic thesis is that economic or moral factors no longer determine family relationships, but that the essential elements are love, affection and emotional commitment. It is claimed that intimate relationships are an end in themselves and that they only continue for as long as they provide emotional satisfaction to the partners. At the same time, it has been stressed that the choice has increased: if a relationship no longer provides emotional satisfaction, ending it and starting a new one is easier than before (due to changes in the economy, legal systems and values); the norms governing a relationship are negotiated individually between the partners. It is typical of these reflections that children are only seen as an element in the intimate relationships of adults. The assumed changes in the directions of family relationships are not examined from the children's angle, as children's emotions and experiences. If the children are mentioned, they are there as the objects of adults' emotions (see, for instance, Beck and Beck-Gernsheim, 1995, pp 37, 127; Giddens, 1999, p 60). From the viewpoint of children's emotions and agency, the reflections are problematic. In the first place, children, being dependent on adults, cannot easily be included in the assumption of the negotiability and interchangeability of close relationships. Carol Smart (1997) rightly points out that it is problematic to construct a theory of reflexive social relationships and a new kind of love without taking into account the children as central partners in social life and close relationships. Second, social problems related to the issues of power between genders and generations, such as violence against children and women, do not fit in well with the general reflections on trends in family and close relationships (Smart, 1997); or, if mentioned, the sociological consideration of violence in familial relationships is generally viewed as a residual category in family studies (McKie, 2002). An exclusive concentration on companionship, trust, self-expression and democracy in the consideration of family relationships is a viewpoint that may conceal the patriarchal, ethnic or intergenerational power relationships that continue to exist in the material and symbolic practices of family life (Chambers, 2001, p 130).

A forum of debate that is very different from the general debate on family and close relationships is provided by research on special issues of children exposed to violence at home/child abuse. These two debates do not easily enter into a dialogue. Because of the lack of dialogue, children exposed to violence at home are easily seen as a divergent social group – often unattached to broader sociocultural contexts. In actual fact, the interface between special and ordinary is porous, as is shown, for example, by Jan Mason and Jan Falloon's interviews with 'normal' Australian children (2001).

Research on violent childhoods has predominantly focused on an examination of the problems, symptoms and emotional difficulties such violence causes to the children. The problem- and symptom-focused research stresses that domestic violence is associated with various behavioural and emotional disorders. According to the studies, the risk is especially great for children with long-term exposure to violence as both victims and observers. Aggression, antisocial behaviour, shyness, fears, psychosomatic symptoms, nervousness, lowered social tolerance, depression, various trauma symptoms and personality disorders are among the typical symptoms of these children and the underlying emotions. It is said that boys customarily exhibit extroverted symptoms, while girls suffer from introverted symptoms. Violence is considered to lower the children's self-esteem and, with some, to lead to the belief that they themselves are justified in resorting to violence. The strongest symptoms have been observed at the toddler stage[2]. Studies of adults convicted of crimes of violence have shown that, almost without exception, they have been shadowed by brute, long-term violence in their childhood homes (Haapasalo, 2000). This has been used to prove that violence is learned through socialisation. The term used is a 'vicious circle of violence', which may be carried over to the next generation (Haapasalo, 2000)[3]. The results of this research, mainly quantitative and often experimental and mapping out causal relationships, rarely offer information on children's emotions and the meanings they assign to them in the here and now – not just as a key to their lives as adults or as justification for the acts of adult professionals.

Problem-focused research tends to generate and maintain an image of the child as a victim of violence. The bulk of this research, anchored in traditional psychology, concentrates on the child as a developing individual (acquiring socialisation). It is more rarely that the sociopolitical character of childhood is problematised by focusing, for instance, on how seeing childhood as a stage of life enclosed in family intimacy helps to preserve the secrecy of violence and thus makes intervention more difficult. From the child's point of view, a crucial drawback in the problem-centred research is that it is very often based on the views of either mothers or professionals dealing with children's problems and emotions (Edleson, 1999). If questions are asked of the children themselves, then ready-made questionnaires or other experimental set-ups formulated for the needs of adult professionals are used. The child's own, specific and naturally occurring ways of experiencing violence in the vicinity and assigning meanings to it have been little researched. Nor has the traditional psychological and psychiatric research of a more general nature on children's emotions highlighted the child's viewpoint. Instead, the child is seen as typically responding to stimuli, without taking into account broader environmental and contextual factors (Kirmanen, 1999, pp 272-3; Hughes and Dunn, 2002). Traditional methodologies focus on quantifying abuse and defining deviancy, with the goal of promoting a normal childhood and functional adults (Mason and Falloon, 2001, p 102). One of the drawbacks of problem-centred research is seen to be its level of generality. Data are needed on the differences between children, the processes of violence and the ways in which children experience violence, which are likely to be different at different times. Similarly, particular situational factors (such as the shelter stage – later stages of life) have not received very much attention. Information is also needed on factors that promote and support children's coping: which things support the child's coping with the crisis of violence, which factors alleviate and reduce the problems encountered by the children and what (positive and negative) means to improve coping do the children possess? This orientation also assigns a more positive role to the child.

From the starting points of childhood research with a social scientific orientation (James and Prout, 1990), it is possible to come to grips with children's emotions by means of new questions and approaches[4]. A child-centred approach to violence requires an openness towards the children's own interpretations of violence and its meaning in their lives. In the following, I shall concentrate on the micro-sociological perspective on children's emotions, but I shall go on to link it to broader macro-sociological perspectives.

Data sets and analysis

The capturing of children's emotions linked to violent close relationships is a sizable ethical and methodological challenge, in the face of which the researcher is forced to look for new solutions and to make compromises. In the following, I shall use one case to open a window to children's emotions in violent familial relationships and the meanings children assign to these emotions.

The case description is based on two sets of data gathered by the children's workers in the shelters. The larger data set consists of texts (28) written by the children's workers, documenting treatment encounters with children, with the conscious purpose of recording as much as possible of the child's own descriptions and narratives[5]. Typically, the children were under 12 years of age, the youngest of them being three to four years old. Another data set used is tape-recorded and transcribed interviews (26) with six- to 13-year-old previous child clients of the shelters who were no longer threatened by violence. In the interviews, the children talk about ways of helping children who suffer from violence and assess the success of the help given to them in the shelters, approximately a year after the helping period in the shelters[6]. Inside the larger data set, I have only concentrated on accounts of emotions by children who have encountered brute violence by their fathers towards themselves and their mothers and who, at the same time, are strongly attached to their fathers. Thus, my scrutiny is not a general representation of the emotions of children who have experienced violence at home. The children's emotions vary, depending at least on the type, degree and duration of the violence, the nature of the child's attachment to their father/their mother's male friend (and their mother), and the stage/degree of recovering from violence. On the basis of a closer reading of the data, I have created a case description based on experiences shared by several children and thus partially fictitious, to avoid the identification of actual children. The description deals with the children's emotions during the process of surviving the stressful phase of life. The description focuses on the children's accounts of emotions identified by me in the texts and in the interviews, on its chronological plot and particularly on the different stages in the plot. I have separated four different stages in the descriptions of emotions linked to the children's process of recovering from violence. In practice, surviving violence, whatever its stages and the associated emotions, is not a linear process, but more like a spiral, containing conflicting emotions. At times, the child goes back to a previous stage and then again moves on towards a new stage. I do not write so much about actual episodes of violence as about the child's accounts of his or her feelings concerning the relationship to the father during the process.

Although the data were recorded by the children's workers, and the later interviews with children were conducted by the children's workers in the shelters, my aim has been to give prominence to the child's own narrative. The notes taken after the encounters with children and the subsequent interviews, and the emotions transmitted through them are, on the one hand, natural institutional encounters with the purpose of helping the children, but, on the other hand, they have been adapted for the purposes of research interested in the children's voice.

The use and description of children's painful experiences were preceded not only by formal consent and gate-keeping procedures, but also by other types of ethical reflection – I am conscious of the power differential between the researcher and the researched, visible at several levels. First of all, I consider that painful emotions are an essential part of violent intimate relationships, and it is important to study them. Silence might only perpetuate the practice of non-discussion, lack of awareness and non-intervention that many of the children in my study have suffered from. Second, my starting point is the children's right to be heard and the revealing of difficulties that shadow their lives. Third, I attempt also to include in my consideration an element of hope: it is possible to overcome painful emotions. However, it is a paradox of a study that immerses itself in the intimate that, despite good intentions, there are no guarantees that the information gained automatically benefits anybody. Information that is used to empower people who have encountered difficult issues may, in another context, be used to justify control and constraints (see

Forsberg and Pösö, 2002). In spite of this ambivalence, I have attempted to write respectfully about the children I describe, to show an appreciation of their own ways of structuring the issue and to look for forms and expressions that would meet this goal as closely as possible.

In writing about the children's emotions towards their father during the process of recovering from violence, I mainly use the present tense and the first person, as if the child were there, telling her or his story to the reader. I have constructed this I-narrative, summarised as a case description, on the basis of the descriptions of the children's turns of speech in the workers' texts and on the basis of what the children have narrated in the interviews. This approach aims, on the one hand, to give space to the child's own narrative and, on the other hand, to distance it from the actual narrators. Nevertheless, the case description attempts to be faithful to what is revealed in the data of the emotional landscape of a child who is attached to her or his father but has been treated violently, as well as of the changes in that landscape. I have adapted the children's expressions so that the style is close to that of fiction.

The case description enables me to contribute to the debate on the new family relationships as emotional relationships. I examine the extent to which the idea of individual choice and negotiation finds a response in the choices of actual children who have experienced violence at home. At the same time, I describe the experiences of particular children in their own words, as an alternative to a more generalising, psychologically oriented research on the problems of special groups.

Children and emotions in the process of recovering from violence

When a mother and child arrive at the shelter, violence has typically been a part of the family's life for years and is generally quite severe. Nevertheless, the child has not necessarily considered the father's behaviour as abnormal, having grown up with it. Repeated violent episodes may have formed a kind of routine that the child regards as a part of the family reality, which he or she is not able to question but which he or she thinks of as a matter of course in family life (cf Peled, 1998; see also Weinehall, 1997). The impression that the family is 'normal' may also exist outside it, at the child's school, for instance. A child may live for years shadowed by violence without an outsider questioning the way of life lived in the family. The latest point at which the child becomes more conscious of the dangers of violence is when the violence at home becomes an issue because of a public confrontation – calling the police, seeking help at the shelter or moving away from home. At the same time, the child's relationship with the father (and mother) undergoes a change. At the public helping organisation, the child's image of the father may be challenged for the first time by an image that there is something wrong with the father. Some children only realise the seriousness and unacceptability of violence at this stage (cf Peled, 1998, pp 8-10; see also Forsberg, 2002, p 44). At this stage, the emotional landscape of a child who has encountered brute violence towards her- or himself and the mother and who reacts to it strongly could be described by the children's expressions "in a labyrinth", "in a prison" or "in a trap". In the following, I shall let the children describe in more detail the emotions associated with this stage.

"In a trap"

> Dad has changed, he only ever thinks of himself. What he did to Mum! I stood there in a state of shock. If I tell someone, he'll kill me for sure. I can't say anything to Dad. I'm trapped and alone; I can't talk to anyone. There's no fun in life. There's only pain – in the brain – and emptiness. That is scary. I would like to die. It is wiser to kill myself than let Dad do it.
>
> There's a pressure at the top of my head, as if someone was drilling into it. Pain in my heart. There's a thunder in my head, a cold spot at the top of my head; my ears are ringing. My nerves are gone to pieces, I'm hiding, in the night, in a labyrinth. Someone is chasing me. I see Dad's angry face everywhere. I can't get Dad out of my head, I see the evil in him all the time, in my eyes.
>
> My head aches. I can't go looking for help.
>
> I don't care what happens to my Dad. Suppose I changed my name and went to live at the other end of the country. So he couldn't find me. Suppose I'd walk as far as I could; far away until I was hungry and thirsty.

As violence gets more brutal and the threat more acute, the fear of one's life being threatened and the anxiety over the consequences of telling others about it reaches a peak. At the emotional level, the child is, as it were, against the wall, trapped with no escape. The children's descriptions depict a deep hopelessness, loneliness, lack of joy, extreme helplessness, pain and emptiness. The feeling that the easiest solution would be to die, to kill oneself, becomes stronger. The feeling that there is nothing you can do against a superior power is tangible. Evil is felt in mind and body – at different points in the body. The children's experiential world is filled with the evil emanating from the father. The only hope is the idea of walking away, of disappearing. The feeling of imprisonment is linked with dreams of escape, of going away. Some dream of a "sunny country" or, less hopefully, only of walking away until hunger and thirst overcome the traveller. Changing one's identity by changing the name and other elements of identity are also part of the dream of not being found out by the father. The child's space diminishes; at the emotional level, the child feels that he or she has no right to exist.

"Ambivalent awakening"

He beats the back of my head and hits my stomach. Mum stands next to him. We never speak of the beating. He never says he's sorry. Dad says that the arguments are my fault. I suppose that's true, for after all grown-ups are honest.

Why aren't I braver, why don't I stand between Dad and Mum? I'm so afraid that Mum will have to go to the hospital or dies. I can't ever ask my friends to come over. I can't visit anyone either. Whatever will happen to Dad now?

It is difficult to talk about what happens at home. I am not used to talking about it. I would like to get revenge somehow. All the other people have it so much better.

Sometimes when Dad's not drinking and he cooks something nice, I can relax a little. I have this one friend whom I can visit.

I feel as if I was grown up already. If only Dad would change!

If only we could all live together again. And there were no arguments.

I wish something happened to Dad. A car accident? Would anyone come to his funeral? What if I killed myself, is there another life? Will I ever see Mum again? I wish I could talk some sense into Dad.

The opportunity of talking about things provided by the shelter makes some children anxious. They do not like to talk about their own father beating them. It is shameful, which is why many children prefer silence – especially since the father may call his blows love. Shame is an emotion that evaluates the self and finds it wrong. In experiencing shame, we bring to light a part of ourselves that ought to be hidden away and excluded. Shame isolates but does not protect; a person experiencing shame is helpless. Shame causes an internalisation of inferiority: "I am not worth anybody's love". At the same time, shame is a power-intensive emotion, for those who are ashamed consider their situation to be deserved. Shame blocks out protest (Ronkainen, 1999, pp 135-7). Shame tells of children's subjugated position and their lack of the right to speak. However, it must be noted that in the children's narratives shame comes up in the context of a positive emotion, that is, commitment. Shame is an ambivalent feeling, because the child also links positive emotions and characteristics with the violent father.

Gradually, as trust is being built, even children with the most hurtful experiences open up and at the same time awaken to their painful reality. The emotion talk typical of the awakening phase are linked to shame, but also to guilt. The child may think that the father's violence is his/her fault; the father may have said as much. Children also feel guilty for not daring to stand between their father and mother in an argument. Thus, at the emotional level, they share the guilt for the violence. In guilt, the self is evaluated as bad. When the child awakens to the realisation that things are not necessarily the same for all other people, anger and the desire to get even with others are also awakened.

The awakening into one's own reality leads to conflicts because of the child's attachment to the father. This being so, the father is never simply cruel and evil in the child's eyes, but carries good and attractive traits at the same time. Because of the attachment, the child keeps hoping that the father will change, and may also hope that the whole family will live together again without arguments. If the child's hope of seeing a change in the father is not realised, a psychological separation from the father may be helped by hoping that the father is hurt or even dies in an accident.

The hopes of injury to the father or fantasies of getting even with other people are generally manifested at a symbolic level, through play, stories or drawings. In this case, the child does not hurt anyone and need not bear the ensuing burden of guilt; the agent may be a fictional character created by the child. The processing of emotions linked to the father at the symbolic level appears to relieve and clarify the feelings of actual children.

"Change"

> Talking feels like you wouldn't love Dad anymore.
>
> I have never thought about Mum and Dad getting a divorce. I have thought that we have a real family. I have also thought that when I grow up I'll be like Dad – only nicer.
>
> This man's gotten into prison; there are no friends there. This guy's been put into a coffin and left there all alone. If only a monster dog came and chased away all the bad things!
>
> What will happen to Dad, what will happen to the rest of us from now on?
>
> Dad's treated me wrong, but I do miss him all the same.
>
> I want to live away from my Dad.

The process of breaking away from a violent father relationship enters a new stage when the child begins actively to desire a change in contrast to the past. The change is not easy when the child is attached to and identifies with the father's positive aspects. The change also brings fears, because it is difficult to know what will happen to the father or other family members in the future. The child processes the change, the coping and the associated feeling of control with the help of symbolic and fictional processes. Through play, made-up stories or songs, the child separates her- or himself from the father by placing him in prison, for instance. The child is psychologically ready to let go of the evil when he or she realises that the father has done wrong and when he or she wants to live away from the father even at the risk of missing him. The child gives up the hope of a change in the father. As the desire for change matures, one way of situating the evil in the past is to 'isolate' the father.

"New directions"

> It's a good thing that I can talk. Play music. Make pictures of my life. Hope.
>
> I don't have to be afraid any longer. It helps when I feel safe and can talk. You get rid of pressures when you can talk.
>
> I'm doing OK now. I've many friends, too. I need not feel pain every day.
>
> I suppose the fear will only die away completely after I've grown up. When I'm grown up, I'll at least be strong enough to stand up against him if he should attack me again.

> Being safe and talking are important. Pressures vanish
> when you can talk. I need not be afraid any longer. I'm
> doing fine and I've a lot of friends.

Talk is given a new meaning now. Talk does not so much signify the
fear of going against the father as an attempt to relieve the feelings of
not being all right. The father's dominance retreats into the background,
while the child her- or himself and her or his feelings come into the
foreground. When violence is no longer a part of daily life, the painful
emotions retreat and the joy, positive attitude to life and important
peer relationships, all typical of children, come into play. In the meanings
assigned by the children, talk receives a broader than usual significance:
talk that relieves may consist not only of words, but of pictures, music,
stories and play. In order for talk to be possible, one must have a secure
setting. As the feeling of security increases, fear releases its grip of the
child. The children with the most painful experiences, however, point
out that the threat linked with the power and strength of an adult can
only completely retreat after the child has grown up enough to stand
up to the father physically if he tries to threaten the child in some way.
This is a poignant expression of how deeply dependent on and
subjugated to adults children may be.

Freedom, marginality, morals and children's agency

Children's emotions

The statements concerning the central role of emotions as factors
shaping family relationships appear to hold true as one examines
family relationships, the associated tensions and pressures towards
change from the point of view of Finnish children of the early 2000s
who have experienced brute violence. The flow, content and shape
of emotions, however, follows a logic different from the post-
modern ideals of intimate relationships between independent adults.
A study of the children's emotion talk also enables a more nuanced
observation of emotions than is possible in more general studies on
the emotional problems of a special group. Children cannot be
placed in the same moral category as the 'confluent love' and 'pure
relationships' deriving from individual choices, which are discussed
in theories on family and close relationships in the post-modern
era. Structural violence that reveals the power relationships between
children and adults is also present in studies that see violence only
as an issue of problematic marginal groups, such as the poor and

those with multiple problems. The latter type of studies refuses to see the violence experienced by children in so-called 'normal' families. However, children of families with a weaker social status have no automatic guarantee of being heard. As a social issue, the structural power relationship between children and adults touches many more groups than just those at the margins of society (Mason and Falloon, 2001).

The secondary nature of children's suffering and the invisibility of their emotions (see the first section of the chapter), is also transmitted by my case descriptions. The child's family shuts in their emotions and experiences – "There's no one I can talk to" – for the child is threatened with punishment, even loss of life, by the father. Other family members are often part of the network of secrecy. The authorities that come into contact with the family may also bypass the child's suffering. In this situation, the only one bearing the responsibility for the pain, grief, fear and suffering is the child. If we consider family and close relationships to be only private spaces for love and affection, and if we see those who have failed to find personal happiness as completely free in their choices, then shame and guilt are guaranteed to form part of the emotional landscape of those who do not succeed. This will also be the case when we start from the assumption that the issue of violent intimate relationships only concerns pathological special groups.

However, my case description also provides material for seeing how the best-case outside interventions may give space for the child's agency, or participation, in the 'negotiation' on family and emotional relationships. However, at that point we are no longer dealing with morals that can be individually and privately negotiated. Nevertheless, outside intervention does not always reach the child – not even in the data sets I used. In her in-depth interviews with Swedish young people who had experienced violence at home, Katarina Weinehall (1997) noted that even though the young were in sore need of one person at least to confide in, to share experiences with and to reflect on them, they were left alone to fend for themselves (see also Chapter Nine in this volume). In addition, the experiences that the young people had had of professional helpers in different contexts were preponderantly very negative (Weinehall, 1997; Chapter Nine in this volume). My data do include children whose bad feelings had been successfully alleviated through the interventions of the children's workers at the shelters. Positive changes require not only that the child is ready for them, but also that the mother or someone who is close to the child at least is committed and supportive, and that the helper is skilled and brave enough to meet painful emotions eye to eye. The help offered has succeeded in alleviating the fear, terror, shame, guilt and powerlessness of some children. With the help of symbolic revenge and anger, the helpless, trapped victim has become a more capable and active child, whose life also includes happier things.

In his book on intimate relationships in the post-modern era, Giddens (1992, pp 104-9), who has been criticised for his abstract, neutral and general orientation, nevertheless considers the case of 'toxic', violent, alcoholised, exploitative parents and admits that there have always been cruel parents. They continue to exist even though it was expected that little by little, with the appearance of modern motherly love, parenthood would become more lenient and the parent–child relationship would become more equal. According to Giddens, the reprocessing of cruel parent relationships – of which my case description may be considered an instance – is particularly important in the post-modern era. This is important so that the child may attain the status of an autonomous and equal human being and that the making of choices and individuality become possible. According to Giddens, memories and experiences need to be rethought and negotiated. I assume, however, that in saying that the freeing and 'healing' of the inner child is important, Giddens is writing about adults (Giddens, 1992). On the basis of my case example, the child's task seemed primarily to consist of achieving a release from the inner adult.

Morals of love and the ethic of rules

The child's emotions, whether reworked or otherwise, are not only personal, but are also intertwined with social structures and power, with an assessment of what emotions are possible in intimate relationships at any given time. In many Western countries, family legislation has also begun to encompass the idea of people's free choice and capability of negotiating the best possible solution even in times of conflict (Nousiainen, 2001a, pp 15-18). Incoherence in legislation and outside interventions can also maintain or create new problems in personal emotional relationships. In Finland, for example, it has been possible up until the present for a man placed under a restraining order vis-à-vis his wife to retain joint custody of their children (cf Chapter Five in this volume). Riitta Jallinoja (2000, pp 68, 88) – based on Bauman – distinguishes between the morals of passionate love, which only bring into focus individual emotion, and the ethic of rules, which is based on justice, the general good and universal rules. Generally agreed rules and norms are needed as a yardstick for justice, since asymmetrical relationships can lead to acts that go against individual basic rights even in the name of love – just as the violent father had justified his acts according to the child in my case description. The partners in a relationship that is only based on the morals of individual love must be equal. The relationship between children and parents is rarely so; at worst, the more powerful partner is able to define too exclusively what is good for the other partner. In violent intimate relationships, the use of power and subjugation are particularly typical. Parallel to the morals of love, an ethic of rules is needed in the case of children and other people dependent on others. The purpose of the ethic of rules is to guarantee that the asymmetry typical of the parent–child relationship does not lead to harmful consequences for the weaker partner, that is, the child. The parent may have the illusion that love automatically makes all acts good, but, in subjugating and problem-fraught relationships, the morals of love do not necessarily bring consequences that are good for all partners (Jallinoja, 2000, pp 109-11).

Nevertheless, the parent–child relationship is always also guided by the morals of love, which require that the parent acts for the good of the child according to her or his own assessment. The ethic of rules, in turn, requires that the partners jointly negotiate what is good for the child, or even resort to more universal norms set up by society regarding the child's good or interest. Universal norms cannot always unambiguously settle what is good for the child; in spite of this, they open a broader discussion space in conflict situations (Jallinoja, 2000, pp 109-11).

Contrary to what is presented in problem-focused research on violent childhood, my case description shows how children suffering from violence do not only express fear, helplessness, shame, guilt and other negative feelings. At the same time, the child may also express a feeling of longing for her or his violent father, or recall the peaceful times and happy moments they have shared. The violent father is not only evil and cruel, but simultaneously has also positive characteristics. The negative and positive emotions are intertwined. What is more, the child's emotions change over time. They are in internal conflict and pull in different directions, until the worst tensions are relieved with time and positive emotions gain the upper hand. The existence of positive emotions does not, however, give us the right to deny the adult's cruelty to the child or to close our eyes to it. Outside intervention, offering the child a new perspective and a new language on violence, may provide a means of escape. Thus, the child is able to structure violence and its associated meanings and emotions in a different way from how things were at home, and a reorientation becomes possible. Violence is categorised as an activity both wrong and evil that no one is entitled to. The means of externalising and distancing violence provide the material for a new moral relationship to violence.

A study of children exposed to violence at home is also a study of the issue of social order and social morals. Recognising the fact that children experience violence and defining this as a problem is part of a wider sociopolitico-moral process of change, in which the significance of violent experiences in close personal relationships has only gradually become of importance. On the level of principle, the rejection of private cruelty to children is a widely shared moral standpoint. However, the concept of cruelty and violence that touches children in the private sphere has continuously altered and become more specified over the past 30 years. The earlier, historical use of violence allowed to persons in authority now stands condemned, while human rights have been extended to apply to children. In spite of this, many myths and fears still uphold conflict situations and the impossibility of intervention. The concept of the family as a haven of security, mutual love and privacy is one of the strongest myths. Even today, violent acts occurring in the private sphere, the family (generally against women and children), are neutralised more easily than violent acts in the public sphere (generally between men), which are classified as crimes. Furthermore, the Finnish legislative system appears to recognise more easily violent acts by strangers in the public sphere, and less easily violent acts within the family[7], which, however, generally leave deeper scars (Näre, 2000, p 120). The social scientific debate that defines family and close relationships and the status of children is one of the phenomena that create and reproduce social order and social morals. Sociological debate that examines changing trends in family and close relationships while stressing the importance of emotions, research that stresses the emotional problems of children in violent families, and childhood sociology research that attempts to capture children's emotion talk on their (violent) close relationships – all these provide different perspectives, different rhetorical spaces to the feelings, children's agency, morals and social order associated with the hurtful close relationships experienced by children.

Notes

[1] The Federation of Mother and Child Homes and Shelters is the largest body providing shelter services in Finland, with a nationwide network of shelters. See also Chapter Three of this volume.

[2] For an overview of problem-centred research, see Edleson (1999).

[3] For a further discussion of the debate regarding the 'cycle of violence' or intergenerational transference of violence, see, for example, Morley and Mullender (1994).

[4] The wave of new openings is represented, among others, by Butler and Williamson (1994), Saunders (1995), Weinehall (1997), Peled (1998) and Mason and Falloon (2001). See also the Children 5 to 16 programme (2001) and Mullender et al (2002). In Finland, the pioneering study of children's experiences of violence is by Riitta Leskinen (1982), based on interviews with children on their arrival at the shelter. Even earlier, a group of child psychiatrists stressed the importance of studying children's personal experiences and an article by Vappu Taipale and her colleagues, published in the early 1970s in the journal *Suomen Lääkärilehti* [*Finnish Medical Journal*], provides an interesting reflection of its period on the basis of a single case, although the child's angle is heavily coloured by psychoanalytic interpretation (Taipale et al, 1971). Recent studies have attempted to adopt a more open angle, concentrating on the activity of children here and now (Pitkäkangas-Laitila and Räisälä, 1999; Eskonen, 2001).

[5] The children's workers were asked to write two different descriptions about the course and possible turning points in the problem-solving process of children in shelters. One was asked to be a progressive and the other a more regressive one in nature. Texts produced according to these ideas were based on client files and children's workers' own notes, which contained a lot of near verbatim notes on children's speech.

[6] The data were originally gathered for an evaluation study (Forsberg, 2002) within a national project to develop the child-oriented helping work of the Federation of Mother and Child Homes and Shelters. The project studied the angle of the children's workers on help provided to children who had suffered violence at home and the children's angle on the help offered.

[7] In Finland, the corporal punishment of children is forbidden by law, and domestic violence constitutes a felony subject to public prosecution.

FIVE

Bypassing the relationship between fatherhood and violence in Finnish policy and research

Teija Hautanen

This chapter has its origin in the question as to why fatherhood and violence in intimate relationships are, in Finland, so seldom treated simultaneously within the same context[1]. My aim is to reflect upon this theme on the basis of literature and to accumulate the reasons for this silence in the Finnish discussion. I will begin by examining the Finnish research on violence in intimate relationships. What features can be found there that make it difficult to notice the fatherhood of violent men? Second, I will focus on motherhood and fatherhood – which features in the conception of these two phenomena prevent the discussion of fathers' violence? Finally, I will turn my attention to problems relating to child custody and contact visitation practices, where, as also indicated in relation to Denmark and Sweden (see Chapters Two, Seven and Eight in this volume), the problems connected with fatherhood and violence are particularly acute.

This chapter is based on violence research and parenthood studies in the field of social sciences in Finland. It mainly draws upon monographs and scientific articles written in Finnish from the 1990s to the present. Both research areas expanded substantially within the social sciences in the 1990s and have continued their growth since the new millennium. Even so, the number of researchers focusing on violence and parenthood is not large and it is quite possible to acquire a thorough picture of their work. Other perspectives and nuances could, of course, be found through empirical research. However, I believe that a literature review can indicate key features in current approaches in Finland to fatherhood and intimate violence. Thereby, some of the themes already touched upon in the previous chapters on Finland, such as the gendering of parenthood and inconsistencies in legislation regarding children post-separation and divorce, can also be explored further.

Analysing violence in intimate relationships and neglecting fatherhood

The ways in which violence in intimate relationships is seen and conceptualised in society have an impact on what is done in practice and in politics (for example, Hearn, 1998, p 15). When researchers or professional helpers work with the kind of violence being practised between adults in close relationships where the perpetrators are mostly men (and the victims are women and/or children)[2], they cannot help making terminological choices. When they give violence a name, they at the same time give it a framework.

In Finland, the term 'family violence' is widely used and it has become an established term, in spite of the criticism directed at it. For example, Teuvo Peltoniemi (1984, pp 26-45) argues that the concept of family violence is broad enough to catch the whole range of violence within close relationships. Referring to North American research on 'family violence' and especially to Murray Strauss and his colleagues, Peltoniemi claims that the more gendered concepts that feminists recommend are too emotional or political. Feminist critics, on the other hand, argue that the biggest problem with the concept of 'family violence' is that it makes the violence seem like an interactional problem within the family dynamics wherein all the family members are deemed equally responsible. Thus, it ignores the impact of gender and power relations. Other concepts have been suggested to replace it, such as marital violence, intimate violence, men's violence, gendered violence, sexualised violence and violence against women (see, for example, Ronkainen, 1998, pp 2-14; Notko, 2000, pp 5-8)[3].

Related to the concept of family violence is the understanding of violence from a family-centred viewpoint that has a strong tradition in Finnish violence work (see also Chapter Three in this volume). A family-centred perspective uses an approach where there is considered to be something very wrong with the whole family – without identifying the perpetrator(s) or the victim(s). As a result, we have a problem-filled family with a number of symptoms, not men, women and children – much less fathers and mothers. If a family violence perspective is adopted, then we even attribute responsibility to the victims for what has happened. On the other hand, a family-centred approach sees all the family members as victims, in other words also men, and this has in turn obscured the responsibility issues (Antikainen, 1999; Partanen and Holma, 2002, pp 200-1).

Besides family-centred perspectives, relationship-centred approaches to men's violence to known women are also widely used. It is, for example, becoming common to use a term that is close to 'marital violence'. The Finnish word *parisuhdeväkivalta* signifies violence between two adults who have an intimate relationship. So, violence is often lumped together with other marital or relationship problems. The victim can also be made to feel guilty when this relational approach is used: she has willingly started this relationship and is concerned with how it works (or does not work). Thus violence turns into 'marital problems' and 'lovers' quarrels' instead of being a crime, or even violence (Husso, 2003, pp 95-9).

Relationship- and family-centredness has a key position in shelter work in Finland (see also Chapter Three in this volume). The first Finnish shelters were founded in 1979 by the Federation of Mother and Child Homes and Shelters, whose origin is in child protection. The principle of considering the whole family became one of the main premises of the work of Finnish shelters. According to Heinänen (1992, pp 84-5), author of the history of the Federation of Mother and Child Homes and Shelters, this implies trying to avoid thinking of the persons involved in terms of the victim and the guilty one. She maintains that violence always involves a serious disturbance in family interaction, and therefore we should not denigrate men or underline the flawlessness of women in violence work. In this respect, Finland differs from many other Western countries, where feminist movements have often been the driving force behind shelter work and where the view that violence is part of the power relations between the genders has been more dominant (see, for example, Eduards, 1997a).

During the 1990s, the family- and relationship-centred gender-neutral conception of violence has become more varied and multi-vocal in Finland, both in research as well as in professional helping work. At the same time, the frequent use of family and relationship therapies as treatment for both the perpetrators and victims of violence has met with criticism. Despite this, Notko (2000, pp 21-2) maintains that the Finnish public discussion on violence in intimate relationships is often marked by the fear of pointing an accusing finger collectively at all men: one can talk about violence against women, but it must be done in a vague manner without accusing anyone; one must be extremely careful not to make generalisations about men. This may lead to the kind of demands in language use that require us to talk about men and women being committers of violence alike in the name of equality.

On the other hand, the concept of 'violence against women' has started to gain a foothold, and much of current research focuses on women's experiences and on their chances of surviving violence. As researchers turn their interest to women, people may think that solving the violence issue is mainly in women's interest. It is true that criminology has all through its history studied delinquent violent men, but violent acts that have taken place in the private sphere have not belonged to the mainstream of its research themes (see, for example, Ronkainen, 1998, pp 6-8). Neither has a gendered investigation of men been common in criminology or social science in Finland. It was not until the new critical studies on men took up the challenge that the theme began to be researched (Jokinen, 1999; Hearn and Lattu, 2002[4]). This field of study is, among other things, interested in how violence is linked to the construction of masculinity and how it may be part of developing as a man and being a man.

I argue here that one of the reasons for forgetting fatherhood in the context of violence is to be found in the family-centred and gender-neutral conception of violence, prevalent in Finland up to the 1990s, which has included a fear of focusing responsibility on men. It is not easy to include fatherhood in the analysis unless one first names men as the most common perpetrators of violence and reflects more closely on the connections between masculinity and violence. However, it seems that sensitivity to gender is not alone sufficient to bring the fatherhood of violent men to the forefront of analysis: in addition, we need to consider the children's position, so as not to let violence become reduced to an affair that only concerns the adults in the family and has nothing to do with parenting.

The children who have grown up with an atmosphere of violence around them have been called forgotten, unacknowledged or silent victims because their experiences have been easily bypassed in the helping systems of different countries (see also Chapters Four and Nine in this volume). More attention has been given to the children and women who have been the targets of violence – and even then physical violence has often gone unnoticed. Little by little, professionals and researchers have started to notice how traumatic just seeing abuse can be for a child, and the effects can be as dramatic as they are for the victims of violence (see Holden, 1998)[5].

Violence statistics reveal that many children encounter violence in their homes in one way or another. The Finnish national survey on men's violence towards women shows that of those women who have been subjected to violence by a husband or live-in partner or ex-husband/partner, 40% think that their children have in some way been exposed to violence, have been the targets of violence or have seen or heard violence (Heiskanen and Piispa, 1998, pp 4, 33). It should be noted that this figure is based upon mothers' reports about children's experiences[6]. However, 42% of the mothers did not know or were not able to tell about their children's experiences, so there may be many more children in Finland who have been exposed to violence than these figures reveal (Heiskanen and Piispa, 1998, p 33). To estimate children's exposure to violence, the researchers at Statistics Finland who carried out the national survey conducted a special analysis of the data and their conclusion was that at least 17% of Finnish children under 18 have seen or been subjected to violence within their own families (Dufva, 2001, p 15)[7].

It has not been until recently that more attention has begun to be paid to children's experiences of living with violence in intimate relationships in Finland. The Child's Time project of the Federation of Mother and Child Homes and Shelters has in particular increased awareness about the position of those children whose lives are overshadowed by violence. The aim of the project has been to bring out the children's special needs and develop new work forms for them. The project has also increased interest in the fatherhood of violent men. In shelters, parenthood has most times meant motherhood. These days, shelters are increasingly accepting the challenge of trying to get fathers involved. It is easier to help the child if the father assumes a positive attitude towards the processing of the child's experiences of violence and the help they receive (Laaksamo, 2001, pp 112-14; Oranen, 2001a, 2001b, p 79).

If we understand violence as a gendered phenomenon and place children in this context of violence, it is possible to focus on violent men's fatherhood as a theme of discussion. And yet, we still need to reflect on the gendered social construction of fatherhood, and of parenthood in general. What is it that obstructs the examination and evaluation of violent men's fatherhood?

The responsible and strong mother-woman

I argue that when a man is violent, otherwise defined as delinquent, an alcoholic or acts in any other way that is perceived as socially problematic, we do not customarily define him primarily as a father. The case is different with women. A 'drug-addicted mother', for example, has become part of Finnish moral discourse; but we may have to wait for some time before 'drug-addicted fathers' appear in that discourse. This echoes the distinction between 'fathers' and 'violent men' highlighted by Eriksson (Chapter Eight in this volume), and the discussion of gendering of parenthood by Keskinen (Chapter Three in this volume).

In everyday life, women's good and bad deeds are often weighed against their motherhood. 'Man' and 'father', on the other hand, are not in the same way socially one and the same thing as are 'woman' and 'mother'. Girls are categorised as potential mothers very early on and, simultaneously, they are saddled with the responsibility for reproduction at a young age. According to Ronkainen (1994, pp 129-130), male sexuality is freed from reproductive responsibilities while women's sexuality and whole womanhood is bound to it. This difference can be seen also in the sex education directed at teenagers: it warns girls in particular about the possibility of getting pregnant (see, for example, Nummelin, 1997). We are worried about the smoking, drinking and drug use of teenage girls specifically because they are future mothers. There is also a great concern about the present low birth rate, and women who have reached their 30s are in turn publicly accused of being materialistic narcissists because they are not fulfilling the expectations set for them to make enough children (to be future tax-payers) sufficiently early. Boys or grown-up men are not to the same extent saddled with responsibility for future or even present fatherhood. That is why a violent man is not self-evidently defined as a father either, even if we know that he has children.

This is, of course, not only a Finnish phenomenon. The emphasis on a close connection that approaches sameness between a woman and mother and between a mother and child has in many cultures a long history, deeply rooted in societal structures (see, for example, Badinter, 1981; Holm, 1993). This is one way of defining the sexual difference. Defining the sexual difference through motherhood has even functioned as women's own strategy in their maternalistic policy making. From the 1800s on, women's movements have used motherhood and childcare as their legitimate tickets to citizenship, to public and political life. Maternalistic ideology, which women have furthered and men accepted, has also been an essential part in the history of modern welfare states. The beginnings of Finnish social work, for example, are in mother and child protection (Anttonen, 1997, pp 173-82; Nätkin, 1997).

In social and healthcare, these maternalistic roots have been combined with a strong emphasis on the role of the mother, found in modern child psychology. Forsberg et al (1994, pp 175-83) maintain that nowadays the practices of Finnish social and healthcare are by declaration gender-neutral, but there is a gender-based difference in professionals' attitudes towards parents that can be seen in their work practices. Even though the intention is to deal with problems that concern the whole family, they are in practice treated as women's problems. The work is often done with the mother and therefore families often shrink into mothers and children. This can lead to a greater understanding of women, but at the same time the work may underline women's responsibility for their families and make them feel guilty. The father's position and importance is maintained in talk, but his physical absence does not as such bother professionals during sessions or appointments. Fathers are not expected to know or remember matters concerning children and the family. Forsberg et al (1994) conclude that, in professional practices, fatherhood seems to be largely rhetorical, while motherhood in turn is very concrete (cf Chapter Three in this volume).

Here I want to point out that there are clear parallels to the UK context. Milner (1996, pp 117-18) maintains that the differing definitions and connotations of fatherhood and motherhood have an impact on how men and women are treated in helping systems, as well as in research. She says that the professionals belittle men's responsibility for violence and shift it onto women. At the same time, women's responsibility for the family, for its wellbeing and for the atmosphere within it, is seen as a lifelong task; and, in practice, the word parenthood very often only means motherhood.

Even when a woman is clearly a victim of violence, many kinds of demands are placed upon her. It is assumed that she has chosen a violent marriage, if she does not, as is expected, get help for herself, her children and her family. She should be active and able to cope, and she should not let subordination, distress and weakness overwhelm her. Researchers in the field have also experienced that readers expect them to focus upon women's survival stories (Ronkainen, 2001a, pp 147-9; Husso, 2003, p 179). The demand for strength is particularly striking if the woman is a mother. The portrait of a hard-working and proud Finnish mother, who can make it on her own if necessary, is depicted in historical data. Even today, we do not want to make room in our cultural truths and meanings for the possibility that a mother might be weak or get tired (Jokinen, 1996, pp 189-92; Nätkin, 1997, p 245).

The recent publication *Naiset, miehet ja väkivalta* [*Men, women and violence*], issued by the Evangelical Lutheran Church of Finland, gives advice to women in dealing with violent husbands:

> You have to stop it at the outset. Do not let him subject you, don't become a victim.... If he does not stop abusing you, you have to have the courage to end the relationship even at the cost of breaking up your family. Because the whole family suffers from the violence, even if it is targeted

at one person. (Suomen ev.lut. kirkon kirkkohallituksen
julkaisuja, 2000, pp 23-4)

In this way, the woman is saddled with the responsibility for ending
the violence, as well as for the wellbeing of the family. The publication
does not advise men to consider the other members of the family.
Instead, they are told: "Each individual is alone responsible for their
own acts. They decide how to behave. But they can also decide to
change their behaviour" (p 24). A peculiar discrepancy arises when
the same pages convey the message that a man is responsible for his
acts alone, but a woman needs to think of the good of the whole
family and therefore has to stop the violence. It is certainly positive
that the Church takes a clear stand against violence, instead of only
speaking in favour of keeping the family together, but these examples
show directly how firmly responsibilities are gendered in the contexts
of parenthood and violence. The advice given to men also illustrates
the normative individualism ("each individual ...") that is an essential
part of the Finnish equality discourse. These kinds of rhetoric limit
the possibilities to use gender-sensitive speech and ignore the fact that
it is men who behave violently in most cases (see Ronkainen, 2001b).

Positive fatherhood

The woman's role as mother contains expectations about her responsibility and strength, which tends to direct our attention away
from the father in connection with violence. Jouko Huttunen (1999,
p 179), one of the most prominent Finnish fatherhood researchers,
also reminds us that indifference regarding the family or children has
not been part of traditional Finnish fatherhood. Gentlemen's agreements
and chivalry have bound a man to his family as late as the 1950s. A
proper man has always borne the responsibility for his acts. The father
has been the breadwinner, the head of the family and the disciplinarian,
who, even if physically absent, was always closely connected with his
family.

Both a weakening and a strengthening of fatherhood have been the
trends in the past decades, according to Huttunen (1999, pp 179-88).
He sees as symptoms of a weakened fatherhood the psychological
lack of a father generated by divorce and separation, some men's
unwillingness or inability to really take responsibility for other people
and men's devotion to work brought about by modern individualism.
The opposite trend is a strengthening of fatherhood, which made its
appearance first in relation to the man as the mother's helper. Later,

from the 1980s onwards, following the North American example, the concept of 'new father' was adopted (cf Hester and Harne, 1999; Chapter Two in this volume). According to Huttunen, it can be used loosely to refer to any challenger to traditional fatherhood (for example, a helping or a participating father). New fatherhood can also mean a new orientation in the distribution of responsibility, based on shared parenthood. The new father is in this case as committed to parenthood as is his spouse, and both of them also bear an equal responsibility for housework, childcare and upbringing in practice.

Both psychological and societal benefits and necessities justify the ideology of new fatherhood. It is seen as beneficial to children, women and men alike. With this new ideology, a child gets two close adults in birth, which is considered especially good for boys. Women no longer need to bear the responsibility for the much-demanding parenthood alone, and their chances to combine it with paid employment in a satisfactory manner have become better. Men no longer need to repress their need for caring, which can open up new possibilities for maturity and a new kind of humane masculinity. In cases of divorce, the father's possibilities to continue a relationship with the children have become better (Huttunen, 1999, pp 188-91; Korhonen, 1999, p 93; Vuori, 2001, pp 356-8). Tigerstedt (1996, pp 266-7) argues that, when becoming reality, fully-fledged parenting is expected to bring new social opportunities and stability to men in particular amid the changing bonds of present-day life. Fatherhood carries, according to Tigerstedt, a 'big promise'.

At the same time, it is often hoped that new forms of masculinity in fatherhood will civilise men, so that they will no longer be violent. Säävälä (2000, p 16), for example, maintains that the negative phenomena belonging to masculinity, such as violence, might disappear if men learn to live with more consideration to other people and if they actively take part in childcare. According to Säävälä, this can become reality in two different ways. The widening of the variety of one's social tools gives new options in conflict situations; and, in turn, new ways of acting generate new dimensions to life.

The ideology of new fatherhood has also been criticised in the Finnish discussions. It has been said that it moves on the cultural or societal level and is too far from the reality of the day-to-day life of families (Huttunen, 1999, p 186). Also, people can still think that a father who cares for his children is too feminine. Even professionals in the field of parenting and education may be afraid that men and fathers will turn into 'men with no balls' amid the pressures of equality and calls for softness (see, for example, Sinkkonen, 1998, p 13).

Vuori (2001, pp 356-9), who has analysed Finnish expert texts, makes the critical remark that it is fathers who mostly reap the benefits of shared parenthood. What was originally intended as an increase in women's possibilities for choice only seems to augment mothers' causes for concern. Men are being encouraged to enjoy their fatherhood, but they are not expected to assume full responsibility. Different family professionals often emphasise that mothers should tempt fathers to fatherhood and support them when they care for the children. Vuori concludes that the new father is being constructed through the mother (cf Smart, 1999; Chapter Eight in this volume). The 'big promise' of the new fatherhood is one of the factors that can push the man's possible violence to the sidelines in research and helping work. This becomes particularly striking if only good fatherhood is underlined and the mere presence of the father is thought to bring wellbeing to the child(ren) (see, for example, Hester and Harne, 1999, p 157; Chapter Three in this volume). An excellent Finnish example of this kind of underlining of good fatherhood can be found in the Report of the Father Committee (Komiteanmietintö, 1999, pp 47-8) set up by the Ministry for Social Affairs and Health. The report says that, in a harmonious marriage and family, fatherhood is generally not a problem. It becomes a problem, according to the report, especially in divorce when the man is put in the unequal position of a defendant, which may lead to his social exclusion. The report does not take up the theme of how social problems and social exclusion, not to mention violence, are related to the quality of the practices of fathers.

The ideals of new fatherhood are indisputably well meaning and offer the possibility of a better life to men, women and children alike. We nevertheless need to ask critically what will follow if we use these ideals in our rhetoric and apply them in various situations in our legal system and in social work and social policy; in situations such as negotiations about children's affairs in connection with divorce.

Problems with child custody and contact arrangements

Great expectations and the sometimes very normative tone of discussions on fatherhood keep the researchers who write about fatherhood and violence on their toes. They have to consider carefully how to treat the theme, so as not to make people think that they are attacking fatherhood and men. The demand for sensitivity to the subject comes up especially when fatherhood and violence are attached to the problematics of custody and contact arrangements. For example, my ongoing research has this kind of focus and several times I have had comments from my researcher colleagues such as "Oh, you are sitting in a minefield". Fatherhood, violence and divorce are considered a flammable combination.

Marjo Kuronen (2003, pp 109-13), who has analysed the Finnish discussion and research on divorce, concludes that the public discussion about divorce has most often been concerned about the poor position of men (as is the case in other places as well, see Hester and Harne, 1999). In particular, there has been much worry about the continuation of fatherhood after divorce. Kuronen says that the most important question has been how to ensure the child's good relationship with the father who is not living in the same household anymore. Discussion and research on women's experiences of divorce or lone motherhood have been quite rare. Also, research on men's and women's parenting practices after divorce is minimal in Finland.

During my own work, I have followed discussions about divorce in the biggest newspapers and popular magazines in Finland and I have noticed that some basic arguments are repeated over and over again. It is claimed that women are better off after separation and that they get custody of the children because female social workers take sides with the mothers. It is also claimed that women often make false accusations about violence and sexual abuse and that professionals always take these accusations seriously. Men's alcoholism and homelessness can be seen as originating from difficult divorces. These kinds of arguments can be found in a broad range of media, and they often define the poor position of men as a serious issue of gender inequality. In this context, it is understandable that speaking of fathers' violence in relation to custody and contact arrangements could be seen as explosive.

Still, divorce is the central point at which the messy relation between fatherhood and violence also becomes focused and defined in public, in addition to being defined in private. However, there are currently no Finnish research findings available on how violence has impacted upon these negotiations and decisions.

In Finnish legislation, there are two main principles about how the separating parents are supposed to arrange child custody and contact visits after divorce (see Kurki-Suonio, 2000). These basic rules also apply to unmarried parents who have been cohabiting. One vital principle is that both mothers' and fathers' parenthood should continue after separation and that it will happen via joint custody and contact visits. The Act on child custody and contact that took effect in 1984 prioritised joint custody in all situations and the right to contact also became central. In her doctoral dissertation, Kurki-Suonio (1999, pp 440-557) has investigated how this law was developed and how it works in practice. She says that the shaping of these ideals is rooted in the psycho-scientific comments and writings of the time that underlined fathers' meaning in children's lives. In Finland, the driving force behind these reforms was the state-directed equality policy, and not the fathers' rights movements as in many other countries[8].

The other basic principle is that the parents should achieve an agreement about the custody of the children, their housing and right of contact. The ideal is written in the legislation and it is also widely carried out in practice (Kurki-Suonio, 1999, 2000). This goal can be reached through family mediation provided in municipal social services and also when the judges probe the chances of an agreement during the court proceedings. This principle is based on the assumption that an agreement between the separating parents is a far better starting point for the future and for the upbringing of the children than litigation (Auvinen, 2002, pp 158-9). On the other hand, lawyers may often feel that these kinds of family issues should not be handled in the courts (for example, Pettilä and Yli-Marttila, 1999, pp 36-7).

Issues concerning the custody of the children, and their residence and contact visits, are mostly dealt with by the social services. Parents can take part in family mediation and the social services can also ratify the contracts the parents have planned. Only about 10% of the separating parents use the court system and only half of this 10% have disputes in the court. In court cases, social workers often present a report that includes a description of the situation and a suggestion for the best possible solution (in a similar manner to court and family advisers in the English courts). In the disputed cases, 80% of the courts' decisions are made in accordance with the social workers' suggestion (Taskinen, 2001, pp 43-5; Auvinen, 2002, pp 113-68). Thus, social workers have a central role in custody and contact outcomes.

The principles I present above – the avoidance of custody disputes and the hope that both parents continue their parenting via joint custody and contact visits – are largely endorsed by public opinion and a variety of professionals. It is not usual to criticise these principles. Nevertheless, some lawyers and shelter workers have expressed their anxiety about these principles, because they see that the rules do not fit situations where violence prevails.

There are several concerns in child custody and contact rights practices (see also Chapters Two, Seven and Eight in this volume). It has been maintained that many women who have been subjected to violence are traumatised and become easily tired by the divorce process. They may agree to accept nearly all of the man's demands, so as to bring an end to the harassment and accusations and to get some peace. Hence, the ideal of equal negotiations does not ring true and the mediation process itself can mean a serious security risk for women. However, the father may continue pressurising and acting violently towards the mother and/or the children via contact visits. These visits may also give the man legal grounds for evading the restraining order imposed on him. Furthermore, joint custody, so popular in Finnish society, has not proved to be a good solution in situations that involve violence and in which the agreement has been made on the man's terms. According to both social workers and women subjected to violence, joint custody offers an abundance of possibilities for badgering, harassment and continuous intervention in the mother's affairs (Lehtonen and Perttu, 1999, p 101; Perttu et al, 1999, pp 22-4, 54; Oranen, 2001b, pp 92-3). However, according to the law, joint custody is prefer-able even in situations in which one of the parents is against it. When studying court cases, it has become evident that some mothers have referred to the father's use of violence as one reason why joint custody has been impossible in practice (Kurki-Suonio, 1999, pp 541-4).

Two tragedies took place in Finland in 2002, with the consequence that the problems of custody and child contact practices were in the headlines for a while. In July, a father killed himself and his three children by setting his house on fire. In October, a mother poisoned her six-year-old daughter. In both cases, there was a pending divorce, and the children were visiting the murderer-parent. In both cases, the other parent claimed afterwards that social services officials had not taken their concern for the children's safety seriously. After the death of the little girl in October, the Ministry for Social Affairs and Health appointed a working group to investigate how to prevent similar cases in the future and how to improve authorities' practices. The report of this working group (Työryhmämuistio, 2003) made several suggestions, beginning with enhancing the position of municipal child protection practices and developing cooperation between the authorities. That supervised contact visits are not equally available in different parts of the country was seen as a major problem. Organising them is not a part of the statutory social services. Another problem was that the separating parents and some of the professionals are not properly informed about the possibilities for arranging supervised contact visits. Judges are not accustomed to suggesting this. The report also mentions that in some cases contact should be fully denied because of the possible dangers or extreme strain caused to the child. Those cases are not specified in the text of this report.

Although the report notes the problems concerning visitation practices, it does not in any way take into consideration the difficulties connected with joint custody.

Although the report of this working group is brief and preliminary, the understandings created in it are not at all inconsequential because further action in the Ministry for Social Affairs and Health can be based on the suggestions made. From the text, it is possible to see that in Finland there is still strong resistance to conceptualising violence as a gendered phenomenon. For example, violence between the parents is dealt with in a gender-neutral way. Likewise, the psychodynamics of custody disputes are approached from a gender-neutral position. In my view, the risk factors concerning the child's safety will not be completely estimated if the evaluators do not carefully take into consideration how violence against women is connected with violence against children or how fathers' and mothers' violent behaviour differs in quantity, quality and dynamics.

Conclusion

In this chapter, I have reflected on the problems of fatherhood and violence in intimate relationships in the Finnish context and explored the reasons for the silence prevailing around this theme. It is important to look for reasons for the silence because it is often exactly in this silence that the most difficult and bitter conflicts exist in terms of research.

I see two factors in the conception of violence in intimate relationships that result in fatherhood being hidden from sight in relation to it. First of all, fatherhood remains unnoticed because we do not always have the courage to say that the violence was committed by men and that they are responsible for it. Second, violence is easily seen as a marital problem between two adults that has nothing to do with the issues of parenting. This means that we are ignoring the situation of children.

In the ways in which parenthood tends to be understood, I have found two further explanations for the fact that fatherhood and violence are seldom discussed simultaneously. The first is the gender complementary construction of parenthood; motherhood and fatherhood are social categories of a totally different character. The commitments and responsibilities of the two genders are defined differently, whether we speak about comfortable and smooth day-to-day life or violence-filled life. Even if new ways to be a mother and a father are developing little by little, the focus of parenthood is still very much on motherhood. Therefore, a violent man is generally not defined through his responsibilities as a father. The second explanation is that fatherhood as a concept is rhetorically strong today, and much is expected of its even greater future development. This too makes the discussion more difficult because, in this age of hope-filled fatherhood discourses, the talk about fathers' violence is very disconcerting. When fatherhood is being defined as solely positive, it is difficult to place violence alongside it.

Lastly, I discussed child custody and contact arrangements in relation to violence in intimate relationships. The guiding principles of Finnish legislation are that parents should try to be reconciled and both parents should have a close and warm relationship with the child, also after separation, via joint custody. From the perspective of violence against women and children, extensive compliance with these principles is really a major problem: for these principles can increase the risk of physical or psychological harm done. At the same time, the public discussion around these issues is often about men's misery after divorce, which further turns attention away from considerations of men's violence.

Notes

[1] This chapter is a translated and revised version of an article previously published in the Finnish journal *Janus* (2002), vol 10, no 3, pp 237-49.

[2] The first and so far only Finnish national survey on men's violence towards women was carried out in 1997. The data were collected by a postal questionnaire and nearly 5,000 women, aged 18 to 74, responded. According to this survey, 22% of Finnish women have been the targets of their present spouse's physical or sexual violence or threat of violence, and as many as half of the previously married or cohabiting women have been the targets of their ex-husband's or ex-partner's violence or threat of violence (Heiskanen and Piispa, 1998, pp 4-13).

[3] For a further discussion of the problems with the concept of family violence, as well as the idea of symmetry in intimate violence, see, for example, Dobash and Dobash (1992, 2004) and Johnson (1998).

[4] In their review of current research on men in Finland, Hearn and Lattu (2002) show that there is a large amount of Finnish research relevant to the study of men but that many of these studies do not provide a gendered analysis of men. Hearn and Lattu also argue that until recently there has

been almost a complete absence of critical studies on men and violence in Finland.

[5] It should be noted that the harm done to children when they witness violence is now recognised in English legislation (2002 Adoption and Children Act).

[6] For a further discussion about the problems with using mothers' reports to estimate the victimisation of children, see Mullender et al (2002).

[7] It should be noted that this figure cannot be found in the original report (Heiskanen and Piispa, 1998) but is often quoted in media and research.

[8] For a discussion of how equality politics and fathers' rights movements have been part of the force for change elsewhere, see Hester and Harne (1999), Eriksson and Hester (2001) and Eriksson (2003).

SIX

Marching on the spot? Dealing with violence against women in Norway

Wenche Jonassen

Little has been done to create new measures for victims of violence or to improve the quality of existing public agencies in Norway. The problems of women exposed to violence seem to be more or less left to be solved by non-governmental organisations (NGOs) through shelters for battered women. Violence against women has been politically acknowledged as a serious social problem for more than two decades. Despite this, there is a long way to go before one can say that services for battered women are satisfactory. What kinds of measures have been taken to tackle the problem during this time? What are the current challenges of working with violence against women? And finally, is there any reason to look to Norway to learn how to deal with problems of violence?

   This chapter describes the development in the field of violence against women during the past 20 years. The aim is to illustrate how political objectives do not in themselves necessarily result in definite measures to solve problems, and, furthermore, how an issue such as men's violence has to be put on the political agenda over and over again before real change can be achieved. The analysis is mainly based on two studies on battered women's shelters in Norway carried out with a 16-year interval (Jonassen, 1987; Jonassen and Stefansen, 2003).

What measures have been provided for women exposed to violence in Norway?

The first shelter for battered women opened up in Oslo by a feminist group and with public funding in 1978. Within a few years, the voices that claimed that women's groups were exaggerating when they presented the extent of violence against women declined. Local women's groups belonging to different political parties challenged their fellow politicians to address the problem. Before long, there was an agreement across political party lines to put the problem on the national political agenda. Women employees (and some men) in state and local authorities showed their solidarity with the women's movement and, later on, the shelter movement, by supporting the demands for establishing shelters. This broad support made things easier when members of the shelter movement applied for funding and asked for cooperation with established public services and other public bodies. In 1986, there were 46 shelters for battered women in Norway. The shelters provide temporary accommodation and protection, offer counselling and advice, impart public and other support, and some have temporary housing possibilities. In addition, some shelters offer support to children. It is of great importance for the shelter residents to have the possibility to meet other women facing the same problems as themselves. In addition, there were 11 telephone groups running consultative services. From 1982 onwards, the state authorities established a funding system for shelters that was based on a 50-50 share between local and state authorities. The sum of money that was granted to the shelters from the local authorities resulted in the same amount of funding from the state. This led to considerable differences, which still exist, in budgets between shelters.

In 1983, a government plan of action, Measures Against Violence Against Women[1], was promoted by a group of representatives from different state ministries in Norway (Interdepartemental arbeidsgruppe, 1983). Battered women's shelters had revealed the problem of violence against women to be greater than expected. Research showed that public measures did not function very well for the target group (Malterud, 1981). A report based on interviews with battered women showed that the shelter for battered women in Oslo functioned better than any of the public agencies with which the informants had been in contact (Nisja and Aslaksen, 1980). Almost two decades later, in 2000, a new government plan of action was put forward (Justis- og politidepartementet et al, 2000). Let us have a look at what has happened in this field during the period between these two plans of action, and what progress there has been since then.

Strengthening shelters for battered women

The 1983 plan of action stated that shelters for battered women were considered to be the most important measure for the target group. Since shelters were unevenly distributed throughout the country, the plan suggested that the establishment of new shelters should take into consideration equal accessibility for women, no matter where they lived. The plan suggested that employees in charge of running the shelters should have a regular salary, while 'volunteers' should get some kind of allowance. Local authorities were encouraged to support the work at the shelters, and at the same time to create better public services for battered women.

Twenty years later, little has changed. Since 1986, only four more shelters have been established. Norway, with a population of 4.5 million people, now (summer 2004) possesses 50 shelters and one crisis telephone[2]. According to the new plan of action on violence against women, which lasted for three years, the shelters for battered women, mostly run by NGOs, were still seen as the most important measure for battered women.

During this 20-year period, the shelter groups have been continuously fighting for their existence. Unlike the shelter movement in many other countries, Norwegian women in principle want all work within the shelters to be paid. They argue that women's work should be taken seriously. To run shelters is an important contribution to solving a social problem that ought to have been solved by public authorities. How far the shelters are able to pay for all the work within them and to what extent they are able to pay salaries, varies a great deal. In 2003, the budgets of the shelters ranged from 11,400 to 1,123,000 euros. In the same year, 40% of the shelters were run wholly by paid staff on regular salaries, while 60% were run partly by paid staff and partly by volunteers with some sort of allowances. Only one shelter was run by a group of women where no one held a regular salary. On average, shelters possess a better economy than they used to have, but many of them have an unpredictable budget situation, and do not know from one year to the next what their financial situation is going to be. A few shelters have been forced to close down. Between 2001 and 2002, 12% of the shelters had their budgets cut (Jonassen and Stefansen, 2003).

All shelters in Norway have been established on the initiative of local groups of women. No consideration has been given to the needs for shelters in different areas according to population, geographical accessibility or any other survey of demands has been carried out prior to new establishments. This has resulted in a very unequal distribution of shelters in different parts of the country. At one end of the scale, there is a shelter in a rural district covering 5,500 inhabitants. At the other end of the scale, the largest shelter (Oslo) covers 510,000 inhabitants. In some areas, women have to travel 300 kilometres to get to the nearest shelter. The number of women residents at different shelters varies considerably – between one and 355 in 2003, for example (Jonassen, 2004).

Public agencies supporting victims of violence

In the 1983 plan of action, social welfare agencies and healthcare agencies were encouraged to improve their services towards battered women by increasing accessibility and raising the qualifications of their staff. The plan proposed that staff should be trained to know more about problems of violence, for example, knowledge about how to identify and meet victims, about perpetrators and about other adequate assistance and treatment strategies. Healthcare agencies were asked to be more accessible and contribute to strengthen women's independence. Staff members were expected to improve their knowledge about battered women and increase their awareness about the consequences of exposure to violence. In addition, the plan advocated the provision of day and night services at the social welfare agencies. Healthcare services were also encouraged to record the extent and type of their clients' exposure to violence. Collaboration between the police, social welfare agencies and healthcare agencies were expected to improve. The plan also suggested that social welfare agencies should test and evaluate different methods of intervention with regard to victims of violence and perpetrators.

In 1986, the first state-run service for rape and sexual assault was established in Oslo. This service was later expanded to become an agency for other victims of violence. In 1990, the state health authorities suggested that all the local authorities throughout Norway should establish a corresponding service (Nesvold, 1997). Initiatives have been taken to establish programmes for rape victims at hospitals throughout the country, but cases are few, especially in rural areas, and this results in the measures falling apart. Norway is a sparsely populated country, and these measures do not seem to be very well known by the general public. A lack of cases creates lack of practice for the professionals who were supposed to operate these relief programmes. The measures seem mainly to work in the larger cities of Norway. In addition, larger municipalities like Oslo have established a service for victims of violence (not just rape) with trained healthcare staff and social workers. Staff members are trained to carry out adequate physical examinations of victims, and they also offer counselling and accompany victims to the police or other support agencies when necessary. Few other cities have corresponding services.

A few local municipalities have offered training programmes on domestic violence to professionals working within public health and social services. In 1998, the municipality of Oslo offered a training programme for employees working with victims of violence, perpetrators and prostitutes. Representatives of services outside the municipality, like the battered women's shelters, the police and family counselling services, were also invited to attend. The training programme led to increased collaboration between professionals in different services within Oslo, and the participants felt more secure when meeting victims of violence and perpetrators than they did previously (Jonassen, 2001).

One of the aims of the new government's 2000 plan of action was to arrange conferences on domestic violence for professionals throughout the country. The plan proposed special training programmes for healthcare workers and for staff at battered women's shelters. Five regional conferences on domestic violence were organised for healthcare professionals, social workers, the police, staff at the battered women's shelters and other NGOs. State politicians intend to increase the level of competence within the field of violence against women, but the money available to do this is very limited and progress is slow.

Shortcomings of family counselling

The 1983 plan of action called upon family counselling services to evaluate methods used in working with those in relationships where violence is part of the problem. Evaluation showed that family counsellors did not see violence as an important issue in conflicts between family members. Family counselling methods derived from a systemic perspective did not seem to work well with couples where one partner was exposed to violence. The 2000 plan of action repeated the request for evaluation of this method within family counselling agencies. Family counselling agencies are now more aware of their shortcomings in working with domestic violence and some have started to work with groups of violent men to stop the abuse.

Monitoring and recording

The government's 2000 plan of action repeated the suggestion from the 1983 plan that public agencies – particularly the police, the courts, social welfare agencies and agencies providing healthcare – should start recording cases of violence against women. The agencies were also encouraged to coordinate the recordings. Some new routines for recording have been developed since 1983. Many different agencies do monitor cases of violence. The problem is that, except for the police and battered women's shelters, they do not use the same kind of recording forms and the monitoring between agencies is not coordinated (Hjemdal and Stefansen, 2003). This means that data between agencies are incomparable.

Violence on the curricula for professionals

An important aim of the 1983 plan of action was to incorporate domestic violence into the training curricula of police officers, healthcare and social workers. The same was suggested in the 2000 plan of action. In spite of repeated suggestions, however, domestic violence is still not on the syllabus when training police officers, social workers, nurses, medical doctors, psychologists, priests, and so on. Oslo University College has offered a limited postgraduate course on elder abuse to professionals, and in the autumn of 2004 ran a postgraduate course on domestic violence that will be offered as a permanent course in the future. Courses on violence are offered at different colleges and universities, but not on a regular basis. It is up to individual students to decide whether they want to include this topic in the curriculum.

Improving the situation of battered women

The 1983 plan of action considered different measures to improve women's financial situation when leaving violent partners/spouses. The plan was also concerned with the need to support women and children who moved out of the shelters, either back to the perpetrator or separated from him. The measures that exist for women leaving violent partners in 2004 are still the same as they are for women leaving non-violent marriages/partnerships. Thirty-four per cent of battered women's shelters offer personal support (by volunteers) to women who leave the shelter. Three out of 50 shelters have an arrangement with social welfare agencies that provide this kind of support (Jonassen and Stefansen, 2003).

Improving housing possibilities

In 1983, the lack of housing possibilities made women stay in shelters for longer than they wished. The 1983 plan of action suggested that the authorities should find ways of improving housing possibilities for disadvantaged persons. The problem still exists in 2004. The number of shelter residents fluctuates from year to year: between 1992 and 2003, it has varied between 2,200 and 2,900 women[3]. The number of days women stay in shelters has on average increased a little: it fluctuated in the same period from 23 to 35 nights a year on average. For many of the women staying in the shelters, it is hard to find an alternative place to live. The problem seems to be especially difficult for women from ethnic minorities. In 2002, only 16% of the shelters had access to a temporary accommodation where women and their children could stay until they found a permanent place to live (Jonassen and Stefansen, 2003).

Children in shelters

The 1983 plan of action was concerned about the situation of children who stayed in shelters. An evaluation report of the shelter in Oslo had shown that many of the children were unhappy due to lack of space, with few opportunities for doing homework, playing, and so on (Nisja and Aslaksen, 1980). The Ministry of Social Affairs was encouraged to work out a proposal for creating measures relevant to children while they were staying in shelters. Very little happened before 1998, at which point a report on children's situation in the shelter in Oslo was published (Olsen, 1998). The report was quite critical about conditions for children in the shelter and members of the shelter movement were exasperated. The author of the report claimed that by focusing on the women (mothers), the staff at the shelter failed to see the needs of the children. The children were witnessing women in crises and traumatised mothers were asked to take care of their children. Reactions to the content of the report seemed to lead to stronger emphasis on the matter, and in the following years the Ministry of Children and Family Affairs granted money for projects to find out what could be done to improve the children's situation. Many shelters altered their routines to improve conditions for children. In 2002, 28% of the shelters had employed staff specifically to work with children. Eighty per cent of the shelters could offer babysitting to women staying in the shelter, and 24% to women who visited the shelter during the day (this might be done, for example, when women needed time to contact other assistance agencies, and so on). Twenty-four per cent of the shelters had a child group arrangement, and 30% offered other activities for children. More than half of the shelters (52%) made arrangements to facilitate contact between children staying at the shelter and their fathers, in cases where the fathers were entitled to see their children (Jonassen and Stefansen, 2003). However, the situation for children at the shelters is still far from satisfactory and is repeatedly put forward as an issue by the shelter organisations and by the Minister for Children and Family Affairs.

Legal improvements

At the time when the 1983 plan of action was written, there existed an arrangement for free legal aid for battered women, and a possibility for the police to institute a victimless prosecution against the perpetrator when victims did not wish to prosecute. Victims of violence were also entitled to apply for compensation from public authorities in cases where the partner or spouse was the perpetrator. Since 1983, some legal changes have occurred that have improved the situation for battered women. The compensation for victims of violence has now been legalised and the monetary limit to which the victim may be entitled has been increased. Abused women from ethnic minorities without Norwegian citizenship may now be allowed to stay in the country if they divorce their husbands. Victims of violence are entitled to have up to 10 hours of free legal aid. Rape victims and other victims of serious cases of violence (penal cases) are entitled to a legal representative paid for by the government (as many hours as needed). Following a legal verdict in 1995, which ruled that a restraint order can be imposed on a perpetrator, the perpetrator is not allowed to approach the house where his victim lives. Since 2002, the perpetrator can be held in custody immediately if the restraint order is broken. Since 1997, victims of violence have been provided with alarms. By the end of 2002, 897 victims in Norway kept alarms and, between 1997 and 2002, 3,052 had been provided with alarms for a shorter or longer period of time. Ninety per cent of the alarm holders were women[4].

New measures following the government's 2000 plan of action

As we have seen, many of the proposals in the 2000 plan of action had already been suggested in the earlier plan of 1983. New measures in the 2000 plan of action, which had not been proposed before, were as follows.

Coordinator of the plan of action

Four different ministries working on issues related to violence against women supported the 2000 plan of action. The Ministry of Justice was given the role of coordinator and a minister appointed accordingly.

In connection with the plan, a committee on violence against women [*Kvinnevoldsutvalget*] was established and given the task of reporting on issues concerning violence against women in Norway.

The committee suggested an alteration of the subsidy arrangement for battered women's shelters, and proposed a new law to secure a minimum standard of equal access to shelters on a national level (Kvinnevoldsutvalget, 2002; Justis- og politidepartementet, 2003). Kvinnevoldsutvalget [Committee on Violence against Women] proposed that staff at the shelters should be given the opportunity to improve their qualifications and the quality of measures offered to children. It also suggested that funding be improved to allow for the provision of staff training programmes corresponding to the increased demands placed on the shelters. The committee also suggested that shelters for battered women should be secured by establishing a law demanding all local municipalities to financially support a shelter. The committee has also made suggestions about improvements and enforcement of the juridical system, and about improving relief measures for victims of violence.

Experimental projects

Three (out of 434) municipalities were given grants to create models on how best to improve relief measures for victims of violence. The experimental projects were funded by the government for a period of three years.

Police asked to increase their efficiency

The police were asked to sharpen their efficiency in solving cases of domestic violence and to expedite cases of violence in court. Generally, cases concerning violence against women have been given low priority by the police (Justis- og politidepartementet, 2003). Another improvement concerning police work in this field was the establishment of domestic violence coordinators in each of the 27 Norwegian police districts. These positions came into force in July 2002. Two years later (in 2004), however, it turned out that only five out of the 27 appointments were full time. The other coordinators were part time or the task of attending domestic violence cases was done in addition to pre-existing duties[5].

Increased protection for threatened persons

The new plan of action recommended further consideration of the question of increased protection for threatened persons, including a new identity. In 2003, about 1,000 persons, most of them women, had been given a new identity.

Research and evaluation

The 2000 plan of action proposed a research project to systematise and adapt the knowledge that has been developed through different measures in the treatment of violent men in Norway. This has been addressed through the book *Menns vold mot kvinner* [*Men's violence against women*][6], in which different clinical and research workers share their experiences from treatment and research done on men who have used violence against their partners (Råkil, 2002).

In addition, a new research programme was established on domestic violence and gender violence. The programme ran from 2000 to 2004 and covered eight projects, with special focus on children and youngsters exposed to violence.

Raising competence of staff in battered women's shelters

Battered women's shelters are still considered to be the most important measure in supporting women exposed to violence. However, the new plan of action says that experience shows that the assistance given at such shelters has certain limitations, especially when it comes to helping victims with psychosocial problems. The plan had recommended a training programme for staff at the shelters to address these limitations. As was mentioned earlier in the chapter, the training programme took the form of conferences attended by professionals and staff from a variety of different services and NGOs. The government paid for one person from each shelter to attend a conference, but the rest of the participants had to pay for themselves. In Norway, there are close to 1,000 people working at the shelters. Only 107 persons participated in the conferences (some of them as lecturers).

Another initiative was for staff at the shelters to be given regular guidance from professionals with high levels of competence in dealing with victims of violence. In 2002, 26% of the shelters received guidance free of charge from local authorities. In addition, 22% received guidance financed by the shelter (Jonassen and Stefansen, 2003). The new plan also stated that battered women's shelters should have a solid and predictable financial basis. The Ministry of Children and Family Affairs was to encourage the shelters to allow local political representatives to be on the boards. Indeed, the Prime Minister of Norway mentioned the shelters for battered women in his new year's speech on TV on 1 January 2003, saying that the shelters were to be given more support. A few days later, however, the Minister for Children and Family Affairs said to the media that there was no money available for the shelters. Again, despite the political intention to support work with victims of violence, it seems as if those efforts are not expected to cost very much.

Old ideas in new bottles

Politicians change and history is forgotten or was never known. Old political suggestions are repeatedly presented in new 'outfits'. The Minister of Justice gave a public speech in 2001 where she presented the proposals of the 2000 plan of action as if for the first time, albeit that she seemed to be sincere and to want to do something to improve the situation for battered women. The same seems to be true of the Minister of Justice in 2004. The current government has decided to follow up the previous government's 2000 plan of action with a new plan of action targeted at combating domestic violence (Barne- og familiedepartementet, 2002).

As far as reducing the problem of violence against women is concerned, there is reason to say that improvements have been limited during the past 20 years. There have been a few changes in the legal system to protect victims of violence and there is now the possibility of higher compensation in cases where violence has caused the victim severe physical damage. However, there is still no regular training for professionals in the field of violence, either through college or university education, and only a few courses on offer to professionals. The competence of professionals in this field has mainly been gained either through the professionals' own experiences with victims of violence or their personal efforts to learn more about the subject.

What are the challenges in the field of battered women?

New groups asking for assistance

There are different aspects to consider when discussing problems of violence against women and what can be done to fight the problem.

First of all, the ethnicity of those battered women who apply for assistance at different agencies has changed during the past 10 to 15 years. All European countries have received migrants from other countries. Throughout Europe, many more shelter residents are migrants and/or from ethnic minorities than before. Liz Kelly (2002) questions the adequacy of shelter models and how appropriately they are staffed for meeting the needs of the women. Can we find new ways to run shelters that will improve their functioning?

In 2003, 45% of the women who stayed in battered women's shelters in Norway belonged to ethnic minorities (Jonassen, 2004). In the city of Oslo, they amounted to 73% of shelter residents, and 89% of those spending the night at the shelter (Oslo Krisesenter, 2004). There is reason to believe that people from minority ethnic groups and other cultures represent a challenge for both battered women's shelters and public support agencies. A large proportion of women from minority ethnic groups asking for support from shelters seem to have poor knowledge of Norwegian, and are therefore in many cases in need of an interpreter. They also need more comprehensive assistance from a larger number of agencies than do ethnic Norwegian women. Extra resources in terms of use of time and money are therefore required to help them. For many shelters, this represents a significant problem and may result in assistance of a poorer quality. In Norway, women from ethnic minorities seem to know little about social welfare and benefit systems, healthcare systems and agencies that can help them if they leave a violent relationship (Jonassen and Eidheim, 2001; Nilsen and Prøis, 2002).

Other previously unseen groups entering battered women's shelters are women who are the victims of 'trafficking', and women from other countries who, with the expectation of a better material life, marry Norwegian men they do not know (so-called 'mail order brides'). Shelters all over the country have residents from within this latter category. Compared with their number in the overall population, they seem to be overrepresented as shelter residents (Smaadahl et al, 2002). In 2003, 29% of shelter residents from ethnic minorities (181 out of 616) were exposed to violence by Norwegian men (Jonassen, 2004). Shelter organisations have been concerned about this development and have suggested to the authorities that Norwegian men who apply to marry a woman from a foreign country should have their criminal record sent to the women in question. However, proposals like this raise many ethical questions.

The need to increase the quality of the shelters

Kelly (2002) suggests that staff working in shelters should listen more carefully to what kinds of assistance women and children are asking for. She gives an example of women in the UK who wanted to stay in their violent relationships while their partners attended treatment programmes. Only when treatment did not work were these women ready to leave their partners. Listening to women, rather than just measuring outcomes of treatment programmes, taught staff working at the shelters something important and profound about the role men's programmes can play in women's empowerment. Even if all evaluations of agency responses give a shelter the highest satisfaction rating, Kelly suggests that there is still room for improvement. In addition to practical support and safety, many women need help with extensive physical and psychological damage. Kelly highlights the diversity of needs expressed by women who have been exposed to violence. This is also an issue in Norway, where criticism of battered women's shelters has been related to the fact that emphasis is mainly placed on juridical solutions; and that the shelters have less to offer women who ask for assistance to work on their relationship with their violent partners (Haaland, 1997).

Keeping society aware of the problem

All over the Western world, there seems to have been an attitude change on the question of violence against women among politicians, professionals and the public in general since the battered women's movement first came on the scene. Kelly (2002) finds that in both industrialised and developing countries there is a growing intolerance of violence against women, and domestic violence in particular. However, efforts to raise awareness on violence against women has to be maintained. The public needs to be continually reminded that violence should not be tolerated. The legal system has shown some improvement in its dealings with women victims of violence, but there is still a long way to go before women can feel respected in the court system when it comes to cases concerning sexual harassment and rape.

To combat violence against women, we still need to highlight the problem through research and through the activity of interest groups. Different political issues receive a different emphasis at different times, and public money seems to be directed towards the problems with the largest headlines in the media. Violence against women, for example, was a hot political issue in the media for a while around 1980; then there was a gap of many years when the problem had a low profile among public agencies. Since 2000, political focus has again been directed at domestic violence in Norway. The lesson seems to be that continual effort is needed to alert politicians to the problem of battered women and domestic violence; and also to produce professionals who are competent, able to relate to victims and who can contribute to solving the problem.

Lesley McMillan is concerned about what happens to shelter groups when they receive state money (McMillan, 2002). She asks whether shelters funded by state authorities will ever stop criticising government policies. Norwegian shelters have always been funded by money from local and central authorities. Their organisations continue to criticise the authorities. It might be true, however, that shelters that have been incorporated into local authorities and obtain their salaries directly from them do seem to try to collaborate with their employers before they go public with issues they wish to criticise. Shelters in Norway used to spend more time highlighting violence against women as a political issue during the first 10 years of their existence. Now their priorities seem to be concentrated on the wellbeing and safety of women who have been exposed to violence, sexual assault or child abuse; as is the case with shelters in Sweden and the UK. At the same time, one of the two Norwegian shelter organisations has hired leaders who seem to have reactivated the shelter movement as a political force. This does seem to depend more on the person in charge of the organisation than on any renewed political engagement of the shelter groups as a whole, but it works. The issues of battered women and domestic violence are in the headlines more often and the spokeswoman of the shelter movement [*Krisesentersekretariatet*] is usually asked for an opinion in high-profile cases related to domestic violence.

Improving services for battered women

Up till now, measures for victims of violence have only to a small extent been based on evaluation and research about what works and what does not work. Women rate their experience of assistance highly if the person providing the service is motivated to help the woman and shows some empathy for her case. If the shelter worker is knowledgeable about problems of violence and knows what kinds of agency can provide help, then the woman feels that she is well provided for (Jonassen and Eidheim, 2001). It is clear from this that a curriculum on domestic violence has to be included in education programmes for healthcare personnel and social workers.

In addition, local authorities have to take responsibility for establishing measures that work well for battered women: for example, provision in areas where the access to battered women's shelters is scarce. Even more important is the task of making professionals recognise the competences that can be used in working with victims of violence, and of providing training programmes on how different agencies can meet the challenges of domestic violence. Kelly (2002) claims that when it comes to professional services in the UK, the problem has shifted from one of silence about domestic violence to one of a refusal to listen and act on the part of those who are told. She points to research showing that institutions have knowledge that they neither recognise nor use.

Improving security

The establishment of shelters for battered women was a great improvement in the way in which women exposed to violence were treated. The availability of personal alarms and the change in the legal system giving police the power to take into custody immediately perpetrators who break restraint orders have added to the women's feelings of safety. Like Canada, Austria and more recently Sweden, Norway has given battered women and their children the right to stay in the home when the relationship has ended – another improvement in the treatment of women exposed to violence.

Slow progress

There are many experiences and incidents to indicate that the intention of tackling the problem of violence exists, but progress is slow. In spite of all the shortcomings, there are still reasons for thinking that things seem to be moving in the right direction. Battered women who turned to different agencies for assistance in 2000 appeared to be more likely to encounter empathetic professionals who were willing to help them compared with battered women in the study from 1987 (Jonassen, 1987; Jonassen and Eidheim, 2001). In addition, the battered women participating in the 2000 study encountered extra assistance from people working in agencies such as banks when they were acquainted with the situation the women were in. Attitudes among police officers towards battered women also seem to have become more positive since the earlier study. In addition, domestic violence has received more attention in the press and other media, more research on violence against women is being carried out within and across countries, and more and more conferences are being held for researchers, professionals and representatives from NGOs working in the field of violence.

As this book went to press, a new plan of action was being put forward by the Norwegian government in June 2004 (Justis- og politidepartementet, 2004). This new plan, entitled *Vold i nære relasjoner* [Violence in close relationships][7], has four main aims:

- to strengthen collaboration between agencies working with victims of violence, and to raise the level of competence of professionals working in public support agencies;
- to make violence in close relationships more visible as a public problem that can be prevented through attitude change;
- to ensure that victims of violence in close relationships receive the necessary assistance and protection; and
- to break the spiral of violence by improving treatment possibilities for violators.

The Minister of Justice claims that 100 million Norwegian kroner (12 million euros) are being granted to fulfil the plan[8]. This sum apparently includes all those measures on domestic violence that were already operational before the new plan was activated. Even if the eventual sum granted is smaller than this, the persisting political focus on this issue is of inestimable value to the cause. At the same time, one has to treat the promises in the latest plan with caution. A brief glance at the outline of the new plan shows a number of features recurring from the two previous plans: for instance, the intention to provide financial security for shelters, to raise the competence of professionals working in public support agencies, and to strengthen collaboration between assistance agencies. Is there any reason to believe they will better succeed this time?

Conclusion

There are many questions that need to be answered after more than two decades of work within the field of battered women. Why has so little been done to fight the problem, in spite of political agreement and several plans of actions on the matter? Why are shelters for battered women the only one measure directed specifically at the target group? Why has no one established a public shelter or other kind of public measure for battered women? Do politicians grant small amounts of money to the cause to dampen down feminist criticism? Do politicians believe the problem does not require significant financial investment? Is the lack of engagement from professionals on the issue due to the fact that the problem is still taboo and therefore too difficult to deal with? Can the reason for lack of interest among professionals be explained by the fact that current research more frequently associates violence with the lower classes of society (see Pape and Stefansen, 2004), so that it has a lower profile than other types of problems? How is it that professionals do not recognise their competence and fail to use it in working with victims of violence? Why is violence not an issue in educational programmes for doctors, nurses, social workers, police officers, psychologists and others? Why are there so few postgraduate courses on violence issues directed towards professionals?

Given Norway's response to the problem of battered women, there is no reason for other countries to look to Norway to find an ideal model for themselves. It seems more as if Norway 'marches on the spot' in this matter. However, the government appeared to be much more serious in its treatment of the 2000 plan of action on violence against women than was the case with the plan of action two decades earlier. Kvinnevoldsutvalget suggested a variety of ways to fight problems related to violence against women. Quite a few of these suggestions are to be found in the new 2004 plan of action on violence in close relationships.

Even though progress is slow, and funding is at a minimum, I do believe that Norway is heading in the right direction as far as fighting the problem of violence against women is concerned. At a Nordic conference on women's movements in June 2004, the director of the division for gender equality at the Ministry of Industry, Employment and Communication in Sweden, Marianne Laxén, asked the audience if they really thought that 5,000 years of patriarchy could be beaten by 30 years of battle by the women's movement. I suppose the problem of violence against women can be looked upon in the same way. The progress in fighting the problem is far too slow, but we are hopefully heading in the right direction.

Notes

[1] Author's translation.

[2] Cf the situation in England and Wales, where approximately 570 refuges, helplines, outreach services and advice centres are organised by Women's Aid in England and Wales, and Rape Crisis (see www.womensaid.org.uk; www.welshwomensaid.org.uk; www.rapecrisis.org.uk, accessed 4 January 2005). There is a shelter, refuge or helpline per 88,000 people in Norway compared with 93,000 people in England and Wales (the population of England and Wales was estimated at almost 53 million in 2003).

[3] Cf the situation in England, where approximately 143,000 women and 114,500 children were supported by the 500 Women's Aid projects in 2001/02 (www.womensaid.org.uk, accessed 4 January 2005).

[4] Information given by adviser Stig Winge in *Politidirektoratet* [the Police Directorate]. Currently (2004), an evaluation of the alarm arrangements is ongoing.

[5] Article in the newspaper, *Verdens Gang*, 24 May 2004.

[6] Author's translation. The book is about the situation in Norway.

[7] Author's translation.

[8] *Dagsavisen*, 25 June 2004 [Norwegian newspaper].

SEVEN

Children's peace? The possibility of protecting children by means of criminal law and family law

Gudrun Nordborg

Det som händer	What happens
är förbjudet	is forbidden
det är så till den milda grad förbjudet	so very forbidden
att det inte finns	that it doesn't exist
ingen tror	nobody believes
på det som inte finns	that which doesn't exist
ingen ser	nobody sees
ingen låtsas om	nobody cares
också jag vet	I, too, know
att det är förbjudet	that it's forbidden
därför händer det	therefore it doesn't happen
åtminstone inte mig	at least not to me

This poem was written by Karolina Kraft (Kraft, 2000, p 21). The forbidden happened to her. The forbidden also happened to her as a mother and thus violence has also affected her children. Many brave testimonies have contributed to the fact that violence, which before was totally private, has been highlighted to such an extent that it has become a public, political issue in Sweden, resulting in a series of reforms aimed at curtailing violence by men towards women and children. But this violence has recently been forbidden! At the same time, a father's right to have access to his children has been strengthened. The legislator prioritises shared custody and increased rights of contact with the children. What are the consequences of this for those who seek to use the law to protect children against continued assaults by the man and father who has used violence?

This chapter will elucidate the changes in legal positions of women and children within intimate relations in criminal and family law when these relations are charged with sexualised violence. I wish to make visible the child in the gendered conflict of the adult world. Ultimately, I seek to problematise the current law in relation to human rights. This chapter begins with a few perspectives on the law before moving on to analyse the possibilities of protecting children, using examples from Swedish law.

The power of the law

Within the Nordic tradition, the written law is a weighty instrument of social control. The articles of the law can be regarded as frozen politics. The words of the law reflect officially accepted values and constructions, including those that pertain to the relations between the sexes and what relations between children and parents should be like. Thus, the law is a powerful political instrument for creating and recreating gender, as it is for creating and recreating the relations between adults and children. The law is power, it distributes power and can break power by re-evaluating what the positions of individuals should be in relation to each other.

At the same time, it is obvious that the articles of the law do not automatically translate the norm into reality and turn 'should be' into 'is'. Karolina Kraft was forced to realise this. In addition, her poem shows that the effect of the law can be such that it contributes to the concealment of what it wants to forbid.

Historically, the law has regulated events within the public sphere, which for a long time was dominated by men. The fact that the law begins to concern private, intimate relationships means that it must handle significances of masculinity and femininity, and also take into account the child's perspective. These are still big challenges.

Only a few generations back Sweden had an extremely patriarchal family model. The man, husband, master had all the power. He ruled over his woman's time, labour, economy, body and sexuality. He, as sole custodian, ruled over the children. He had the right to use violence for educational purposes, that is, corporal punishment, towards his woman and children. The family was a lawless space. The will of the man, the father, *was* the 'law' for women and children. About 150 years ago, a long series of enforced, cautious reforms was begun in Sweden that loosened a number of patriarchal bonds[1]. Today, women have the same formal rights as men. The existing rules have been opened to women. But these rules, which have been created by and for men, have rarely been changed to also fit the living conditions of women. The reforms are contradictory (see, for example, Eisenstein,

1988). The rules both presume and conceal the fact that man/ masculinity is still the norm. The paradox can also be seen in the way that the law is based on the assumption that the sexes are alike, while society at large still positions and values women and men differently.

Despite this, it is important to emphasise that the development of relative equality has reduced the significance of sex. The opportunities for women and men, girls and boys both publicly and privately have increased. Many of the borders between what has been seen as traditionally female or male can now be crossed. Perhaps this is exactly why the body and sexuality have become more visible, often in combination with power and violence. Perhaps this is also why children, particularly girls, are sexualised more clearly within advertising, toy production, and within 'high culture' as well (cf Mellberg, 1997).

It took a long time before protection and rights connected with women's right of self-determination on their work, body and sexuality became political issues. Only from the 1970s onwards are the latter questions fully included in the political agenda. The women's movement was a significant force in lobbying for this. The demands were supported particularly by research produced by women and they could be handled by a growing group of female politicians. Thus, a requirement for the reforms to happen was that women gained formal political and financial rights and used them. However, without support from a number of men, the reforms would not have been possible. In Sweden, women are not yet represented in politics in relation to their proportion of the population.

Women's experiences have led to changes in the legislation. Women have become actors in the public sphere. Children are not yet there. However, the stories of many women have included experiences from their own childhood. Others describe experiences as mothers trying to protect their children (Mellberg, 2002). Through deeper insights into women's experiences of violence, the vulnerability of children is also exposed.

Children's century?

The 20th century was proclaimed as the children's century by, among others, Ellen Key. While women 'have gained' rights and status as individuals, at least resembling those of men, children are still at the beginning of this process in relation to adults. There are two reforms in Swedish criminal law that are particularly valuable from the viewpoint of children: those concerning incest and corporal punishment. Up to 1937, both parties were considered responsible in incest crimes. This attitude reflected, among others, the view that all sexual activity outside marriage was a sin and, at the same time, criminalised. Tendencies towards changes in these attitudes started appearing in the 1860s. Only in 1937 did this contribute to the acknowledgement of the child as victim and the adult as the sole responsible perpetrator because of the imbalance of power in cases of incest. There still are suspected perpetrators who claim that the little girl had been seductive or wished to be sexually initiated. This might result in discontinuation of a preliminary inquiry or mitigation of the sentence (see, for example, Swedish court case *RH 1991*, p 92; Diesen, 2001, p 88). Blaming the victim, which is particularly common in cases of sexual crime, might thus still be successful even when the victim is a child.

Corporal punishment of children was forbidden in Sweden in a much-debated but successful reform passed in 1979. The family law was then altered so that violence for educational purposes no longer formed an exemption from the rules on assault and battery. Corporal punishment has decreased, but child abuse has not ceased. A study of the number of instances of child abuse reported to the police suggests a growing number of cases, which is probably due to a diminished tolerance of violence against children. At the same time, some of the myths about who subjects children to violence are being challenged (cf Chapter Ten in this volume). There is an overrepresentation of first-generation immigrants, but not of second-generation immigrants. And "the higher the level of education of the perpetrator, the more often there are several victims in the family" (BRÅ, 2000, pp 15, 31).

Research results based on material collected around the turn of the millennium show that children suffer several cultural and legal disadvantages. Of the crimes reported to the police in Stockholm, not even one tenth of reported sexual assaults on children led to legal proceedings, and the number was even lower in the case of child abuse (Diesen, 2001, pp 78, 93). What is more, the frequency of charges showed a decreasing trend. One partial explanation of this is the problem with evidence in cases of crimes committed within the private sphere, another is children's 'procedural disadvantage', since Swedish legal proceedings are usually based on videotaped interrogations of the child, while the defendant adult is present in court. An even more serious fact is that one third of the children were never interviewed for the preliminary investigation. Furthermore, many investigations were closed without the suspect having been interviewed, and some prosecutors closed all their cases, even when there seemed to be good evidence and the suspect had confessed to at least some of the reported crimes. Christian Diesen points out a possible reason for this: failing competence and hesitance when facing extremely unpleasant crimes. Another researcher within the same project, Helena Sutorius, studied psychological experts and experts within the judicial system in processes concerning sexual assault of children. She found that representatives of both professions displayed examples of prejudice, arbitrariness, lack of objectivity and speculation. In addition, interpretations were often made from an adult perspective. One example is "the failing credibility of the child in relation to the father's proven unimpeachability (no prior convictions, well-established…)". In another case, the court noted that "the girl had proven injuries that cannot be ignored", but the man has "denied the description of the deed and behaves calmly and objectively, and shows genuine indignation over the accusation" (Sutorius, 1999-2000, p 129). A positive feature is, however, that the study showed a certain increase in quality over time. Perhaps future reforms can strengthen this trend.

Women's peace and children's peace

In 1998, decisions on several reforms were taken on the basis of the government's proposition *Kvinnofrid – Women's peace*, or the later accepted official translation *Gross violation of women's integrity*[2] – which, to a large extent, was based on the final document of a committee convened to report on violence against women, which was published in 1995 bearing the same title. This was the result of the first and, so far, only public inquiry working from the perspective of women in Sweden. The reforms included prohibition of the buying of sexual services, that is, buying prostitution. It was also decided that the wording of a law should not only use the male pronoun in accordance with the normative male dominance of legal language, but should be formulated to address both sexes. Furthermore, a new crime was introduced, which takes into account the process of normalisation of violence in an intimate relationship where a series of violations results in reduced self-esteem and debilitation of the victim. For the first time, the experiences of women form the basis of the norm in criminal law. This is a new feature within Swedish legislation and an innovation in post-modern law (Nordborg and Niemi-Kiesiläinen, 2001). It results in an improvement in the legal standing of women who are exposed to violence by men, and, at the same time, this reform also includes protection for others who are subjected to violence in intimate relationships. The first paragraph of the article covers, for example, violence in homosexual relationships and children exposed to assault by a parent – this I want to call children's peace.

The wording of the law is consciously gender-neutral, while also exposing the violence of men against women. One and the same norm with the same basic prerequisites applies to all intimate relationships, while the nomenclature in the classification of the crime depends on the specific constellation of the perpetrator and the victim. This system of wording the law facilitates statistics and research into which are the most common victim–perpetrator constellations and frequency of cases concerning other parties. The article is included in Chapter Four of the Penal Code, which concerns crimes against freedom and peace, while Chapters Three and Six, also referred to in the law, concern crimes against life and health, and sexual crimes. The article currently reads as follows:

> BrB 4:4a: A person who commits criminal acts as defined in Chapters 3, 4 or 6 against another person having, or have had, a close relationship to the perpetrator shall, if each of the acts form a part of an element in a repeated violation of that person's integrity and suited to severely damage that person's self-confidence, be sentenced for *gross violation of integrity* to imprisonment for at least six months and at most six years.
>
> If the acts described in the first paragraph were committed by a man against a woman to whom he is, or has been, married or with whom he is, or has been cohabiting under circumstances comparable to marriage, he shall be sentenced for *gross violation of a woman's integrity* to the same punishment. (SFS 1999:845)

There are, as yet, few cases of crimes against children's peace, which might be explained by the fact that children are exposed to such serious violence that the cases fall under other legal paragraphs, but it might also be due to children not receiving enough attention from the police and others within the judicial system.

New laws are not enough

The reform of women's peace involves more than the creation of new articles in the law. The government has emphasised that stricter legislation as such cannot solve the serious social problem that men's violence against women constitutes. "It is currently well-documented, both in research and other literature, that the violence that men direct against women has often originated in and been nourished by prejudices and notions about the superiority of men and the subordination of women" (Prop, 1997/98: 55, p 2). The government has also pointed out that the understanding of "the connection between male cultural values and violence against women" (Prop, 1997/98: 55, p 23) must increase. This has led to demands for changes in basic education and for continued education specifically based on established knowledge about issues of power and violence in intimate relationships. This also resulted in the government giving the Crime Victim Compensation and Support Authority[3] a commission to conduct a study of the extent of men's violence against women. This investigation resulted in the report, *Slagen dam* [*Captured queen*], which attracted much attention (Lundgren et al, 2001).

Individuals within structures

The reforms concerning women's peace are based on conscious structural perspectives in the current power relations between the sexes. These perspectives have not been maintained by later Swedish public inquiries, such as those of the committee on sexual crime (SOU 2001:14) and the Committee Against Child Abuse (SOU 2001:72). Both describe perpetrators and victims from an individual perspective. It has, nevertheless, been made clear that the power relations between individuals vary, particularly in cases of children's exposure to and relations with adults. The need for power and control are also named as factors influencing assaults. This, too, is important in relation to the classic free (male) individual of the law. All this results, among other things, in an important suggestion for a new crime: the rape of children, which no longer has to involve physical violence or threat if the victim is under 15 years of age.

However, individuals not only have varying degrees of power in relation to each other, they are also part of social, cultural and structural contexts. This pertains both to perpetrators and victims as well as to the people around them. Inspired by, among others, Nea Mellberg (1997, 2002), I claim that the structures must be seen as a (changeable) framework within which assaults are made possible, happen and are then interpreted and encountered by the surrounding world. This latter claim is of great relevance for representatives of the judicial system and the social services. It influences the investigation of crimes and legal proceedings, the interpretation of the prerequisites of the law and the valuation of evidence, as well as the crime victim's opportunity to be treated with respect.

Children in the vicinity of violence

In a separate chapter, the Committee on violence against women focused on the exposure of children growing up in environments where violence is a recurring element. At that point, the reference material available mainly comprised findings from international research (for example, Christensen, 1988). Since then, there has been further study of children's circumstances in a Swedish context. For example, Katarina Weinehall's doctoral thesis *Att växa upp i våldets närhet* [*Growing up in the proximity of violence*] (1997) illustrates in an alarming way the vulnerability of the adolescents; even in cases where they have tried to attract the attention of all around them (see Chapter Nine in this volume). The report "... *och han sparkade mamma*" ["... *and he kicked Mummy*"] describes discussions conducted over two years with 45 children who have experienced prolonged violence in their families (Arnell and Ekbom, 1999). The report gave rise to the important question within legal policy as to whether children who have seen violence against their mother should be regarded as witnesses or as victims of mental assault. I will return to this question below.

These reports, as do other research documents, point to the fact that the most difficult experiences of the children are connected with silence and concealment concerning the violence and assaults, and also with the lack of intervention by other adults (see Chapters Four and Nine in this volume). The silence surrounding the assaults means that the children's traumatic experiences are rendered invisible and invalid. The children carry the burden of a secret personal catastrophe alone.

Reform?

The Committee against child abuse topicalised the question of whether children who witness violence are victims of a crime. The studies of the committee show alarming data: "about 10 per cent of all children have at some point experienced violence at home and about 5 per cent experience it often" (SOU 2001:72, p 26). The study suggested an extended definition of child abuse and wanted to include mental abuse in cases where, for example, "the child had been forced to witness (see or hear) violence in his or her immediate environment, or live in an environment where violence, or the threat of violence, is a recurring element (p 24ff). However, the definition was not suggested to be valid in criminal law, despite its having been established that children are generally more exposed and vulnerable than adults, and that children are exposed to more serious risks pertaining to their health and development "at least in the case of recurring violence" (p 334ff). The argument of the study against criminalisation is that:

> Since the mental abuse of children perpetrated by adults usually takes place at home where the risk of being caught is very small, it must also be regarded as doubtful whether an extended criminalisation actually would have a deterrent effect. However, it is, above all, questionable if changes in the criminal law are an appropriate method to convince grown up persons to treat children with the respect they are entitled to. (SOU 2001:72, p 335)

So, the government bill does not accept the suggested definition of child abuse, but arguments around children who are badly treated. The final proposed bill, which was passed by the Parliament, does, nevertheless, contain a more severe punishment in cases where a crime has been committed with a child watching or listening (Prop, 2002/03:53). This might contribute to the process of making children visible, but it does primarily reflect the adult perspective as an indication of the additional vulnerability of a woman if her children are present at the scene of the violence.

So, children are left deserted by the criminal law. The family is given priority over the rights of children. The private sphere closes as a continued lawless space around the child, as it has done for women for so long. Children do not obtain their own redress.

From the child's perspective, an obviously better alternative is to give children clear legal protection by introducing a new section in the criminal law stating that it is a crime for someone to let a child watch or listen to the assault of a person with whom the child has a close relationship, or to expose the child to a real risk of seeing or hearing such assault (cf the Domestic Violence Act in New Zealand, passed as early as 1995). Only then does the child acquire status as victim of a crime with the given right to a legal counsel for the injured party, who can look after the interests of the child during the preliminary inquiry and the trial, including the child's right to claim damages. This could include compensation for infringement of personal integrity, which is currently totally excluded. In Swedish law on damages, this compensation can only be awarded to persons who are victims of a crime in the traditional sense; and, as to its amounts, it has developed into a very important form of compensation. If they existed, children's damages could also cover costs for treatment and therapy. In addition, this criminalisation could strengthen children's rights within family law.

The changing family

Divorce was effectively introduced during the 20th century. Gradually, the legally accepted grounds for divorce were extended and 'free divorce' was introduced through a reform of 1973. Since then, the desire to separate is reason enough. At the same time, the question of which spouse has caused the marriage to fail has ceased to have any legal significance.

Violence

Only later, towards the end of the 1970s, were problems concerning widespread violence against women made visible. Sexualised violence was documented in all social classes and began to be regarded as a social problem. Nowadays, 70-80% of all divorces are initiated by women (Dahlberg et al, 1990, p 119ff). Their reason for doing so is often their husband's failing to recognise equality in everyday practices, which can also take the form of violent repression. According to the report *Slagen dam [Captured queen]*, 35% of the women who have left their husbands have experienced violence and threats from their partner (Lundgren et al, 2001).

When problems connected to violence were made visible, it was found that there was no provision in family law to deal with them, apart from the possibility of obtaining divorce, which, as such, is important. Previously, the spouse who was held responsible for the divorce could be placed under various sanctions, such as loss of the opportunity to gain custody of the children and the obligation to pay damages to the other spouse. After the 1973 reform, there was no means of limiting contact or of demanding the payment of damages. It could be argued that the abrogation of the focus on responsibility primarily resulted in the husbands being exempted from their responsibilities, both for their acts of oppression and the violence that many of them have performed (Nordborg, 1999). Thus, adults can now separate from their partner freely. It is increasingly seen as desirable to effect friendly separations – but not to separate from the children. The child–parent bond replaces marriage as a permanent (heterosexual) family bond[4].

Joint custody

From a historical perspective, joint custody is a relatively new phenomenon in Sweden. It was only in 1920 that married mothers obtained the same rights as their husbands to be custodian of their children. And the father's right to joint custody has been extended so that it is no longer necessarily conditional on being married to the mother. Since 1977, joint custody can continue after a divorce and be valid both for couples living together and for those living apart. So far, the parents must be in agreement. Statistics show that the percentage of cases of joint custody after divorce almost doubled over a short period. In 1983, 44% of all children of divorced parents were in joint custody; in 1992, the corresponding figure was 82% (SCB, 1989, 1992; see also Norborg, 1997). Thus the reform on joint custody had a great impact.

However, the governmental investigation on child custody conflicts (SOU 1995:79) suggested that a court could also decide on joint custody 'against the wish of one of the parents'. The investigation's remit was to analyse its findings and make recommendations from the perspective of gender equality, but, in fact, it dissociated itself from this remit by "emphasizing that issues concerning children and what is best for a child in disputes centring on custody, living or meeting are not a question of equality between the parents, i.e. the sexes" (p 43). The gender-neutral wording had, nevertheless, a gender-specific motivation: "that the father can participate in the custody even if the mother opposes this" (p 9) (cf Chapter Two in this volume).

Since it ignores the status of power between the sexes, the result can, in fact, be described as an 'equality sharing' of the children between their mother and father through joint custody – supplemented by the threat that if the mother opposes this, the father might get sole custody. This is the case despite the observation that disputes are increasingly connected with serious problems of, for example, accusations of violence and sexual assault (p 62ff).

Children's rights

Data found on violence conflict dramatically with the norms that should apply to children. Corporal punishment of children was made illegal in Sweden in 1979. The Parental Code [*Föräldrabalken*][5] accentuates this in a beautifully formulated aim: "Children have the right to adequate care, security and a good upbringing. Children are to be treated with respect according to their personality and distinctive character and are not to be subjected to corporal punishment or other insulting treatment" (*Föräldrabalken*, chapter 6, article 1). The following section says that the custodian is responsible for this, both through his or her own behaviour and by ensuring that the child is treated well by others.

The UN Convention on the Rights of the Child aims to prioritise what is best for the child and emphasises children's fundamental right to "a personal relation to and direct contact with both parents" – a right that is often referred to. It is important to note that the text continues with " except when this is in conflict with what is best for the child" (article 9, section 3). The UN Convention on the Rights of the Child accentuates the parents' responsibility for their child, not their right to the child. In addition, the Convention emphasises children's need for legal rights in a number of articles. One in particular highlights children's need for protection "against all forms of physical or mental violence, injury or assault, abandonment or negligent treatment, assault or abuse, including sexual abuse, while the child is in the custody of both or one of the parents" (article 19, section 1).

After a well-publicised case of so-called sabotage of the right to contact (Swedish court case *NJA 1989*, p 335), a new article was introduced in the Parental Code emphasising that the court should pay particular attention to the child's need for close and good contact with both parents. A rigid interpretation of the criterion of contact with both parents resulted in a new intervention by the legislator. The aim then was to emphasise the need to "take into account the risk that the child [...] is exposed to assaults, is abducted or otherwise maltreated" (*Föräldrabalken*, chapter 6, article 2). The wording of the law was to be "a request to courts, parents and other parties involved to pay direct attention to the significance of the fact that children are not harmed" (Lagutskottet 1992/93 LU22, 22). The committee also wrote that it "need not be beyond all doubt that the child is maltreated" but "it is enough that there are concrete circumstances indicating that there is a risk that this is the case".

This underlines something that should be evident. The strict requirements of evidence needed in a criminal case, where it must be 'beyond reasonable doubt' that the suspect is guilty of a crime for him or her to be sentenced, are not applicable in child custody cases. When the issue is to judge questions pertaining to custody and right to contact, it is the best interests of the child that are most important. The probability of the risk of harm to the child is what needs to be judged. This child-centred perspective has since been reintroduced. Both the Committee on Civil Law and the Health and Welfare committee pointed out that "it is very important that children are protected in all ways against assault and abuse" (Lagutskottet 1997/98 LU12, p 30). In addition, the Committee on civil law stated that "in cases where one of the parents exposes a member of the family to violence, harassment or other insulting behaviour, shared custody against one of the parents' will should not be possible". On the right to contact, the committee again accentuates the importance of judging the risk of harm to the child and adds: "The assumption of the Parental Code that it is important for a child to be in touch with both parents even when they live apart does not mean that it would always be in the child's best interest that contact is achieved" (Lagutskottet 1997/98 LU12, p 4).

To what extent courts of law and social services take this child perspective into account is continually under discussion. Women's shelters claim that their biggest problem is that information on violence and assaults by fathers is not taken seriously (Nordenfors, 1996; Lundström et al, 2001). Critical voices are also raised within child and adolescent psychiatry (Lindberg, 1999-2000; Metell, 2001). In practice, it seems that neither social authorities nor courts of law think that a father's violence against, or sexual assaults on, the mother disqualify him as custodian (Dahlberg et al, 1990, p 87; Rejmer, 2003). Thus, the violent man and the father are not regarded as one and the same man (Eriksson and Hester, 2001). This can have serious consequences for the children, regardless of their sex. For girls, there is an increased risk that they will be exposed to the same kind of sexualised violence. Both girls and boys risk being influenced by attitudes of contempt for women.

There is only one precedent (Swedish court case *NJA 2000*, p 345). In that case, the mother complained of a deeply rooted conflict where her husband had exposed her to prolonged physical assault and had occasionally also beat their children. He had been sentenced for one incident that involved seizing her by the throat in the presence of their daughter during a contact visit, while school staff panicked and locked themselves and the son in another room. The man was given a protection order. In the custody case, the man admitted to having punished the children, not by using any "brutal violence" but by "spanking their bottom" and sometimes slapping their face. The Supreme Court stated that "this crime of assault was committed in an agitated situation a year and a half ago" and therefore could not be regarded as meaning that the father was currently unsuitable to be custodian. However, the Supreme Court continued: "The assault must, nevertheless, be seen as an example of the difficulties the parents have had to solve problems concerning their children[...]. There is such a serious and profound conflict between the parents in that they are unable to cooperate on questions concerning the children". Therefore, the mother was given sole custody of the children.

This statement, like many from the lower courts, is characterised by the violence being minimised, reinterpreted and 'dissolved' from the context. It is also one of several examples of violence being regarded as a relational problem, with the responsibility for it being laid on both the woman and the man. It is also often the case that mothers who talk of assaults on themselves and their children in connection with custody disputes are met with suspicion. Women may therefore feel that their testimony will not be held to be credible. But it could be that the assaults are the reason for the woman breaking out of the relationship and that it is only after the separation of the mother and father that a child can begin to feel secure and start speaking of her or his experiences.

Contact – right or obligation?

The right to contact is described in terms of the rights of the child. The regulations in the Parental Code mean that:

- both parents are responsible for the child seeing the other parent;
- the other parent can demand contact through the legal process;
- the parent with the right to contact can get a court order to the effect that the right be fulfilled, usually through sentencing the other parent to a penalty of a fine, but ultimately through the police collecting the children;
- the parent with the right to contact can get the custody transferred to her, or himself, if the right is not effective because of the other parent's opposition – so-called sabotage of contact;
- a parent with the right to contact who has been made custodian can get the verdict put into effect, ultimately by means of the police collecting the child.

If we alter the perspective to see which demands the child may place on the contact parent, we find that the law provides no such regulations. The first point above does emphasise that both parents are responsible for the right to contact. But if the contact parent fails the child by evading that right totally or to the extent prescribed by, for example, a verdict or an agreement, which I call refusing contact, there are no legal solutions on offer. Instead, a lawless space opens up and it is impossible to claim that the child has the right to contact. The right to contact is a parental right. If we connect this to the fact that the majority of contact parents are fathers, the right to contact becomes mainly a right of the father.

Several bodies to which proposed measures are referred for consideration, for example, the Faculty of Law at Stockholm University, have suggested sanctions by fines for parents with the right to contact who fail their children. The government response was that "[t]here is a risk that contact that must be forced by sanctions might influence relations in an undesirable way" (Prop, 1997/98:7, p 60). I agree, but why is this risk not considered if the child has to be forced to see the parent with right to contact? The effect is that the right to contact is voluntary for the parents. For the child, it is an obligation[6].

Violence

One research project on contact issues in relation to violent fathers in Denmark and England resulted in a recommendation that after an assault on the mother by the father, it should not be assumed that it is in the child's best interests to continue seeing the father (Hester and Radford, 1996; see Chapter Two in this volume). In Swedish legal usage pertaining to contact, the most problematic cases have concerned suspected sexual abuse of the child. In an earlier survey of verdicts, I found a verdict by a Court of Appeal that involved a true judgement of the risk from a child perspective among many verdicts from lower courts that lacked both aspects (Nordborg, 1997, p 188ff). The verdict still appears as unique and worth citing[7]. The mother demanded that the child contact should be cancelled because the father exposed his children, a seven-year-old girl and a nine-year-old boy, to assaults, and she had been raped by him on several occasions. In the prosecutor's opinion, no crime could be proven. In the case concerning contact, the following, for example, is quoted from the statement by a child psychiatrist: the girl "names her father as the one who has touched her bottom with his penis", describes "games with sexual features that make her agonised" and "a game in the shower where she says she has also been peed on". The boy describes games with penises used "as some kind of symbol for shooting guns" and that he has "been caressed or touched on his penis by his biological father". The investigators found the children's stories to be realistic and serious. Testimonies by the mother and other persons could also be said to support the conclusions of the investigation. The District Court argued that it had no information as what the children "more precisely had told the investigators" and found the videotaped police interrogations – one with each child – to be the most reliable evidence, stating that "the [father] possibly played with his children in a way which is not appropriate". The father was granted contact with his children every other weekend, in accordance with what he had applied for. The mother appealed against the verdict and asked one of the child psychologists to be interviewed as a new witness. The Court of Appeal wrote that regardless of what the police interrogations "might be thought" to show, "it must by proof of other investigation [...] be regarded as demonstrated that the children had witnessed or been exposed to sexual acts by the [father]. In addition, the children have felt mentally imbalanced after contact with their [father]. What has now been said, indicates a considerable risk that the children would be harmed in continued meetings with their father". The father was not granted child contact.

The same kinds of problem recur in later legal usage. In a referred case in the Court of Appeal, a father had been prosecuted for sexually abusing his daughter (Swedish court case *RH 1999*: 74). The District Court disapproved of the prosecution, but the mother was still convinced that he had sexually abused their daughter. The Court of Appeal found that the mother had opposed contact with the father without acceptable reasons: "There is therefore no doubt that she has failed her responsibility as a parent". In a collective consideration, "the Court of Appeal, for its part, feels no doubt that it is best for [the girl] that the custody of her is transferred to [her father]". The girl was then 10 years old and had during the previous four years only had sporadic contact with her father.

As custodian, the mother is responsible for her children being treated well both by her and by others. At the same time, she can be forced to leave her children with their father despite serious concerns about abuse and even if she knowingly fails her children. When the principle of the child's best interest is interpreted as a demand for contact with both parents, the mother who questions the father's contact with his children by definition is a bad mother. The norm for fatherhood is different; even a violent man can by a court of law be regarded as an adequate father (cf Eriksson and Hester, 2001).

Summary and strategy

Far too often, the courts of law adopt pure criminal case approaches in civil law cases on custody and contact. There have, as a rule, been greater powers of insight for adults than for children and for fathers than for mothers. The following table is intended to clarify the differences to which attention must be paid, along with a gender perspective, in the two different types of case (Table 7.1).

The mistake I regard as most frequent is that if a crime has not

Table 7.1: Important but ignored differences between criminal cases and cases of custody, contact or residence

Criminal case	Case of custody, contact
Who: an adult	a child
What: possible crime	the child's best interests
that is, a specific incident	that is, an overall judgement of the contact
Aim: legal rights	legal protection; risk that the child is harmed
Requirement: beyond	judgement of probability
reasonable doubt	

resulted in prosecution or a verdict passed as guilty, this is interpreted as if 'nothing has happened'. Even if there has not been enough evidence to support a crime, there might be reason to judge various signs of the child being harmed. If a crime against the mother is proven, a paradoxical situation might arise where she is granted certain protection against continued assault by a protection order, while the children are expected to spend time with the same man. Should children not be entitled to at least the same protection as adults?

The power of men over women and children was, for a long time, based on marriage. The marriage has gradually lost its significance and stability. Nowadays, fatherhood appears as the 'institution' that can give men power over both children and their mother. As with marriage earlier, it is not a given fact that men and fathers use their power in a destructive manner. However, the function of the law should be to provide protection against those who do so.

There are national and international developments taking place to give women and children the status of individuals equivalent to men's. While human rights issues have traditionally concerned protection against the state, they also now include demands on protection by the state, even in exposure in close relationships. The UN Women's Convention is a tool for introducing a gender perspective into the law. If the whole UN Convention on the Rights of the Child is taken seriously, several gendered relationships are problem-atised together with a child perspective. Through human rights, the life experiences of women and children can gain legal relevance. Then the demands on motherhood and on fatherhood could be equal and the protection of children would be prioritised both in criminal law and in cases of custody and contact.

Notes

Translation into English: Heidi Grankvist.

[1] A table of a large number of reforms pertaining to women's history is found in Nordborg (2001, p 52ff).

[2] The first official translation of the crime was 'breach of women's peace' (SOU 1995:60, p 443). This wording has a historical background in Sweden, linked to reforms during the 13th century in order to protect the family against violence towards their women from men outside the family. The contemporary reforms are focused on protection of the woman as an individual and especially within the family.

[3] The Crime Victim Compensation and Support Authority has three areas of responsibility: to decide on state compensation for criminal injuries, to administer the Crime Victim Fund and to act as a Centre of Competence (see www.brottsoffermyndigheten.se).

[4] Homosexual love has gradually gained increasing legal support and can be registered as a partnership with rights corresponding to those of a married couple with one exception: children (Nordborg, 1995). However, a controversial Bill was recently passed that could give homosexual couples the right to adopt children (Prop, 2001/02:123).

[5] It is worth noticing that the name is still the Parental Code and not the Children's Code, which would be implied with the change from an adult perspective to a child perspective.

[6] The child's wish is to be taken into account "with regard to the child's age and maturity" (*Föräldrabalken*, chapter 6, article 2b) and putting it into effect must not happen in principle if the child is 12 years or older, or is regarded as having reached corresponding maturity (*Föräldrabalken*, chapter 21, article 15). It appears to be rare that children under 12 years can influence the outcome of a legal process.

[7] Verdict by Svea Hovrätt (Swedish Court of Appeal) *DT 27, 1996-05-29*, in *case T 1748/95*.

EIGHT

A visible or invisible child? Professionals' approaches to children whose father is violent towards their mother

Maria Eriksson

This chapter points out some of the contradictions and dilemmas associated with current Swedish attempts to create gender equality – including shared parenting and a 'new father' – and attempts to promote children's interests. In legal cases concerning custody, contact or residence in Sweden, a particular group of social workers, the so-called family law secretaries (word-for-word translation), conduct the investigations that form part of the basis for the court's decision. Furthermore, the family law secretaries also lead cooperation talks – that is, mediation – with separated parents who want to settle conflicts involving children. The practices of this group of professionals are crucial for children's safety and wellbeing post-separation/divorce when the father has been violent towards the mother and/or the child. In what follows, the work of these professionals in cases where there is a history of violence by the father towards the mother is discussed. Furthermore, the chapter explores how family law secretaries perceive the child's situation and needs when the child's father has been violent. The aim is to shed light on the position of abused children in court mandated investigations concerning custody, residence or contact.

The chapter is based on research into Swedish family law and policy, and how fathers' violence is dealt with (Eriksson, 2003)[1]. The research consisted of three interlinked studies of what constructions of age, gender and kinship mean for the handling of fathers' violence against mothers/co-parents and children. The first study built upon public documents from three policy areas ('violence in close relationships'; 'parenthood, separation and divorce'; and 'children at risk'), and investigated how the issue of violence from fathers is handled in social policy. The second study built on thematically structured interviews with abused separated mothers and investigated what the father's or co-parent's violence means for the everyday life of mothers post-separation, and how the violence is handled by the mothers. The third study built on thematically structured interviews with family law secretaries and investigated how these professionals handle violence by fathers. This chapter draws primarily on the interviews with family law secretaries[2].

Violent fathers in Swedish social policy

Since the Second World War, there has in Sweden (as in most Western countries) been an increase in divorce, and later separation by cohabiting parents. The policy response has been to modify the nuclear family as an institution. What I call 'the separated nuclear family' has been the particular outcome of the recent development of the law and policy on residence, custody and contact (Eriksson and Hester, 2001; Eriksson, 2003). Swedish family policy today presupposes shared parenting and a high degree of parental cooperation post-separation or divorce (see Nordborg, 1997; Chapter Seven in this volume). Face-to-face contact is generally presumed to be 'in the best interests of the child'.

The policy regarding the separated nuclear family is based primarily on the notion of the child's right to close contact with both (biological) parents (in line with the UN Convention on the Rights of the Child). Swedish family law takes heterosexual, biological parenthood as its point of departure (Singer, 2000). Rights and obligations that used to be ascribed to biological parents – which were independent of the actual care or contact with the child – are today rights and obligations of custodians only (Schiratzki, 1997, p 344). Since most biological parents are presumed to be custodians, the emphasis on joint custody can be interpreted as a reconstruction of parenthood as fundamentally biological (rather than social or psychological) – of kinship as blood ties (cf Stone, 2001). Furthermore, it seems as if in practice it is primarily fatherhood that is reconstructed as biological. Even though most separated parents share custody (that is, they share the legally sanctioned decision-making rights as regards children), mothers normally are the main carers when the parents live apart, especially in cases where the children are very young (SCB, 2003). The legally sanctioned decision-making rights of fathers tend in other words to be more disconnected from actual care than are the decision-making rights of mothers.

As regards violence, there is an increasing recognition in Sweden of men's violence against women as a social problem (Eriksson and Hester, 2001; Wendt-Höjer, 2002). Furthermore, in the 1990s, the issue was the object of important law reforms: Swedish legislation today acknowledges violence in heterosexual relationships as gendered, as primarily violence by men against women (see Nordborg and Niemi-Kiesiläinen, 2001; Wendt-Höjer, 2002; Chapter Seven in this volume). However, the policy on violence against women has tended to focus on protection and support to women and to a limited extent to children. Violent men are seldom in focus as parents and they can thereby avoid being held responsible for the wellbeing of their children (cf Peled, 2000; Eriksson, 2001).

As regards policy on contact, custody and residence, the issue of men's violence has to only a very limited extent been discussed in relation to (continued) parental cooperation and the wellbeing of children post-separation/divorce (Eriksson and Hester, 2001). In the preparatory works to the law[3], it is mentioned that there are cases where the general principles of joint custody and unsupervised face-to-face contact do not apply, but very little attention has been given to these exceptions and there are no guidelines for the handling of these cases. Despite the growing recognition – in politics and policy – of the gendered features of violence in heterosexual relationships, fathers are still to a large extent constructed as essentially non-violent (Eriksson and Hester, 2001).

Family policy and legal practice

This socially constructed gap between 'violent men' and 'fathers' means that the overlap between men's violence towards women and men's violence towards children, as well as the special problems facing mothers leaving violent fathers (see Chapter One in this volume), tend to slip out of focus. There is no established critical discourse on violent fathers that mothers – and others involved – can use to hold violent fathers accountable in a post-separation or divorce context, or to push violent fathers to change (cf Chapter Three in this volume). The development of legal practice in Sweden needs to be investigated further in this regard. However, so far the presumption in practice seems to be that a father who has been violent to the co-parent is a good enough custodian and contact parent until proven otherwise (Eriksson, 2001; see also Boqvist and central government Children's ombudsman, 2002; Rejmer, 2003; Chapter Seven in this volume).

To judge from legal practice, Sweden has chosen the rule of optimism (Dingwall, 1989) and is thereby exposing both children and mothers to far greater risks than, for example, is the case in New Zealand (see Jaffe et al, 2003; Chapter Seven in this volume). In spite of an official ambition to promote gender equality and children's rights, the separated nuclear family seems to make possible the reproduction of father-power based on blood ties to not yet adult children (Eriksson, 2003).

Professionals' approaches to children with violent fathers

The practices of family law secretaries are crucial for the safety and wellbeing of both children and mothers post-separation or divorce. Yet, do these professionals relate violence by fathers towards mothers and/or children to their work methods? If so, how?

At a more general level, the interview accounts can be seen as expressing two different models for the work of family law secretaries, with two different points of departure for the assessment of future custody, contact and/or residence arrangements[4]. In model one, the separated nuclear family is placed centrally and fathers' violence against mothers is constructed as having little relevance. In model two, violence against women is placed centrally (for an elaboration, see Eriksson, 2003). However, when the family law secretaries' narratives about children's situations are taken as the point of departure, it no longer makes sense to divide the respondents into these two groups. All respondents were asked about children's victimisation and one of them responded as follows:

> Well.... I don't know. Is there such a connection? I don't even know if there is, is it? [...]
> *Maria: But that's not your picture, like?*
> Noo.... I can't really say that. I can't really say that. What is more common is that the children have been hit without the woman being hit. The children are the victims so to say. Primary victims.... But that's another problem. It's a desert around children in conflicts. Children who in addition have seen ... violence between their parents, it's even worse for them. And there are ideas that you pass on this pattern if you don't talk about it. That's really important, to talk. To give [them] permission to talk.

These answers are typical. The family law secretaries state that they have come across few cases where both the mother and the children have been physically abused by the father. These professionals tend to talk about fathers' violence against mothers or co-parents and fathers' violence against children as unconnected phenomena. Some make an explicit distinction between the two violent activities and argue that even if a man is violent to his partner "he doesn't have to be mean to his children".

The separation between fathers' violence towards mothers and their violence towards children can also be seen in the respondents' presentation of their work methods and routines. For example, physical and sexual abuse of children is portrayed as something that professionals must take into account and the respondents say that they have a duty to report suspected abuse. In such circumstances, the child's situation must then be investigated properly according to the Law on Social Services (Socialtjänstlagen [SFS 2001:453], chapter 11, article 2). However, none of the respondents talked about routinely making a report or initiating an investigation as soon as they find out about violence in the adults' relationship. If fathers' violence towards mothers and fathers' physical and sexual abuse of children are presumed to be separate phenomena, this is understandable: a father's violence towards a woman partner or co-parent is not in itself perceived as an indicator of risk.

Even if fathers' physical violence towards children is not perceived as very common, respondents state that they can certainly imagine that it happens. By contrast, a distrustful frame for professionals' interpretations of mothers' narratives on child sexual abuse can be seen in this empirical material. This frame is constituted by notions of mothers suspecting child sexual abuse because of their own childhood victimisation; a wave of incest allegations in Sweden in the late 1980s and early 1990s; and alleged abuse used by mothers to win custody cases. In her research into the situation in Sweden of mothers whose children are abused sexually by fathers, Nea Mellberg (2002) shows how mothers can move back and forth between different interpretations of reality before drawing the conclusion that their child is being abused. The question is whether there is space for such a process when mothers encounter family law secretaries. To judge from the interviews discussed here, the construction of child sexual abuse as a reality seems to require a previous court verdict, strong bodily signs on the child and/or a mother who is consistent throughout the investigation process. If this is the case, sexually abused children whose mother (the non-abusing parent) is working through the issue of abuse parallel to the legal case concerning contact, custody or residence might end up without protection due to professionals' lack of awareness about the complexities of discovering child sexual abuse.

It is assumed that fathers only display emotional or psychological violence towards children in an indirect sense. In some interviews, the father is portrayed as a problem for the child only when the mother is physically present, since it is then the children are assumed to be – or are at risk of being – witnesses of violence and consequently subjected to psychological violence. In other interviews, the mother's physical presence is not placed so centrally, although the victimisation of children is associated with some form of mother presence. The psychological violence towards the child is constructed as a 'byproduct' of the father's attempts to reverse the separation or regain control over the mother. To put it another way, when the family law secretaries talk about cases where fathers are violent towards mothers, 'psychologically abused children' exist but not 'psychologically violent fathers'. The assumption that fathers who are violent towards women are psychologically non-violent to children is also made clear by the respondents' description of their practices. For instance, they do not mention assessing what the use of violence to women means for a father's attitudes and practices in relation to his children; nor do they mention systematic risk assessments prior to contact.

The presumption of contact: children's need of the father

Generally, the interviews are marked by the presumption that contact is in the best interests of the child. This presumption is tied to the notion that children need two parents when growing up: the 'developing child' (see, for example, James and Prout, 1990; Smart et al, 2001; Chapter Four in this volume) needs a mother and a father. Heterosexual parenthood is the point of departure for all the family law secretaries[5]. The interviews with this group of respondents underline how closely the construction of child development as dependent on a two-sex/gendered environment is tied to the naturalisation of gender complementarity and heterosexual parenthood. As mothers and fathers "are" different and "have" different care to give, children need both parents and have a right to contact with both of them.

The general need for and right to contact also applies to children who have experienced violence. A recurring theme in the interviews is children's need of contact with the father who has been violent to the mother: "children see themselves as part of both" parents, they "need to get a realistic picture" of the father and "see that he doesn't just have negative aspects". Even though "you always have to make an assessment of the individual case", there is a presumption among the family law secretaries that no contact at all might be more damaging for the child's development than having contact with a father who has been violent towards the mother, or the child:

> If you could manage to arrange contact with good conditions, which are safe for the child, then it creates a possibility for the child to kind of work through what has happened and also to keep a realistic image of the parent.

Here, contact with the previously violent father is portrayed as in itself therapeutic for the child, the condition being that it is arranged in a safe way[6]. Yet, how do investigators assess whether the child is experiencing contact as physically, sexually and/or emotionally safe?

Are the child's experiences made visible?

According to Swedish family law, professionals conducting an investigation on custody, residence or contact should, if it is not totally inappropriate, investigate 'the child's view' and give an account of it to the court (*Föräldrabalken*, chapter 6, article 19). The child's wishes are taken into account in the legal process – with consideration of age and maturity (*Föräldrabalken*, chapter 6, article 26).

The 'standard' way of working with children as presented in the interviews can be outlined as follows. It consists of three or four encounters between the family law secretaries involved and the child: two visits to the home with the mother and father respectively and one or two sessions with the child by her/himself or with the siblings at the family law/social services office. Some of the respondents talk about conversations (not accompanied by a parent) with four-year-olds and older children, but most talk about such sessions with school-age children (six) and above.

This standard method is neither portrayed, nor stands out, as suitable for making children's own experiences of, and perspective on, violence visible. Some professionals say they neither ask children directly about experiences of violence nor talk with children about the violence in the adults' relationship already known by the investigators. In some interviews, this is explicitly stated to be in the best interests of the children: because children should not be used as "sources of information"; because the family law secretary task is defined as doing investigations but not therapy and "you cannot set too much in motion" when you do not have any follow-up contacts[7].

The conversations these investigators have with the (school-age) children concerned seem primarily to be aimed at satisfying the demands of family law (that is, to document the child's wishes). Consequently, the family law secretaries' interpretations of appropriate contact arrangements and the father–child relationship in cases with violence are not grounded in the experiences and perspective of the child concerned. What, then, forms the basis for the professionals' interpretations?

Constructions of the child and interpretations of children

Swedish family law deems children competent enough to make their voices heard (cf Schiratzki, 1997; Singer, 2000). However, some of the interviewed professionals portray the demands of direct dialogue with children as difficult to handle. The dilemma the family law secretaries talk about – that they should talk to children, and at the same time not put children under pressure or use them as sources of information – can be interpreted as a conflict between a focus on competence as regards children's wishes (expressed in the law) and a construction of children as dependent, primarily on parents (cf Singer, 2000). A 'competent' child is in conflict with a 'dependent' child.

In the interviews with the family law secretaries, a focus on needs and protection, rather than competence, is presented as professional:

> It's part of the responsibility as parent not to put the child in a situation where the child has to choose. It is not reasonable to say that 'now we have not managed to deal with this, we can't agree about anything and now you have to take responsibility for this by choosing between us'. That's totally ... you cannot put those demands on a child. That's part of the parental responsibility.... It's important to deal with it this way, I think, when we do these investigations. In relation to the child too. That's an unreasonable choice. It is.... Of course you act in accordance with the UN convention of the rights of the child, and children's rights and all that.... You can't let the child solve something that first the parents, then the parents in cooperation talks, then the court has failed to, to put that on the child.

Note that the child's choice is presented as something problematic throughout this quote. To express a wish and to choose when you are a child with parents in conflict is constructed as taking responsibility for adults' problems, not as, for example, exercising a right to influence your own destiny. Here, children's 'right' is constructed as the right to be spared a situation where you have to make choices: the right to not having to choose and especially to not having to waive the right to contact with one parent.

In this sense, the professionals do not give children a real choice: the only reasonable wish a child can have is to have contact with both parents. This is also made visible by the professionals' way of talking about children's choice as regards contact with a father who is violent towards the mother. When the professionals discuss wishes from children that are in accordance with the needs of the 'developing child' – and the child wants to see the father – children are presented as competent and their wishes authentic. For example, children's longing for a father who has been violent is portrayed as something unproblematic, genuine and 'given'. The issues of children's survival strategies, fear and/or identification with the perpetrator that are discussed in research and among Swedish practitioners working with children's experiences of violence (see, for example, Christensen, 1990; Metell, 2001) cannot be found in these interviews. However, children's wishes not to see their father tends to be presented in another way:

> You have to investigate thoroughly, is it the mother who doesn't want to? Since, I mean, the mother can make the children to, not want at all. That's the first thought like, I think you carry that with you, the first thought when they say that the children don't want to, I think 'is it the mother who doesn't want it?'. And it's clearly so that, or I have never experienced that the mother really wants it [contact], but the children don't.

When particular children's wishes are in conflict with the needs of the developing child – they do not want to see their father – children tend to be portrayed as dependent on, and influenced by, their mothers. The possibility that children might not want to see their father because of experiences of violence – that they, for example, are trying to protect themselves – is not discussed by these professionals.

These family law secretaries seem to be prepared to encounter children with problems associated with a general dependent (child) position, and children whose needs are more or less identical with the needs of an abstract 'developing child' (cf Hester and Radford, 1996; Chapter Three in this volume). However, they are not as prepared to encounter the experiences, emotions and strategies of particular children who have been – or are – subjected to physical, psychological or sexual violence by a father who is also violent towards the mother. Consequently, there seems to be less space for some child subjectivities in encounters with these professionals. How do abused children themselves experience and tackle investigations on contact, custody or residence? That is an urgent question for further research[8].

Mother-centred families?

To judge from the interviews with the family law secretaries, it is not just abstract notions of the developing and dependent child, but also gendered constructions of parenthood that play a crucial role in the assessment of appropriate custody and contact arrangements (cf Hester and Radford, 1996). How, then, are fathers who are violent towards women assessed as parents of children?

The family law secretaries' perceptions of fathers are made visible through their contrasting perceptions of mothers. The professionals' statements convey a picture of abused mothers as not fully adequate parents: abused mothers can – in different ways – neglect their children (cf Chapter Three in this volume). The respondents talk both about a general tendency among mothers to be occupied with their own problems, and about a more specific inability to recognise the children's need of contact with the person who has abused her. All respondents engage with this notion of abused mothers as neglectful and inadequate parents, with the 'inadequate abused mum'[9].

Is the father's use of violence presumed to have any consequences for his parenting skills? It is notably harder for the respondents to express themselves when asked about 'violent men as dads'. The interviews also show that the talk about fathers is marked by pauses, restarts and argumentation back and forth to a much larger extent than is the case with the talk about mothers. One recurring theme is insecurity about how violent fathers actually are as parents:

> [Pause] I haven't got a very good idea about that actually. [Pause] Well, they have them … they do things, but…. No, I don't know actually. It's more what, what the mother … in that case she is very believed, if you say. In principle she can say, 'I think it should be like this and that way I think the contact will work'. Well the ones I've had, they have been perfectly capable to judge. And it's not for me to say whether it is too much or too little or … no. But then, of course you have to ask how they [the fathers] are as parents.

I mean, it's some kind of barrier that they don't have, and
children are provoking you....

In spite of the statement "you have to ask how they are as parents", the
respondent says that she does not have a clear image of how violent
fathers function as parents. This quote is typical in that it is the mother's
image of the father that is brought to the fore. Another example comes
from a respondent who stated that mothers have difficulties in separating
the child's need of the other parent from their own feelings. However,
the generalising statements about mothers are not paralleled with similar
statements about fathers. When asked about 'violent men' as 'dads', the
respondent said:

> Well, that's not possible to say generally, since there are so
> many different levels of violence. You can't say ... there are
> mothers who have been subjected to really serious violence,
> but who still aren't worried that the children fare ill with
> the other parent. Again, you can't generalise, you have to
> see that every case is unique.

In this quotation, the level of physical violence is in one sense assumed
to be of importance for the assessment of the father as parent. However,
it is made clear that even if the father has been very violent to the
mother, he does not necessarily qualify as harmful to the children.
The mothers' lack of worry is here given a central place in the
assessment of the fathers' harmlessness to children. Both of the
respondents quoted above transfer the responsibility for assessing the
fathers' parenting skills – and possible risks for children – from
themselves to the mothers concerned. It can be added that in the
interviews it is not just the mother's view of the father that is given a
central place in the talk about violent fathers as parents, but also
children's love and longing for their dads.

   A father's use of violence against his (woman) partner is in other
words not given the same obvious implications for his parenting skills
as is a mother's victimisation by her (man) partner. All respondents
convey a clear image of how abused mothers "usually" are as parents.
However, when they talk about violent fathers, the mother's view or
the children's feelings tend instead to be in focus. The 'gap' that can be
seen in policy and in the legal discourse can, in other words, also be
seen in the interviews from this group of respondents. A discursive
figure comparable with the inadequate abused mother cannot be found
in these interviews: the 'inadequate violent dad' does not exist.

The logic of the mother-centred family model

The overall responsibility for children's wellbeing, emotional and other needs, as well as protection, is primarily associated with mothers, not with fathers. That is why the issue of violent fathers' parenting skills slides out of focus. A complementary construction of parenthood dominates the interviews: it is constructed as fatherhood and motherhood (cf Chapter Three in this volume). It should be noted that this gender-complementary construction of parenthood has implications also for the child's 'place' in family relations. The following quotation exemplifies how the mother is given a central place in family relations and how the father–child relationship is constructed. One family law secretary talks about a man who is "lethally dangerous" (to the mother):

> This mother, with this lethally dangerous man, for example, he has been an excellent contact parent for this little boy, so far. Since this child has been rather small. You can think that with his psychological status there might be some conflicts, as the child grows older. Since older children are more difficult to handle and suddenly have bigger needs of their own. So far it's been okay.

The "lethally dangerous" father or co-parent is here presented as an excellent contact parent for the child, at least as long as the child is young. He is also portrayed as potentially dangerous for the child: "with his psychological status". That he – despite this – can be an excellent contact parent is logical if his parenting is mainly presumed to entail "doing things with the kids" and being complementary to the mother's responsibility for care and protection. Here, the father becomes an adequate contact parent through the mother's main responsibility. The speech context – the mother as custodian and father as contact parent – can be interpreted as contributing to this construction. He would probably not be presented as an excellent custodian or residential parent: his excellence depends on a custodian with main care responsibilities.

In the example discussed above, the mother is implicated in the child–father relationship. The presumed model for family relations can be characterised as 'mother-centred'. The mother is constructed as the central person and she is presumed to act as a facilitator of the child–father relationship (Figure 8.1) (cf Smart, 1999).

Figure 8.1: A mother-centred family model

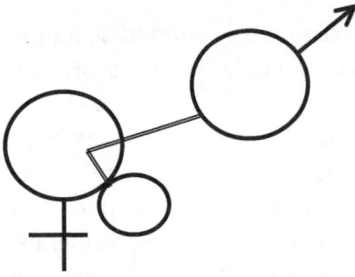

According to the logic of the mother-centred family model, a father–
child relationship independent of the mother does not really exist.
One interpretation of the lack of focus on the violent fathers' parenting
skills can be that the respondents tend to 'think with' the mother-
centred model and use it as an interpretative frame when talking about
violent fathers as parents and in relation to children. Against this
backdrop, the association between the victimisation of children and
some form of mother presence (discussed in a previous section)
becomes understandable. The tendency among some respondents to
shift the responsibility for the assessment of the father from themselves
to the mothers concerned can also be interpreted as an expression of
this logic. Motherhood includes being responsible for fatherhood (cf
Smart, 1999; Vuori, 2001; Chapter Three in this volume), also in
encounters with the social services and other authorities.

The logic of the mother-centred family model seems to imply a
responsibility for the father–child relationship post-separation or
divorce. When asked about how contact between violent fathers and
their children usually works, some respondents emphasise that it can
work if the mother is helping the child to deal with the encounters
with the father, that is, acting as an emotional 'buffer' between the
children and their father. It should be added that it is also apparent
that mothers should mediate the father–child relationship in a
'measured' way: mothers can be interpreted as being both 'too much'
and 'too little' of a buffer. The powerful position of mothers in a mother-
centred family model should not be abused. More precisely, a good
mother does not shut the father out. Here, a structural tension becomes
obvious: a good mother does not shut the father out, and a good
mother protects her child – also against the father (see also Eriksson
and Hester, 2001; Mellberg, 2002).

'Doing' fathers peaceful and (some) children invisible

As shown above, the family law secretaries tend to construct children as dependent, developing and in need of guidance and protection from adults. A protective welfare perspective is evident in the interviews with these professionals and children become objects for adult intervention (cf James and Prout, 1990; Alanen, 1992; Smart et al, 2001). However, the respondents' welfare perspective on children seems to be selective. The professionals mainly focus on children's vulnerable position 'in general' and not a specific vulnerability due to physical, sexual and/or psychological violence from a father who is also violent towards the mother.

This is partly a consequence of how and when the respondents use different constructions of family relations. One family law secretary described a case where she knew that the father had been violent towards the mother, and where it was difficult to talk to the child:

> During the investigation it became clear that the man had abused the woman. They were separated. And then when the boy should come here, he came with his mother. And then he didn't want to come in. So I said that 'well you could just come in and sit down and I'll talk to your mam'. And she almost dragged him into the room. He didn't say a peep.... And afterwards I got it because then the dad rang and said, 'you had promised that I should come too, when he would come and talk to you'. That he wanted dad and mam to sit in the waiting room. To be able to come here and talk. And he found it really difficult this. At the same time, he had chosen to be more and more with his dad.

The problems are here presented as an expression of the child's wish to have both his father and his mother present at the family law office. Yet, the problems could just as well be explained by the father's behaviour. Against a backdrop of knowledge about violence towards the mother, just as reasonable an explanation would be that the father had put the son under pressure, manipulated and/or threatened him – so that he would not talk to the investigators without his father present at the family law/social services office – and so forth. However, such interpretations seem not to come easily to the fore. It is also worth noting that the child is described as having 'chosen' to be more and more with his father (that is, is represented as competent to choose).

Figure 8.2: A symmetrical family model

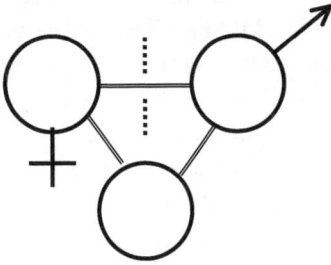

Such a choice, however, could just as well be interpreted as a consequence of the experience of violence. Children's behaviour and emotions are in other words focused on selectively. They are associated with the child's relationship with both of the parents, but not with experiences of violence or victimisation due to the father's behaviour *targeting the child*.

When talking about fathers' violence, parenthood and parenting, the professionals make use of a mother-centred family model as an interpretative frame. In this model, both age and gender are constructed as difference: the child is represented as dependent on adults, primarily upon the mother. When taking the child's wishes and needs as their point of departure, the professionals make use of another one: a 'symmetrical' family model. In this model, gender, and to some extent age, is constructed as sameness. The child is to a larger extent represented as an individual and as competent. The latter model forms the basis for the separated nuclear family institutionalised in policy (see also Eriksson, 2003). According to this, the relationship between the child and each parent should normally continue post-separation or divorce. The marriage or sexual relationship and the child–parent relationships are presumed to be independent (Figure 8.2) (cf Smart, 1999).

This switching between interpretative frames depending upon what is put in focus is of central importance for how reality is represented. Through the switching between interpretative frames, the professionals are 'doing' fathers peaceful (that is, not violent) and abused children invisible[10]. Since the family law secretaries tend to use a mother-centred model when talking about violent fathers as parents or in relation to children, the fathers' attitudes and behaviour to children slip out of focus. The child–father relationship tends to be talked about and interpreted from the (general) child's perspective. To put it in another way, the professionals make the (general) child–father relationship visible, but not the (violent) father–child relationship.

This selective, or interchanging, use of interpretative frames contributes to the 'gap' between violent men and fathers – between violent fathers as 'co-parents' and 'parents to children'. The symmetry in parenthood seems in practice to be created not with similar caring or parenting abilities as the point of departure, but in the child's need of both parents, of the (biological) father and mother.

Through the interchanging use of interpretative frames, the question of what to prioritise – the child's need of safety and protection, or the need of both parents post-separation or divorce – becomes a non-question. The construction of kinship as blood ties is also left as a 'given'. Consequently, the child's relationship to the violent biological father does not have to be questioned, nor the father's wish to have contact with the child. Thereby the family law secretaries can avoid taking a stand; they can avoid challenging patriarchal power. In doing so, the professionals contribute to the everyday reproduction of father-power based on blood ties to not yet adult children in Sweden.

Notes

[1] It builds upon a doctoral thesis in sociology that reports the findings from the research project *In the best interests of children: Gender, violence and parenthood at separation and divorce* (1997-2001), which was funded by the Swedish Crime Victim Compensation and Support Authority.

[2] The respondents were self-selected – they volunteered after receiving information about the research – and the respondent groups consist of 13 mothers and 10 family law secretaries (they were not involved in the same 'case'). The latter group consists of eight women and two men from eight workplaces. The respondent group is probably not representative of the average group of family law secretaries, but more qualified.

[3] The Nordic idea of law is 'continental' in the sense that written laws are considered to be the primary legal material. In the Nordic courts, the role of preparatory works is quite central in the interpretation of the laws. The preparatory works are often rich in statements about the aims of the acts and often also about how the acts should be interpreted (see Nousiainen, 2001b).

[4] Cf Hester et al (1997) on the different models for the work of court welfare officers.

[5] At the time of the interviews, it was not possible for homosexual couples in Sweden to be assessed for adoption (as is the case today), and the debate on gay and lesbian parents seen in Sweden in recent years had not yet begun.

[6] Cf one of the professionals in Hester and Radford's (1996) study who similarly talked about children seeing violent fathers as therapeutic – as 'facing the demon'.

[7] The presumption is that the non-abusive parent – the mother – should seek other help for the child from agencies within the social services or health system that provide counselling/therapy.

[8] This has begun to be investigated in the UK (see, for example, Mullender et al, 2002), and in 2005 I will start a Swedish research project on this specific issue with funding from the Crime Victim Compensation and Support Authority.

[9] In some interviews, a counter-image of such a negative image of abused mothers can be found. However, these respondents do also engage with the notion of the inadequate abused mother.

[10] It should be noted that my focus on social practices and the construction of reality is inspired by the 'doing gender' perspective as developed by Candace West, Don Zimmerman and Sarah Fenstermaker (West and Zimmerman, 1987; West and Fenstermaker, 1995).

NINE

"Take my father away from home": children growing up in the proximity of violence

Katarina Weinehall

In this chapter, my focus is young people's narratives of growing up in the proximity of violence. The discussion draws on my research into experiences of violence in families, which constituted the first major research project on men's violence against women and children's experiences and perspectives of violence in Sweden (Weinehall, 1997).

Sweden is generally perceived as a country where principles of gender equality and justice are prevailing and Swedes also like to think that. Sweden is a leading country with regard to these issues. Nonetheless, national studies show that violence in intimate relationships in Sweden is extensive (see Lundgren et al, 2001; Chapter One in this volume).

A battered woman does not always live alone with a violent man. Many of the women also have children. The man who perpetrates violence could be her present or former husband or partner. He could be the child's father or stepfather. When a man/husband/the child's father abuses the child's mother, events may take place in total secrecy, inside the home, and become a family secret (Weinehall, 2002b). There are seldom any witnesses to the violent episodes other than the children. To be forced to witness the mother being battered by the father or stepfather means that the child is psychologically abused. Research confirms that many such children are also physically abused. A battered woman's child is, compared with other children, 15 times more likely to be physically abused (SOU 2001:72, p 300).

About one fifth of the population in Sweden (around 1.9 million people) are children and young people less than 18 years of age (www.scb.se/statistik – Statistics Sweden, 31 December 2004). They are generally thought to have good living conditions, and to be well taken care of by their parents. For some of these children, however, circumstances are not as good; the home is not a peaceful place to be in (Weinehall, 1999). According to Save the Children in Sweden, about

190,000 to 200,000 Swedish children are thought to have experiences of violence at home (Arnell and Ekbom, 1999, p 32). This corresponds to the numbers presented by the Committee against child abuse, which points out that 10% of Swedish children have experiences of violence at home and 5% of children experience it often (SOU 2001:18, p 12). There is no doubt that men's violence against women also hits children hard (Jaffe et al, 1990; Hester et al, 2000; Christensen, 2002; Weinehall, 2002a).

The research

The research on which this chapter is based was a qualitative study providing in-depth knowledge about how children experience and are affected by domestic violence. The study was longitudinal, with 15 young people sharing their stories with me during a five-year period when I followed and documented their descriptions of what it is like to grow up in a home where the father or man perpetrated violence against the mother or woman (Weinehall, 1997).

I interviewed 15 young women and men. Ten of the informants were girls and five were boys. All of them were 15 or 16 years old when the interviews began. Barely half of them grew up in a nuclear family with their biological parents. In 10 families, there are more than two children, and seven of the informants are the eldest or second eldest child in the family. Ten of them lived with their biological mothers up to their teenage years. Sometimes the biological father also lived with them, at other times another man and not necessarily the same man every year. Most of the informants are accustomed to regular disruptions caused by separations, reunions and household moves. A majority of them have not lived in the same place for more than two to three years at a time.

The study was grounded in feminist theory, seeing gender and power relationships between women and men as structuring social relations. The purpose of the study was to gain knowledge regarding the conditions related to socialisation in the proximity of violence through listening to, interpreting and attempting to understand the children and young people's narratives about life when violence is an everyday occurrence. I wanted to obtain a picture of the conditions under which these girls and boys grew up as described by them and by concentrating on in-depth studies of a few individuals. A narrative approach was chosen in the interview setting in order to allow interaction and to ease the process of disclosure for the informants. The premise was that each of the informants would relate her or his own truth, that is, describe a picture of life as he or she has lived it. Thus, truth is here a contextual and relational concept.

In order to ensure the safety of the children and young people concerned, the interviews were conducted in the greatest possible secrecy and far-reaching security measures were applied. The interviews progressed in steps from background information to the most private and sensitive questions about the violence that had taken place in the home. The number of interviews was determined case by case; the interviews were concluded when no or few new aspects emerged.

All of the informants witnessed violence in the family. Thirteen of them were also victims of physical violence. Five of the girls, but none of the boys, were victims of sexual assault. In eight of the families, the mother had been sexually assaulted by her partner (see Table 9.1).

In 14 cases, the primary perpetrator of violence in the family was the biological father. In seven of the families, another man associated with the family (stepfather) also perpetrated violence. In eight cases, the biological father alone was the perpetrator. In three families, the mother was also violent towards the children. In 11 of the families, the father or stepfather abused/used alcohol or drugs and in four of those families, the mother also abused alcohol. In no instance was the woman the only adult substance abuser in the family.

The sample was contained via schools, youth centres, sports facilities, and so on. The teenagers who decided to participate in the study may, in light of other research, be seen as a group with particular

Table 9.1: The perpetrators, the assaults, and the alcohol/drug use/abuse children were exposed to at home

Gender	Perpetrator of violence (F = father, S = stepfather, M = mother)	Victims of sexual assaults	Whether child is a witness (W) or victim (V) of physical abuse	Alcohol or drug abuse/use
Boy	F + S	–	W +V	F + S
Boy	S + M	M	W +V	S
Boy	F	–	W	F + M
Boy	F + S + M	M	W +V	S + M
Boy	F	M	W +V	F
Girl	F + S	M + girl	W +V	–
Girl	F + S + M	M	W +V	S + M
Girl	F	–	W +V	–
Girl	F	Girl	W +V	F
Girl	F + S	Girl	W +V	–
Girl	F + S	–	W	F + S
Girl	F	M	W +V	–
Girl	F	M	W +V	F
Girl	F	Girl	W +V	F
Girl	F	M + girl	W +V	F + M

circumstances compared with other victimised children. The informants report a larger amount of alcohol abuse (11 out of 15 families), a higher level of physical violence directed against themselves (13 out of 15 children), and a greater share of sexual violence towards the girls (five out of 10 girls) than is shown in other studies. In one national Swedish study, alcohol abuse is not a feature of the violent man (Lundgren et al, 2001, p 71), whereas in my sample, the man abused alcohol in 11 of the families. In the same national Swedish study, 18% of the women report that they had been physically abused and 20% sexually abused before the age of 15, that is the same age as my informants (Lundgren et al, 2001, p 8). In a study from the US, the abused mothers reported that 28% of the daughters had been exposed to sexual violence by the husband or father (Roy, 1988). Compared with these numbers, there is a higher degree of victimisation of the children in my informant group.

Young people's narratives – everyday violence in the home

There are many areas of commonality within the young people's stories about daily family life. These include their descriptions of what they believed to be normal family life while they were growing up. For them, this was a family with a drunken and belligerent father who battered the mother and sometimes the children as well. They describe a home environment lacking in structure and fixed points of reference such as established mealtimes, bedtimes, and so on.

The children experienced violence in highly divergent ways. Most of them consider the psychological violence to be the absolute worst. The family rules were dictated by the father and were difficult to abide by, as many of them were unexpressed and often changed at random. The environment was experienced as wholly unpredictable. The children never knew when or why a violent situation might arise:

> When mum had made a stew and we used a spoon to fill our plate.... If anyone got a bigger piece of meat than dad, we were all beaten.

The informants described how a constant state of preparedness prevailed within the family prior to the violent incident and how near total silence reigned afterwards. The teenagers narrate how the family members adjusted their behavior according to the man's rules in order to avoid further violence, if possible.

When the informants described their own feelings and their relationships to their parents, they related both positive and negative judgments, more positive towards their mothers than their fathers. All but one girl were convinced that their fathers were capable of killing them and the rest of the family. All experienced threats described as concrete and realistic. Thirteen of the 15 young people believed that they were alive only because their mothers were able to protect them from the violence of their fathers/other men:

> He was going to kill me, for sure. I know this. But to the very verge of death, only the times he's been really drunk. He's the most dangerous when he's piss-drunk. Then he's got no idea where to draw the line. Then he's not satisfied with hitting us until he has control. Then he could as easily have killed us.

The young people expressed a broad range of emotions. Fear was common to all. The girls more often stated that they felt threatened than did the boys. All were and had been afraid of their fathers, not always because of what they might do to them personally, but rather for what they might do to their mothers and siblings:

> I was so afraid that something would happen to mum ... that my dad would kill my mum ... he used to choke her all the time ... and she turned blue. I was frightened.

All of the young people narrated that they were burdened with feelings of shame, guilt, betrayal and distrust. All of them stated that they felt they were the reason for violence occurring at home:

> I thought it was my fault. Just for existing ... that there was something wrong with me ... it was me they were fighting about. That was what I was feeling all the time. I felt it in my head and in my heart. I felt it the most when they were fighting. I was afraid and thought it was my fault.

The conditions in which they grew up forced the children to formulate various strategies to cope with their situations. They described how they coped with violent events by using different strategies at different ages. When they were younger, passive strategies were presented as necessary as the children were too weak to act and intervene in violent events. The older children had access to a wider range of coping strategies and possible actions. They narrated how they were able to act either by keeping away from home or by staying at home in order to monitor events. They were also able to choose to run away from the entire situation. Making their choices in each situation brought about great inner turmoil:

> I had to check it out. I stayed at home to watch out for my mother ... and it was necessary because my father acted like a fucking idiot. It's almost like having a killer living in the house. You have to watch him so he won't do anything!

When the children made no concrete intervention into a violent situation, they coped with their situation, though in a less conspicuous manner. They described how they tried to forgive their fathers for their violent actions or to keep their feelings in check by refusing to reveal them. Remaining silent, keeping a tight rein over their emotions and the situation were active strategies employed by all of them. Denying reality by fantasising about it, dreaming up a new reality or lying about the situation were strategies used rather frequently by most of the children. However, directly harmful strategies such as intoxicating themselves with alcohol and drugs or attempting suicide were also used.

Managing difficult childhood conditions

The children had been silenced in order to conceal the family secret. The secret was made invisible; it was not permitted to be recognised as a reality and in this way was rendered invalid. Invalidation is more than making something invisible, and very different from mere denial. According to Leira, "invalidation shows that the phenomenon has disappeared for the subject; and completely for the environment" (Leira, 2002, p 286).

It takes both strength and courage to manage difficult childhood conditions as these young people were doing. They describe how they strived to make the invalid valid by writing about it, studying facts about violence and substance abuse and attempting to retain their reason:

> He cannot get into my mind. He can't control my thoughts!

They described attempts to make the invisible visible by running away, going to the police and asking for help, starving themselves or bingeing and, by various means, attracting attention that would lead to change:

> I thought about doing the usual, running away from home and being searched for by the police and all that ... but I just couldn't handle it one more time. I could go to the police myself, after all.

They narrated how they tried to make the evil disappear; they prayed, they forgave and they attempted to create a state of peace and quiet in the home through denial.

Nevertheless, the young people, despite these attempts, may at times have lost their fight for the right to talk about their lives and thus interpret their own reality. Once they had defined their victimisation as enduring, they began to have thoughts of suicide and of killing their fathers. Once the fight appeared to be decided so that preferential rights to interpretation always seemingly fell to the father, the children were prepared to give up:

> I thought I had nothing left then ... so I picked up the razor blade and cut.

The young people denied the reality that they knew existed. They described that they made up scenarios in their minds where they themselves were in the centre of a happy family and surrounded by friends. Longing, wishes, hope and love were usually directed away from the time and place in which the young people found themselves and towards another time, anywhere else but there. Their illusions mostly focused on living in a secure family in the future. All of the young people wanted to have an ordinary father, a good father. They said that in their dreams they wished for nothing more than a different father. They had wanted attention from their fathers but chose to do without rather than take the chance that they would provoke violence. Most of them stated that they hated their fathers. This hatred was often associated with a wish for, and plans for, revenge. Ten children occasionally nourished a wish that their fathers would die or have felt that they wanted to kill their fathers. For them, having a different father implied that there would be no violence in their daily life.

Looking for explanations

The picture communicated by the young people is that the violence was unpredictable, constant and frightening. The children harboured intense feelings of inner loneliness. They did not feel that they truly belonged to the family, their class at school or even the world. They belonged to emptiness, to loneliness. All of the narratives shared a common core language as they spoke of feeling:

> ... alone ... invisible and unimportant ... nobody sees that I exist ... nobody cares about me ... terribly abandoned and left out....

The young people stated that they had no one in whom they could confide; yet they clearly expressed a need for this to be a possibility. There was no support to be found in their surroundings, so they were forced to create support from within themselves. At the same time, they were taking on a lot of responsibility. They had to protect their mother and siblings and became wholly caught up in caring for others. They took on a responsibility much too big for a child or young person to bear. They suppressed feelings and looked for alternative solutions that often exposed them to further danger. When the adult world did not talk to them about the violence, they were forced in on themselves to search for explanations.

One explanation the children had for the violence was that their mothers and fathers might have been taught by their own parents that life should be this way. The boys stated that they did not want to become like their fathers and the girls were determined not to accept situations like those of their mothers. So the young people appeared to establish goals to live a different kind of life, to behave differently than their parents and to seek out strategies to avoid becoming like them. However, despite these goals and statements, the boys described that they had on occasion been drunk and hit their girlfriends and believed that the girls deserved to be hit. The boys explained their use of violence by saying that the girls goaded them into it, thus relieving them of responsibility. The boys resisted seeing themselves as batterers in these situations. For many of the girls, their relationships with their boyfriends were more important than their self-esteem. Half of them said they had been subjected to physical violence by their boyfriends; in several cases, the violence was life threatening. The girls nevertheless remained with their boyfriends even after having been humiliated and abused by them. Girls who were battered by their boyfriends most often found explanations that, in their eyes, removed the burden of guilt from their boyfriends, such as alcohol or drugs. Instead, the girls blamed themselves.

The young people stated that they did not want to assume the patterns of their parents, yet they did. It was difficult for them to shake off their childhood experiences and they did not know why the violence in their childhood homes occurred. They said that they believed the causes of violence are to be found in alcohol and drugs, and they believed help would be available from agencies in this matter, which they realised they could not tackle by themselves.

Thus, the young people appeared to hold some individualised notion of there being a 'cycle of abuse'. They described that there was something "sick" about their fathers; there was something wrong with them mentally. The young people, who themselves were often beaten but never understood why, believed that their fathers' violent behaviour may be ingrained in their personalities, that they may be burdened by their own difficult childhood experiences. They believed the situation may have resulted from a lack of intervention:

> Maybe if someone could talk to my father, unburden his feelings and make him less angry....

Finally, the young people narrate their acknowledgement of their own need for help. This poses a difficult question for the lonely child. Were their circumstances sufficiently difficult for them to seek help? And even if the answer was yes, asking for help was also a difficult and dangerous step to take. The young person had to overcome the fear of breaking the demands of silence and solidarity towards the parents.

The step taken towards seeking help, towards climbing out of the morass created by the culture of silence, was a long and arduous one for the young people to take. They had to believe strongly that something was going to change for the better as a result. Their expectation in seeking help was to become visible and to be listened to:

> To meet someone who believes in me and in what I say ... someone who can offer some help and put a stop to the violence.

It was usually violence at home that prompted them to seek help:

> Mother is beaten and she needs help.... Help me to take
> care of my siblings.... Send my father to an alcohol clinic
> to sober up.... Take my father away from home....

Invisible reality and lack of support

All of the children tried to get support from various (statutory and voluntary) agencies. The picture they provided of the Swedish welfare state is not a flattering one. The teenagers described a lack of support and responses from welfare professionals that sometimes even put them at direct risk of further violence.

Social services agency

All of the children narrate how they have tried to get support from the social services. Some visits led to concrete actions. One girl told the social worker that there was an acute situation:

> Father was drunk and mother was battered, lying on the
> floor bleeding. All the children were also abused ... and
> the social services made a house call four days later.

One girl asked the social services agency for someone to talk to because of the violence at home. The answer from social services personnel was that she could talk to her relatives. The girl explained to the social worker that the relatives were on her father's side. She needed an uninvolved professional:

> The social worker said that if I was strong enough to make
> claims I was strong enough to arrange such a contact by
> myself.

One boy talked about several visits to his home made by social services personnel. He explained how his father would set the stage for the visit, either by using a manipulating charming manner or by being aggressive:

> Either way ... the social services personnel were no help
> at all to my mother and myself. My father could continue
> being drunk and abusive.

Some visits, as the young people described them, led the social workers to repeat the disclosures of the children to their parents, despite promises not to do so, and thus increased their risk of violence:

> After the talk they reported the conversation to my parents ... my dad exploded and then the violence at home increased.

The children needed someone to talk to, someone to ease their feelings of guilt and responsibility. However, they described how their stories were not taken seriously:

> I always think about how my siblings are doing. I want to protect them from all those evil things that my dad is doing to them ... but I feel powerless. I don't have the right to take the little ones away from home. And the social services do nothing! It takes all my energy to worry.

> I told him that my little brothers and sister ... they fare badly by all the violence. He [the social worker] asked me if that was all I had to say ... and then there was nothing more to it.

> She told me not to exaggerate. 'You have a lively imagination', the social worker told me.

The young people described that as soon as a meeting with a professional agency person had occured, their illusions would be shattered. They found it very hard and inconsistent that the help they needed, and appeared to be available, was not offered to them. Their questions remained unanswered and most were not even taken into consideration.

The young people stated that they became negative and doubtful and their image of social services personnel as possible support persons changed:

> That is what I mean ... the social services ... how do I explain this ... you want to tell them ... and then they don't listen. They have no ears at the social services!

> Cowardly social workers are the worst. They make more damage than others. They hurt you so deeply when they start poking into your life and then don't do anything. You

feel powerless.... The powerlessness is the worst.... When you can't even trust the social services!

At the social services ... if you have an opinion of your own ... they don't tolerate that ... because they are the ones to decide. And then you get angry at the social agency ... you must not get angry at the social agency, because then you get no help at all.

Teachers

The young people spoke about the way they had been treated by teachers at school. Even after the children told them about sleepless nights due to violence at home, the teachers spoke ironically of the informants' "ignorance" when they confessed to feeling exhausted and failed to pay attention in class:

There was fighting at home that night ... dad was wild ...
I had been awake the whole night and I was tired to death.
I told the teacher exactly the way it was. I told her so she should understand. And she said I was very lazy ... and not so talented ... and should not blame my shortcomings on others....

Another example was a girl who talked about an occasion when she had not done her homework. She narrated how the teacher kindly stated that she could do it later because she had been home on sick leave for a few days. The girl found the teacher good-hearted and decided to tell about the violence at home:

'That is no reason not to do your homework', was the answer.

The young people describe how they try to get attention from their teachers in different ways:

I have suffered from a lot of anxiety ... I am a lone wolf and the teachers don't like that ... and when one teacher was nagging me ... I throw things around, broke a chair, kicked a hole in the door and went out.... There was nothing done to it afterwards. I had been looking forward to some talking ... but my outburst was all unnecessary.

The conditions under which they grew up gave the young people frames of reference that differed from those of their peers. They had little or no insight into the types of interpersonal relationships practised in other families. The experiences caused them to 'grow up' earlier than their peers. The young people thus ended up occupying a place apart from their peers, where they were regarded as deviant and were teased, beaten and bullied. The pattern recurred even when they moved and changed schools. They described their attempts to get help from their teachers in such circumstances:

> I told one teacher I wanted help to stop the violence at home. The teacher didn't care the least. I became angry and went to the loo and locked myself in. But that is the way it is ... the teachers, they don't care....

> They don't do anything, the teachers. They don't dare ... because if they do, then the pupils get on to them and chastise them. The teachers don't dare to act against the pupils; they don't say anything and they don't do anything. So ... I knew the bullying was my own problem, not theirs.

The children expressed their feelings – that one should not confide in teachers – and stated that they had had negative experiences of doing so. The fact that the adults at school discounted the events was perceived more as a confirmation of the child's worthlessness than as a betrayal.

Police

The young people related that they had positive contacts with the police who were the people who offered most help. The police's responses and actions were in line with children's needs and wishes:

> I want to keep in with the police. Because ... if there is something happening I really want for them to trust me. The police are the most important protector you have got.

> Mother did not have the courage to say no properly. So I had to call the police myself. The police are doing their job. They put an end to the violence; they take care of my mother and my siblings. I can relax for a while. When they had taken dad away it was peaceful at home. The police ... they are the solution to the insanity at home.

The young people were grateful to neighbours when they intervened and called the police.

Child and adolescent psychiatry clinics

Personnel from child and adolescent psychiatry clinics (known as BUP in Sweden) also offered the informants help. However, sometimes they arranged for the whole family to unite and discuss family problems and this was not perceived as safe by the young people concerned:

> I could see mother was scared ... I was also afraid the whole time ... afraid I should disclose something I was not allowed to.... I was terrified to meet my father's eyes. No one was honest and told the truth ... so the meetings made no difference ... and my stomach kept aching.

At other times the clinics arranged individual talks with a professional child psychiatrist. The informants said that they took great risks when they started talking but would do so because they had come to a point where they needed someone to intervene, to help. Yet that help was not necessarily forthcoming:

> At the clinic they say that I am strong to have been able to manage such a great deal and still got as far as I have. They did not offer any more appointments.... I was going to keep on doing as usual. But I could not manage any more ... and I told them so ... but they did not listen with that ear.

> At that place the whole thing was fake in a way ... and it felt like I didn't want to talk to someone ... like some sort of a defence ... because if I talked to someone ... when I went out of the place I was seized with remorse for even talking.... I felt worse after such a meeting and nothing changed for the better at home ... so what was the use?

> They gave me a contact person at BUP ... but that was no use. He asked the same question every time ... and I answered ... and I thought that now we are moving forward ... but the same question every time over and over and over again ... as if my answer was not good enough ... or

was not the right answer. I didn't bother to go there after a while.

The young people described how the staff at the child and adolescent psychiatry clinics did not live up to their expectations, and that this increased their distrust of agencies even more.

In the end, all of the young people stated that they felt negative towards the authority figures, whether social workers, child psychiatrists, school psychologists or counsellors. The statements applied after they had met the agency personnel and given them a chance. They were most negative towards public officials from the social services department followed by personnel from the child and adolescent psychiatry clinics. The young people described how they felt they had been thwarted, disregarded and violated by social services personnel. Only one informant described contact with social services as having been positive, while three had good experiences with child and adolescent psychiatry clinics. Teachers were generally regarded as betrayers only in cases where the children expressly asked for help and did not receive it.

Outer conditions and inner reality

In the families' homes, *the outer conditions* are characterised by the proximity of violence. The man's dominance and violent actions create a threatening atmosphere and his demands for silence in solidarity are driven forward using dictatorial techniques. The family members live under constant oppression and the woman is kept in place by relatively covert subordination. In 13 of the families, the mother is not the only one abused. Almost all family members are victims of violence by a male perpetrator and several girls and mothers are subjected to sexual assault. The informants in this study are not only witnesses, close enough to observe the violence; they are also physically subjected to violence. The children are thus much closer to the violence than they would be if they were merely observing it. The children in this study do not only observe what is happening; they are drawn into it totally. Violence surrounds them. Everyday life for these children is characterised to the greatest possible extent by the proximity of violence (see Figure 9.1).

The symptoms and effects visited on the children by violence are usually not connected to the physical, sexual and psychological violence practised in the home. The taboo against speaking out and gaining acknowledgment of their experiences impedes confirmation of the

Figure 9.1: The increasing emotions and accumulating bad life conditions the lonely child gets no help to cope with

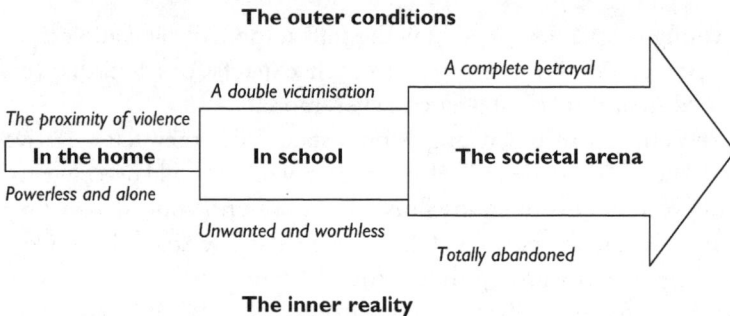

The outer conditions

A complete betrayal

A double victimisation

The proximity of violence

| In the home | In school | The societal arena |

Powerless and alone

Unwanted and worthless

Totally abandoned

The inner reality

informants' *inner reality*. The silence and consignment to invisibility leads to isolation and a feeling of being totally powerless and alone. The young people's attempts to overcome their living conditions make it clear that there are no real opportunities for action. They perceive themselves to be powerless and these circumstances seem also to lead to a constant inner vulnerability. In order to avoid the pain of the 'open wound', the children find strategies to conceal their lack of a skin. They create a protective carapace through strategies that seem to ease the pain.

The significance of the negative effect of violence on the young people's wellbeing is reinforced when they are in arenas outside the home. The presence of violence is the reality that is reflected in their souls and constitutes the frame of reference for possible thoughts and actions.

When the young people are not in the home, the demand to keep the violence a secret weighs constantly on them. Of necessity, this leads them to keep a distance between themselves and people they encounter outside the home. The young people consider themselves to be more mature than their peers and are perceived as being different by them. In school, this difference may be perceived as a threat to the other children and it is possible that this is the root of the bullying these young people endure. The fact that they are subjected to insults by their peers and are neglected by the adults at school reinforces their feelings of alienation and being unwanted and worthless. Their inner experience tells them that they do not count. Their inner feelings of distrust of the adult world that are created in the home are reinforced by their experiences of being let down by adults at school as well, thus creating a situation of double victimisation. The violence perpetrated by the father in the home is mirrored by victimisation at school. The children do not seem to have strategies for coping with this further victimisation. Their vulnerability has left them with fewer resources for avoiding violence and victimisation in situations outside of the home.

The strain of responsibility and survival is exhausting for these young people, leading them to compromise their inner world and to go outside the family to seek help. The outer conditions in the societal arena then emerge in perfect clarity. When they contacted the agencies, the informants did not get the help they needed but were instead rejected and neglected. The agencies could have intervened but generally chose not to do so. The interviewees state that the professionals did not regard their problems seriously. Most visits to agencies came to nothing. Seen from the perspective of the victimised child, the professional actors collaborate to make the problem invisible, to keep the crimes hidden and to allow the child to be forgotten. The actions of adults mean that society's planned helping measures are unusable. When the young people encounter this complete betrayal from the adult world, hopelessness settles in followed by a feeling of being totally abandoned.

Rejection and neglect as a message to children

Those young people are not only silenced, invisible and forgotten; they are also neglected and rejected. The help, so badly needed and so difficult to ask for, was not offered. Why do agency personnel not feel it is their responsibility to help such children? They seem to lack the courage to look and listen; they do not take on board the young people's reality. Instead, the young people encounter negligence, invisibility and 'hide-and-forget methods'.

If the child or young person who breaks the taboo of silence encounters insightful listeners, the 'spiral' of validation can begin (Miller, 1986). According to Leira, validation must be the main goal of interaction. The validation spiral is the name of the construction created through affirmation and recognition in the cooperation and relationship between the helper and the service user (Leira, 2002, pp 286-7).

If the child or young person who seeks support finds a true friend or partner, the loneliness lessens. If the child or young person who seeks help encounters adults and professionals who dare to let go of the fear and see the child's reality, that child is granted worth in their own eyes and in the eyes of the world. Her or his powers of resistance can be mobilised, inner strength confirmed and the path towards a positive self-image opened. Then the child or young person has a chance to overcome the situation and keep the spark of life burning.

Professionals' careless treatment of victimised children or young people sends them a message, the message that they do not count. When the children perceive the full extent of that, they lose hope. Their distrust of the world around them is consolidated. The consequence of the rejection is that they end up without any hope for the future.

One of the few escape routes possible to the child is to wait for the day that their father dies. Eleven of the 15 informants stated that they will not be able to feel good as long as their fathers are alive: "my life doesn't start until my father is dead!". Alternatively, the child could choose to give up his or her life. Quite simply, the children's coping strategies are either to try to bear the situation until the father dies or to attempt suicide themselves. The outer conditions limit the opportunities to handle the inner reality.

Listening to the victimised child or young person should be part of agency personnel's official duties. Listening opens up possibilities. Apart from supporting the child or young person in acute need, agencies may help put an end to violence in future generations. If only agency personnel would listen, and help find ways of supporting and protecting the child's inner and outer world, life for these victimised children could take a different turn.

TEN

Neglected issues in Swedish child protection policy and practice: age, ethnicity and gender

Keith Pringle

The creation of the welfare state in Sweden as an idea (in the 1930s/ 1940s) and then as practice since the 1950s has undoubtedly been a huge achievement. It is remarkable that a country with a relatively small population and only recent industrialisation could create one of the most comprehensive welfare systems in the world. However, Sweden's welfare system is not, and never was, paradise (Pringle, 1998). In this chapter, I will draw on a recent study of children's welfare in Sweden (Pringle, 2002) to suggest that the Swedish system, and the society that contextualises it, is permeated by discriminatory power relations associated with ageism, racism and sexism; and that these can also be seen as operating within the policies and practices of child protection.

Such a view runs counter to the prominent and positively oriented social policy analysis of Esping-Andersen (1990), who argues that welfare systems that approximate to the 'social democratic' welfare regime type (like the Nordic welfare systems) are the most progressive. However, Esping-Andersen's assessment was largely restricted to a class analysis of welfare systems, and was also limited by its focus on income transfers. More recently, some feminist and profeminist commentators have sought to broaden the ambit of welfare under scrutiny to include, for instance, aspects of social care such as day care for children or services for elders (Anttonen and Sipila, 1996). Yet even that broader approach has restricted itself largely to (albeit important) issues of employment and labour in the workplace and the home (Sainsbury, 1999). In this chapter, I want to take the debate further by looking at the performance of the Swedish welfare system in terms of the way it responds to violence against children. Such a broadening of the critique also further problematises the idea of the Nordic welfare regime being, in any simple sense, 'welfare progressive' (Chapter One in this volume).

The Swedish study

I pursue these themes through analysis of part of a recently completed major qualitative study of age, ethnicity and gender in the Swedish child welfare system (Pringle, 2002)[1]. The data consist of written verbatim transcripts from semi-structured and audio-recorded interviews with 37 respondents. The study centred mainly (though not exclusively) on health, day care and social work/social care services. Respondents were drawn from a range of constituent actors in that system: parents; welfare professionals; welfare managers; local and central government politicians; central government policy makers and public administrators; academics prominent in research on related issues. The sample was purposive, and chosen to explore various themes in detail and from different perspectives (Denzin and Lincoln, 1998). For instance, the majority of parents I interviewed were from within a range of minority ethnic groups within Sweden because one of the intentions of the project was to explore ethnicity in child welfare.

The stated objective of the research was to elicit the views of respondents on:

- the positive and negative qualities of the child and family welfare system, as defined by them; and
- the major challenges faced by the system in the next five to 10 years and their assessment of:
  - the strategies by which they expected those challenges to be addressed, if any; and
  - the strategies that they would advocate.

By this means, the intention was to explore the varying 'discourses' used by participants to make sense of the child and family welfare system and of their experiences (from a range of positions) within it. The term 'discourse' in sociological and methodological literature is open to contest (Ashe et al, 1999). Here, my usage follows from social theorists such as Foucault and Laclau and Mouffe (Laclau, 1990), whereby discourses are sets of meanings that are "constitutive of social subjects, organizing social relationships into conceptual frameworks" and therefore analysis "is concerned with investigating the variable 'discursive formations' that make it possible for certain statements to be made and attitudes to be held, while others are excluded" (Ashe et al, 1999, p 64; Fairclough, 2001). As utilised by Laclau and Mouffe (Laclau, 1990), discourses are central to processes of social construction whereby 'reality' (including of course social reality) is constantly mediated in our apprehension of it. Moreover, again following Laclau and Mouffe (Laclau,1990), I do not suggest in this chapter a sharp separation of 'action' and 'meaning'. Actions, as well as language, may be constitutive of discursive objects (Ashe et al, 1999) – and discursive formations may themselves constitute social practices or contribute to processes of social practice.

It is also important briefly to mention one of the theoretical perspectives that has influenced my interpretation of the data. Increasingly, it seems impossible to fully understand the dynamics of any social division without having regard to how that form relates to at least some other forms of social division in specific situations. In saying this, I share the doubts of West and Fenstermaker (1995) about oversimplistic 'mathematical' or 'additive' approaches to such relations. I also share their view that more developed perspectives that focus on the complex intersections between different forms of power are also insufficient. With them and a number of other commentators (Acker, 2000; Eriksson, 2003), I prefer to emphasise the way various forms of oppressive relations of power (in the present case focused around gender, ethnicity and age) *mutually constitute one another* in complex and often contradictory ways. In this chapter, I try to sketch some examples of these processes.

In what follows, by focusing on violence towards children and using primarily the interviews with professional, policy and research respondents, I focus first on an example of what I consider to be systematic aspects of ageism towards children in the Swedish child welfare system. Then I go on to provide examples, within the same frame, of the ways in which combinations of ageism, sexism and racism constitute one another in that system.

Ageism in relation to children

I suggest from my analysis that a considerable number of children in Sweden may well be seriously oppressed within that system, most commonly by acts of omission – typically by silencing or ignoring the voices of children (Pringle, 2002). The issue of physical abuse and the lack of attention to children's perceptions in that context is one of the best examples of this. Because those processes of oppression appear to be so widespread and so 'systemic', I argue that the Swedish child welfare system could be characterised as ageist. Elsewhere, I have argued (Pringle, 1998) that all European child welfare systems are to some extent ageist. The surprise in relation to the Swedish child welfare system is that despite the system's global reputation for being child-friendly [*barnvänligt*], it should be so ageist. It may in many respects be better than many others: but what does that then potentially say about those others?

Although the respondents in my study who were policy makers and researchers in varying respects voiced critical views about a spectrum of welfare professions, social work seemed particularly singled out by a broad range of respondents, in particular the training of social workers. There were several aspects to this critique. It was suggested that much current training for social workers often failed to make them sufficiently alert to, and able to deal with, cases of suspected child abuse of various forms, including physical abuse and neglect. This point was occasionally associated with another serious critique that many social workers too often do not seem sufficiently to talk with, or listen to, children. And in several cases this was largely attributed again to the inadequacies of social work education in Sweden – where social work students are not routinely taught how to communicate directly with children.

Such issues were raised in a general way and also, in some cases, more specifically. For instance, several practitioner respondents mentioned to me that in parental separation and custody cases some social workers tended to: (a) not appreciate that children who have witnessed violence by one parent towards another (predominantly violence by men towards women) and/or been abused themselves by their parent (predominantly the father figure) very often need considerable help; (b) insufficiently recognise the considerable risk that an abusive man partner might also be an abusive father; (c) not work directly with children on issues of violence.

Interestingly, there are alternative, more effective practice approaches in Sweden relating to the recognition of child abuse, working with children and, indeed, the issue of violence in cases of separation and custody – but these alternative approaches tend to be highly limited in availability and have often been developed outside the state sector, which is, of course, still hugely dominant in Sweden. One example of such effective practice, which avoids the criticisms made of social workers noted above, is to be found in the recent account of the therapeutic work of Barbro Metell and Birgitta Lyckner, who are private practitioners and educators of welfare professionals (Metell, 2001). There are four features of their practice that make it stand out within the Swedish context: first, their focus on recognising that children who have witnessed violence in their parents' partnerships and/or been subject to violence themselves in the context of those partnerships, need urgent help; second, their willingness to accept that, in a significant number of such cases, the children will themselves have been directly abused, most often by the father figure; third, their emphasis on the importance of doing direct work with children both individually and at a group level; and, last but not least, the importance they attach to involving the non-abusing parent (generally the mother) in their work, recognising that trust in the mother–child relationship is essential and that the non-abusing parent has a unique potential for helping their child outside the extremely time-limited boundaries of the therapy room. Also worthy of note in this respect is the work of Ami Arnell and Inger Ekbom, based at the non-governmental organisation *Rädda Barnen* [Save the Children Sweden], on interviewing children who have witnessed violence in the family (Arnell and Ekbom, 1999).

At the more general level, we might ask ourselves why communicating directly with children seems, according to the reports of a large proportion of my policy and research respondents, to be so often a skill apparently absent in the repertoire of many Swedish social workers operating in the field of child welfare – who instead tend to rely to a large extent on what parents tell them about their children. As we have seen, it may well be that one major reason for this is a lack of training. But then the critical question becomes why Swedish social work training has not placed a higher emphasis on this sort of work, especially given the supposed child-centredness of the Swedish approach. By contrast, professional training of social workers in England tends to include some training on communication with children, if only limited to one session – and for those intending to practise with children, it is usually a more central training component. After all, it is almost self-evident that unless children are really listened to, then the harsh realities of the lives of many children cannot be understood or addressed. So, in the context of the theme of this chapter, we may ask the following questions: how is it that, in a country that is world famous for being child-friendly, many social workers do not seem either able and/or willing to engage directly with children? And how is it in such a country that many children suffering traumatic experiences go unnoticed and/or unassisted? The very systematic nature of this 'neglect' by Swedish social workers in the specific field of child protection suggests the possibility of those elements of ageism in the child welfare system that my study uncovered more broadly (Pringle, 2002). By using the term 'ageism', rather than a less powerful term, I am suggesting that discrimination against children within Swedish welfare institutions may be both systematic and systemic.

Some of the above issues were also addressed in the influential

Swedish report of the parliamentary committee on child abuse (SOU 2001:72). The committee requested: better training for a whole range of welfare professionals including teachers, focusing on the need for more social work education; extension of the mandatory reporting laws; more, and more detailed, guidance for health and social authorities; the establishment of a centre or centres of research and practice excellence; and a law on collaboration along the lines of the English *Working together* documentation that seeks to systematise procedures for ensuring cross-agency collaboration. This latter point illustrates how in many respects the Swedish government is looking towards the English model of child protection for inspiration. This also emerged very strongly and consistently in my interviews with Swedish child welfare policy makers. Such a tendency towards the English model can be viewed as both potentially positive and negative. On the one hand, some English-style protocols might be useful in Sweden, especially in relation to collaboration and training. However, as commentators on English child protection have emphasised (Thorpe, 1994; Parton, 1997; Pringle and Harder, 1999), that model has been (and remains) heavily flawed, even in its own terms – for, its massive concentration of resources on investigation and assessment leaves relatively few resources for therapeutic assistance while many cases of child abuse (especially child sexual abuse) are missed by professional agencies and most child sexual abusers are never brought to justice.

The committee's report also makes critical points about physical abuse, points that were again developed in my interviews. For instance, methodologically sound research with various constituencies (including children, young people and parents) commissioned by the committee seems to have convincingly demonstrated that, since the introduction of the Swedish anti-smacking legislation in 1979, the routine use of corporal punishment has genuinely become a rarity. That is, the opposition to smacking children has become the dominant mainstream discourse and practice in Sweden. This, of course, is quite different to the state of affairs in England, where the government has decided, on the basis of public opinion, to outlaw smacking only in instances where it may cause mental harm or bruise the skin. However, the Swedish committee report also confirms the views of several policy-oriented and research respondents that severe physical abuse does still exist in Sweden, albeit at a low absolute level, and that the welfare services have generally not been successful in identifying or responding to it; partly again because of a lack of focus on children themselves as informants, and partly because of a tendency for many welfare professionals (not least social workers) to adopt a 'rule of optimism' about the behaviour of parents[2].

In concluding this section on primarily age-based discrimination, my interpretation of the discourses provided by my policy, practice and research respondents gains weight from the following considerations: there was a high degree of unanimity within and across these three constituencies about the age-discriminatory nature of the welfare system; the coherence of these critiques; and the degree to which my respondents drew on a range of consistent research findings to support their critiques. In fact, one of the policy-maker respondents, from within a non-governmental organisation, suggested to me that I should entitle my study '*Where is the child in the Swedish child welfare system?*'.

Gender and age

Interestingly, the relative unanimity that characterised the discourses about age and discrimination in the data from professional, policy and research respondents was strikingly absent when issues of gender and ethnicity were addressed in the interviews. Here much more diversity and debate was apparent, both between different respondent constituencies and sometimes within them. This contrast between the way age, on the one hand, and gender and ethnicity, on the other hand, were discussed perhaps in itself suggests something important about these issues in their Swedish context, or at least in the context of the Swedish child welfare establishment. In the remainder of this chapter, I focus on a few examples drawn from the field of Swedish child protection that illustrate the way my professional, policy and research respondents discussed topics where issues of gender, ethnicity and age were relevant in various combinations.

Some policy makers and leading child welfare researchers among my Swedish respondents suggested that child sexual abuse was a more limited issue in terms of prevalence than in some other countries such as the UK. I discovered that the number of prevalence studies concerning child sexual abuse carried out in Sweden seemed to be considerably less than the number carried out in the UK and the US over the previous 20 years. Nor did many of my respondents in the policy and research constituencies express the view that there was an urgent need to increase empirical research knowledge in this field in Sweden[3]. Some of my Swedish policy/research respondents sought to explain why they felt that child sexual abuse was not such a major issue in Sweden, including abuse in welfare settings. They cited factors such as the alleged relative openness of Swedish society or the heavy involvement of parents in day care and residential care. In the UK, child sexual abuse generally and also in welfare settings has now been recognised as a major social problem (Pringle, 1995; Utting, 1997).

It is curious that a strong discourse about the possibility of child sexual abuse being a social problem in people's own homes and in welfare settings does not seem to be on the agenda, as evidenced in a number of my interviews, nor in the official or semi-official Swedish literature. This is despite comparative evidence that would suggest that all countries should re-examine their assumptions about relative safety when it comes to child sexual abuse, and treat with caution low estimates of prevalence[4]. Moreover, a recent survey in Sweden of violence towards women (Lundgren et al, 2001) also looked at childhood experiences of violence. Since the issue of child sexual abuse was not the main focus of that study, its findings on child sexual abuse should be regarded as indicative rather than definitive. Even on that basis, however, the results suggest the need to carry out a comprehensive Swedish study of child sexual abuse. Thirty one per cent in the sample of 7,000 women who replied to the postal questionnaire reported experiencing some form of physical or sexual violence before their 15th birthday, and 20% of the sample, that is, one in five, reported sexual violence. By comparison, the statistics quoted in the recent reports by Sweden's National Board of Health and Welfare (Socialstyrelsen, 2001) were nowhere near as high, with only 7-8% of women (that is less than one in 10) and 1-3% of men (less than one in 30) said to have been sexually abused at some time in their childhood or adolescence.

Sweden possesses, for its economic size, a very highly developed research infrastructure – in many ways, one of the most impressive in Europe. Why is it, then, that, relatively speaking, so few resources have been invested in researching the size of the problem of child sexual abuse?

While powerful international evidence and suggestive national data regarding the size of the problem in Sweden were largely ignored by my policy, research and practice respondents, at the same time a number of those same respondents positively endorsed other discourses about child sexual abuse that were based on extremely questionable research foundations. And the same pattern could be found in official documentation. One example is the discourse about female child sexual abusers. The official literature states that:

> Most sexual abuse is committed by men. Women are
> believed, according to various surveys, to commit between
> five and 15 per cent of all such offences. These figures are
> uncertain, and it is believed the hidden statistics can be
> higher where female offenders are concerned....
> (Socialstyrelsen, 2001, p 13)

The same putative inflation of the numbers of female abusers occurs
in other official Swedish documentation (Eriksson, 2003). An almost
identical discourse appears in a number of my interviews with practice,
policy and research respondents when I asked them who sexually
abuses children in terms of gender. The answer I sometimes received
was that it was mainly men or boys but with the strong proviso that
the numbers of women abusers is an underestimate. Interestingly, the
research evidence cited by my respondents for this belief in a hidden
pool of female abusers was usually the same and mainly derived from
the United Kingdom. In particular, respondents cited the study of
female abusers carried out by Jacqui Saradjian (1996). Yet all of this
cited evidence consists of studies with small non-representative samples
that, though largely admirable in themselves, do not provide any
quantitative evidence to support the idea of a hidden wave of female
abusers. In fact, a series of prevalence surveys, primarily in the US and
the UK, over a period of almost 20 years have generally, and largely
consistently, estimated the number of female abusers as a proportion
of all child sexual abuse perpetrators at 5-10% (see Pringle, 1995;
Itzin, 2000a). Of course, it may be that in the future higher statistics
for women will be discovered. However, we must base our judgements
on what we know, not on what we might (or indeed might not)
know in the future. In my analysis, I was therefore interested in why
the notion of hidden female abusers should enter into so many of my
interviews with policy, practice and research personnel as well as into
official and semi-official literature. And why is it that when the very
clear and irrefutable evidence of a heavy 'male preponderance' among
sexual abusers (boys as well as men) has to be stated by my respondents
and by the National Board of Health and Welfare, some feel obliged
to add this qualification about women, even though it has little basis
in current empirical research?

I am also interested in why there is such a contrast between this
state of affairs and the far more negative discourse in many of the
interviews about the importance of exploring the size of the problem
of child sexual abuse in Sweden, despite considerable circumstantial,
and some direct, evidence that there is a need for further and more

sophisticated Swedish prevalence surveys. One interpretation is offered here. Can it be that the Swedish child welfare 'establishment' tends to discount discourses suggesting that considerable numbers of Swedish adults and teenagers may be sexually abusing children? And is there particularly a strong discounting of discourses that suggest that considerable numbers of Swedish male adults and teenagers may be sexually abusing children? If so, then we may be seeing a very clear example of the way sexism and ageism constitute one another, in this case reinforcing a powerful silence in Sweden about a massive global problem (Pease and Pringle, 2001).

We can see the same phenomenon in relation to the topic of parental separations, child custody and post-separation childcare in Sweden. A considerable body of international research, largely (but not exclusively) from the US and the UK, has demonstrated that there is a considerable overlap between men who abuse their partners and men who abuse their children physically and/or sexually (Hester et al, 2000; Chapter One in this volume). Moreover, in an increasing number of countries, the legal systems are incorporating these kinds of findings into their operations. For instance, in the UK, the Department of Constitutional Affairs (previously the Lord Chancellor's Department) has actively made use of this research base.

When I asked my practice, policy and research interviewees whether they were aware that such an overlap existed between men who may both abuse their partners and their children, they generally told me that they were well aware of this research, that such an awareness was quite widespread in Sweden, and that they fully accepted the findings of this research. However, when I asked the policy and research interviewees whether they could see any implications of this research for the Swedish legal/court policies and practices on custody after parental separations, on the whole there was considerable denial that a significant problem might exist or at least should be considered as a possibility to be investigated. In a few interviews, I would say the attitude was more than denial. For instance, the response of some interviewees was to emphasise that women tend to make false allegations against their ex-partners in custody cases (but without providing other than media-based or anecdotal evidence of this).

The research field in relation to the whole issue of separation and custody is a complex one and is dealt with more fully in this volume in Chapters Two, Five, Seven and Eight. So I will only refer to it briefly here. The situation specifically in Sweden has been extensively and critically reviewed (for further details, see Eriksson, 2002, 2003; Chapter Seven in this volume). In presuming what is in the best interests of the child, the Swedish courts generally presume that this will be joint custody and/or unsupervised contact. Summarising some of Maria Eriksson's analysis, she suggests that even where a man has a known history of violence towards his partner, the burden of proof is generally left with the woman to demonstrate that he is not a good enough contact parent or custodian (Eriksson, 2002). Given the research summarised above, some other legal systems, most notably New Zealand's, have adapted the law to give women in such situations considerably more focus on safety than is the case in Sweden (see Eriksson and Hester, 2001; Jaffe et al, 2003; Chapter Eight in this volume). Moreover, some Swedish research and policy-relevant documents have suggested that men's violence is an issue that needs to be taken seriously in the context of separation and divorce (BRÅ, 2001; Lundgren et al, 2001).

Given this situation, it seems significant that the more critical discourses about separation, custody, the judicial system and fatherhood – utilising research findings often known to, and accepted by, my policy, practice and research respondents – were not generally recognised by my respondents as being of central concern in relation to the Swedish context. At the very least, one would imagine that there should have been urgent calls by them for further research into, for instance, the vulnerability of children to victimisation from parents after separation generally and, of course, in particular where parents already have a history of violence towards their former partners and/ or children. The fact that this was often absent from my interviews can be interpreted once again as an instance of ageism and sexism coalescing in a particularly powerful and silencing manner.

Ethnicity, gender and age

In terms of my discussions with welfare professionals, the topic of physical violence by minority ethnic group parents towards their children was often raised as one example of a specific and very serious social problem in Sweden. Indeed, a considerable number of my policy, practice and research interviewees made an explicit and strong connection between minority ethnic groups and physical abuse because of their alleged cultural practices in relation to corporal punishment of children.

However, as we have seen, during the course of my fieldwork the Swedish parliamentary Committee against child abuse issued its report on physical abuse in Sweden (SOU 2001:72). One central finding was, as already noted, that while levels of physical abuse do seem to be very low in Sweden compared with many other countries, severe physical abuse still occurs in a small percentage of families. In the context of ethnicity, however, the important feature of these findings is that there seemed to be no direct correlation between cases of severe physical abuse and the ethnicity of abusers once the variable of poverty and economic disadvantage had been taken into account. The question mark this again raises is why some discourses are privileged and common in the interview data while others are not, especially since the common ones are not necessarily based on better quality evidence than the silenced ones – quite the reverse sometimes. However, it needs to be added that a minority of the policy, practice and research interviewees in my study did actively seek to counter the idea that physical abuse was simply an issue of ethnicity. Even so, the relatively common focus by the respondents on minority ethnic groups, and Muslim minority groups in particular, in relation to physical abuse requires explanation. One potential explanation may, of course, involve processes of discrimination centred round ethnicity. Moreover, in so far as such processes draw attention away from physical abuse perpetrated by members of the majority ethnic group on their own children, we can say that they are also constituted by considerations of ageism: for it seems that it is much harder for some of the respondents to recognise the risks of violence run by children from within the majority ethnic community in Sweden than is the case for children from within the minority ethnic communities.

Furthermore, we can also bring issues of gender centrally into this picture. In my interviews, it was noticeable that one of the very few contexts where many of the professional, policy or research respondents directly alluded to, and endorsed, discourses about abusive patriarchal relations was when they referred to the situation of women and children within minority ethnic group – and, again, primarily Muslim – families. As Maria Eriksson has recently demonstrated (2003), the same patterns can be found in recent official documents, such as parliamentary committee reports, relevant to child welfare. Once again, this focus on minority ethnic group families taken together with a marked lack of focus on oppressive practices within majority ethnic families implicitly directs attention away from white Swedish men.

This situation is paralleled by recent media discourses in the Swedish press and television, where the emphasis is generally placed on the alleged abusive patriarchal behaviour by men within minority ethnic families compared with white Swedish families where men's behaviour is generally assumed to be benign.

While I am not arguing against the idea of taking cultural practices and beliefs into account, I do want to introduce two important qualifications about such explicit public discourses and the more implicit ones of some of my respondents and the official literature. Both qualifications relate to the idea that, while cultural practices and beliefs may be relevant in cases of violence, we should not assume that these practices and beliefs are separate from the cultural practices and beliefs of the dominant 'host' society. First, where culture (as a specific set of beliefs and practices) may be relevant to the genesis of violence, we always have to consider the possibility that those beliefs and practices may be the complex outcome of an interaction between an 'arriving' culture with the cultural beliefs and practices of the 'host' society (Maria Eriksson, personal communication, 2002; see also Kamali, 1997).

Moreover, we need to recognise that patriarchal relations of power (albeit somewhat differently configured) are clearly the prerogative of both the Swedish majority culture and minority ethnic group cultures. Let me take statistics available on lethal violence committed by adult men on their female partners in Sweden (BRÅ, 2001). In the period 1990-99, 88% of the victims (144 women) and 84% of the perpetrators (139 men) were from within Europe: 70% and 63%, respectively, if we confine ourselves to Swedish victims and perpetrators. Regardless of how far the statistics represent precise proportionate or disproportionate numbers for each ethnic group, the general point is that most lethal, gendered violence in Sweden is committed by men from the dominant ethnic majority on women from the same group. This fact seems to be (strangely?) absent from most public media discourses in Sweden about minority ethnic groups. Of course, these statistics relate to adult violence rather than parent-to-child violence. Even so, they surely cast doubt on simplistic arguments that portray minority ethnic groups as the sole repositories of men's violence in Sweden.

Taken as a whole, I would argue that both the explicit public discourses noted above as well as the more implicit ones within my interviews and the official literature are clear examples of the manner by which power relations centred around the dimensions of gender, age and ethnicity may mutually constitute one another in complex and sometimes contradictory ways.

Conclusion

In the case of both gender and ethnicity, it seems striking that a number of my 'professional' or 'expert' respondents seem to have avoided consideration of discourses that might challenge basic assumptions about Swedish mainstream society and its welfare system; discourses that, in terms of the research available, warrant more focused debate and evaluation. At the same time, a considerable number of respondents gave emphasis to certain discourses that are not well grounded in empirical research but do reinforce the image of Swedish mainstream society as essentially harmonious.

In the course of this chapter, I have made some reference to England by way of providing a contrast with the Swedish context in some respects. It is important not to overstate the positive case for English practices. As many of us who have worked within and researched the English child welfare system know, that system is deeply permeated by sexism, racism and ageism (Pringle, 1995). Nevertheless, in certain important respects compared with Sweden – and other Nordic welfare systems (Pringle, 1998; Pringle and Harder, 1999) – the English system seems more positive.

I have developed an instrument for comparative analysis of welfare systems focusing on the degree to which they focus on violations of 'bodily integrity' that are major welfare issues. The instrument consists of a series of key questions that need to be addressed in relation to welfare systems and the societies that contextualise them. In terms of the massive problem of men's (and boys') sexual violence to children, using this instrument it is possible to make a case for saying that Esping-Andersen's well-known welfare typology can almost be turned on its head – at least if one asks the following questions to judge a welfare system:

- To what extent has there been research on the issue nationally?
- To what extent is there professional and policy awareness about the scale of the problem and its gendered nature?
- To what extent are welfare professionals trained to address the issue?
- To what extent are their services directly related to the issue?

On all these counts, despite severe and probably increasing problems in the English welfare system, that system still appears more advanced than the Swedish one (see Pringle, 2002); and some other Nordic systems would probably rate even worse than Sweden in terms of the above criteria. For instance, we can also use the latest data available from two EU-funded research projects[5] to illustrate the validity of the point above regarding comparative levels of research within different countries (see Hearn and Pringle, forthcoming; Pringle et al, forthcoming; and the project database at www.cromenet.org). Those recent reviews of academic studies, official statistical data and government/policy documentation relating to men's violence in

Sweden and Denmark (respectively, Balkmar, 2005a, 2005b, 2005c; Iovanni and Pringle, 2005a, 2005b, 2005c) when compared with a similar review of the UK (Pringle, 2001a, 2001b; Pringle et al, 2001) show a very clear pattern: compared with the UK, there have been far less relevant data produced on child sexual abuse in Sweden and even less in Denmark.

Moreover, I suggest that, to a greater or lesser extent, the same argument could be made about a broader range of other social issues relating to bodily integrity, including both men's violence towards women[6] and the extent to which various welfare systems address racism. In relation to the latter issue, I provide one example. On the whole and with a few specific exceptions, there is no real equivalent in any of the Nordic countries to the training on how to challenge racism and ethnic discrimination as part of social work practice that, despite recent pressure to downplay it, remains relatively prominent in all social work professional qualifying courses in England. Indeed, the concept and practice of 'anti-discriminatory' training more generally (that is, addressing a range of power relations including those associated with gender, ethnicity, age, sexuality, class and disability) is largely absent in welfare training across the Nordic countries, whereas it also remains relevant within English welfare training (see Dominelli, 1998 for a similar comparison between the UK and 'continental' Europe).

Although the arguments above are based on empirical research, of course we need more studies to further confirm and explore this relative inversion of Esping-Andersen's model when we are addressing welfare and societal responses to violations of bodily integrity.

Nevertheless how are we to explain such a situation when we know that societal commitment to welfare in terms of the resources devoted is far higher in Sweden (and indeed all the Nordic welfare systems) than in England (Arts and Gelissen, 2002)? To put it crudely, how can one of the worst welfare systems be relatively good and one of the best be relatively poor when it comes to issues such as child sexual abuse, violence to women and addressing racism?

No doubt the explanation for this paradoxical state of affairs is complex and many faceted. Here I offer one aspect of the explanation that I would argue is central: (a) on the one hand, the greater collectivist and consensual ethos of social institutions in the Nordic countries seems to promote a more entrenched commitment to welfare structures compared with the relatively individualistic and conflictual ethos of such institutions in England; (b) on the other hand, it may be that this same individualistic and conflictual institutional ethos has permitted greater recognition in

England than in the Nordic countries of some profound social divisions associated with gender, 'race', age, sexuality and disability.

In other words, precisely the same dynamics that promote the greater resourcing of the Nordic systems may be those that limit the Nordic systems in their ability to acknowledge and address social divisions, and vice versa for the English welfare system and the society that frames it.

Of course, some of the terms in this hypothesis need further deconstruction and clarification for which there is no space here. Moreover, these ideas require far more detailed consideration, elaboration and indeed research to explore the complex societal contextualisations of 'individualism' and 'collectivism'. Despite this need for further elaboration, I still believe the hypothesis holds value in helping us to understand why some discourses around a range of power relations are more open or more closed, more spoken about or more silenced in various cultural locations.

Notes

[1] The project was funded by the UK Economic and Social Science Research Council (Award Number R000223551), with the fieldwork primarily completed by October 2001.

[2] For a classic statement, and analysis, regarding the dangers of 'rules of optimism' among professionals, see Dingwall (1989).

[3] Some felt that problems of definition made estimates of prevalence generally unreliable and unhelpful. I was therefore surprised that no one seemed to have replicated (or indeed often heard about) the research of Liz Kelly and her colleagues in England (Kelly et al, 1991), where, in a retrospective study, those problems of definition were tackled directly and made central to their methodology.

[4] In an overview of then existing prevalence surveys of child sexual abuse across the world, Finkelhor (1991) concluded that major discrepancies in prevalence rates between different locations might well often be due to the use of contrasting methodologies rather than 'real' differences. Generally, he concluded that the more sophisticated the methodology, the higher the prevalence rate discovered regardless of location.

[5] These two projects are: the Framework 5-funded Thematic Network on Men [HPSE-CT-1999-00008]; and the ongoing Framework 6-funded Co-ordination Action on Human Rights Violations (CAHRV) [Project PL 506348].

[6] The EU projects mentioned above also provide direct evidence relating to this issue of men's violence towards known women.

ELEVEN

Tackling men's violence in families: lessons for the UK

Marianne Hester

This book set out to examine Nordic approaches to tackling men's violence in families, by studying policies, practices and issues arising from the contexts of Denmark, Finland, Norway and Sweden. The previous chapters have engaged in a variety of ways with these issues, looking in particular at parenting in the context of men's violence, children's perspectives on living with domestic abuse, professionals' responses and the responses and discourses of policy makers. The book began with a caution regarding the nature of the Nordic welfare systems. While these systems may be seen as successful when compared with those of other countries with respect to many aspects of welfare in general and the criminalisation of violence against women in particular, at the same time they have failed to address other aspects that are of critical importance to women's and children's safety and wellbeing. In particular, the lack of incorporation of domestic violence by professionals and policy makers of children's experiences and needs in circumstances of domestic abuse – where the mother is being abused by her partner/ children's father – highlights even more starkly the contradictions in welfare policies that are supposedly 'child-centred'. The intervening chapters have provided much detail and discussion of the developments and contexts that have created these welfare approaches and contradictions. In this final chapter, I look at some of the main strands that have emerged from the previous chapters, their relevance to current developments in English family policy, and the lessons that may consequently be drawn for a wider audience.

I will begin by briefly outlining some of the key developments in English policies and practices with regard to the tackling of men's violence in families, and will use the lessons and conclusions from the Nordic examples to reflect on these[1].

Policy developments in England

Compared with the experiences of the Nordic countries, in England the move to tackle men's violence in families began earlier, from the beginning of the 1970s, with the nationwide development of refuges to house and support women and children fleeing violent men and limited legislation providing civil protection. However, it was not until the 1990s that both the state and other agencies began to take a more prominent role and that 'mainstreaming' – as discussed by Jonassen (Chapter Six) in relation to Norway – became more evident (Hague et al, 2000; Skinner et al, 2005). Since the mid-1990s, and especially since the Labour government came into power in 1997, there has been a discernible shift in the development of policies aimed at tackling men's violence in families in England, linked in particular to the criminalisation of domestic abuse. A range of policies and related discussion papers concerning domestic abuse have emerged, aimed at creating more coherent approaches across agencies, extending and tightening civil remedies and criminal procedures, and dealing with child contact.

New legislation enacted in the mid-1990s included a strengthening of Civil Protection Orders for Domestic Violence (1996 Family Law Act, Part 4), and the 1997 Protection from Harassment Act, which linked civil and criminal justice and recognised psychological and ongoing harassment. Since the late 1990s, a plethora of new guidelines and legislation with direct implications for women and children experiencing men's violence in families has emerged under the auspices of the Labour government. For instance, the revised Home Office Circular 19/2000, aimed at the police, placed renewed emphasis on so-called 'positive policing' with focus on arrest and better evidence gathering. The Crown Prosecution Service received new *Guidance on prosecuting cases of domestic violence* (Crown Prosecution Service, 2001) emphasising the construction of cases, where possible, on evidence other than that of the victim. Criminal justice and other agencies have been encouraged to increase partnership working, to support and provide safety for victims (Taylor-Browne, 2001). Most recently, a new Domestic Violence, Crime and Victims Act (2004) further criminalises domestic violence, increasing police powers of arrest and strengthening responses to breaches of protection orders. Yet despite these many developments, the policy response appears to be piecemeal rather than being a coherent approach to tackling men's violence. Before the new Labour government came into power in 1997, the promise was of an overall intervention strategy on violence against women, including domestic violence (Labour Party, 1997; see Skinner et al, 2005). A further policy document, *Freedom from fear* (Women's Unit, 1999), followed once the Labour government came into power, but this did not provide such a strategy and none has been presented as yet. The context of debates surrounding the Domestic Violence, Crime and Victims Bill was also a lost opportunity in this respect. This Bill exemplifies the piecemeal and often narrow approach taken. As Skinner et al (2005) point out, it merely takes a criminalising approach, without incorporating the wider statutory base for support needed to resource services related to domestic violence. Also, despite much debate and pressure both from outside and inside Parliament, the Bill has not included other vital issues such as recognising post-separation domestic violence in the context of child contact. A strategy, or plan of action, such as that in Norway, has thus not been replicated in the English context (Chapter Six)[2].

As Wenche Jonassen points out in Chapter Six, having a government strategy to tackle men's violence in families is still not a guarantee that action will follow. She talks about the renewed push by shelter organisations and others that has been necessary for the Norwegian plan of action to be implemented, and the consequent re-emphasis on tackling domestic violence that has taken place in Norway in recent years. There are two main lessons to be learned from the Norwegian experience that I want to highlight here. The first is the importance of continued pressure on the state to ensure that a strategy on violence against women is achieved, and also activated. The second is how women's shelters and refuges, able to provide a range of specially targeted support to women leaving violent men, have been shown to be (and should be) a central part of any strategy to tackle men's violence in families.

Gudrun Nordborg (Chapter Seven) also looks at government strategy to tackle men's violence, in this instance the Swedish *Kvinnofrid* legislation. She shows how this is a potentially coherent approach to tackling men's violence, and one that is not merely confined to violence in families. The Swedish example of the *Kvinnofrid* provides lessons for a wider strategy that the UK government could do well to copy. Not only does the Swedish approach offer a realistically gendered approach to tackling men's violence in families and beyond, it also – as Nordborg suggests – opens up the possibility of incorporating safety and protection for children as well. Currently, the practice related to the *Kvinnofrid* legislation does not actually incorporate children, and, as Nordborg shows, this is indicative of the general marginalisation of children in Swedish approaches to tackling men's violence. Keith

Pringle (Chapter Ten) further reminds us of the difficulties of incorporating both gender and age in policy initiatives, and the need for vigilance as regards ensuring that neither policies nor resulting practices discriminate on the basis of, for example, gender, age, or ethnicity.

Policy on children and contact

With regard to child contact and post-separation violence, policy discussion has been ongoing in England since the late 1990s via government consultation papers and moves to develop new legislation. The debates in many respects echo those outlined in this book regarding Denmark, Finland and Sweden (Chapters Two, Five, Seven and Eight), although the possibility of harm to children where there has been domestic violence has been acknowledged to a greater extent in the English policy documentation (Hester, 2002). Recent legislation has incorporated a clause to the effect that witnessing violence to one's carer may constitute significant harm to a child (2002 Adoption and Children Act, Section 120). However, the problem areas highlighted in the earlier chapters in this book in relation to professional and policy discourses remain very much apparent in the English context, that is:

- seeing as separate issues violence by men towards women and violence by men towards children;
- construing a gap between 'violent men' and 'fathers' so that violent fathers become invisible;
- blaming mothers for lack of contact between children and fathers; and
- not incorporating children's voices and perspectives.

Moreover, in the English context, a shift (back) towards the (more abusive) Danish and Swedish models appears to be in progress.

During the late 1990s, following much pressure from women's organisations and based on evidence from research, the English judiciary began to look more closely at the problems of children's contact in circumstances of domestic violence (Eriksson and Hester, 2001). A report on the topic was issued from the Children Act Sub-Committee (1999) of the Advisory Board on Family Law acknowledging links between domestic violence and possible harm to children, and that this needed to be addressed in cases relating to children's contact with a violent parent. This approach was reflected in case law, exemplified by a set of cases considered by the Court of Appeal in June 2000 (*Re: L* (A Child), *Re: V* (A Child), *Re: M* (A Child) and *Re: H* (Children)), where a cautious critique of the contact presumption previously operating in the courts was also evident. While involving very different circumstances of race/ethnicity and family relationships, these four cases all concerned fathers who had previously been denied direct contact with their children against a background of domestic violence and who were all appealing this. In all instances, the denial of direct contact was upheld.

The cases *Re: L* (A Child), *Re: V* (A Child), *Re: M* (A Child) and *Re: H* (Children) were heard by four Appeal Court judges. Despite the outcome, the judges were not, however, unanimous in their views of children's contact with violent fathers. Two differing perspectives could be discerned. On the one hand, the President agreed with the plea in the report of the Children Act Sub-Committee (1999) for courts to be more aware of the possible effects on children of domestic violence, "both short-term and long-term, as witnesses as well as victims", and of the impact of violence on the residential parent (Crown Court transcript, 2000, p 1). As she says in the trial report, highlighting the connection between violence to adults and to children:

> There has, perhaps, been a tendency in the past for courts not to tackle allegations of violence and to leave them in the background on the premise that they were matters affecting the adults and not relevant to issues regarding the children. (Crown Court transcript, 2000 p 10; original text stressed in bold)

On the other hand, one of the other judges, Judge Thorpe, reminds us of "the danger of the pendulum swinging too far against contact where domestic violence is proved" (Crown Court transcript, 2000, p 12). These perspectives and potential contradictions have continued to be played out in English case law, with wildly differing outcomes (see, for example, *Re: G* (2002) EWCA Civ 1547, *Re: L* (2002) 1 FLR 621 and *Re: R* (2003) EWCA Civ 455).

While the report of the Children Act Sub-Committee (1999) and the outcomes in *Re: L* (A Child), *Re: V* (A Child), *Re: M* (A Child) and *Re: H* (Children) may be seen as indicating a shift from the ideological to a more pragmatic approach, discussed in Chapter Two, the contradictions indicated above are already paving the way back towards the ideological approach. This is exemplified by yet more consultation papers on child contact. In 2004 the government published its consultation paper *Making contact work* (subtitled *The facilitation of arrangements for contact between children and their non-residential parents; and the enforcement of court orders for contact*). This was followed by the White Paper *Parental separation: Children's needs and parent's responsibilities* (2004). Underlying both of these documents is a strong re-emphasis on contact being in the best interests of children. The concern is in particular with the "cases where agreed contact arrangements are not adhered to without the agreement of the non-residential parent". Echoing the 1995 legislation in Denmark, discussed in Chapter Two, the suggestion is that active facilitation (mediation/conciliation) should be used in such cases and that there should be a strengthening of the legal enforcement of contact. The latter is especially concerning, being a direct reflection of the legislation in Denmark and Sweden with regard to 'sabotage', discussed in Chapters Two and Eight (cf Eriksson and Hester, 2001). It echoes the underlying assumption in the Danish and Swedish legislation that women deliberately set out to prevent fathers from caring for children (see, for example, Burgess, 1997). Yet, as the Danish and Swedish experiences suggest, such an approach is only likely to increase the abuse of children by violent fathers. The fundamental problem continues to be the failure to systematically consider safeguards for children in relation to contact (as in New Zealand) (see Jaffe et al, 2003; Chapter Two in this volume). However, any systematic safeguards, such as risk assessment, are not included in the White Paper, and (as indicated above) nor have they been included in other relevant legislation such as the recent 2004 Domestic Violence, Crime and Victims Bill.

Parenting

As Chapters Two, Three, Four, Five, Seven, Eight and Ten indicate, central to issues regarding children and contact are constructions of the family and parenthood, as well as children's positioning within the family. In Chapter Four, for instance, Hannele Forsberg reminds us of the changing role of the family, in particular the emergence of the 'new family' discourse with an emphasis on intimacy rather than economy as its rationale. She argues that such a view of the family is likely to "conceal the patriarchal, ethnic or intergenerational power relationships" – issues that are also key in Maria Eriksson's elucidation of how Swedish professionals involved in decisions about child contact arrangements construe a gap between 'fathers' and 'violent men' (see also Eriksson and Hester, 2001; Eriksson, 2003). A tenet of the 'new family' is 'equality' between parents, a discourse that many of the preceding chapters show to be highly problematic because it is unrealistic where men are violent to their partners and/or children. Yet the 'new family' – and the 'new father' associated with it – is in many respects at the heart of the social democratic project of the Nordic countries, and also of the Labour Party in the UK. It is perhaps not surprising, therefore, that an apparent contradiction exists in policies in both the Nordic countries and England between ideas of gender equality on the one hand and issues related to safety and wellbeing on the other. Moreover, the contradiction appears even starker in the Nordic countries because in these countries the policy debates on gender equality have been focused to a greater extent on the gender division of work than on violations of bodily integrity (see, for example, Eduards, 1997b). In the UK, the problem of men's violence against women has a longer history on both the policy and research agendas (Hearn, 2001; Pringle, 2001a, 2001b; Pringle et al, 2001; Balkmar, 2005a, 2005b, 2005c; Iovanni and Pringle, 2005a, 2005b, 2005c).

Voices of children

In Chapter Ten, Keith Pringle points out that policies against smacking in the Nordic countries are some of the most progressive internationally, and that they have had a positive impact on the physical abuse of children. However, other issues concerning men's violence against children have been largely ignored. This context has made it difficult for children's voices to be heard with regard to sexual abuse and in relation to the impact of domestic abuse (see also Chapters Four and Nine). In England, the consideration in research and policy of child sexual abuse and the abusive impacts of living with domestic violence has a longer history than in the Nordic countries, although these issues have often been dealt with separately, by different agencies, and using different perspectives and approaches (Hester et al, 2000; Pringle, 2001a, 2001b; Pringle et al, 2001; Balkmar, 2005a, 2005b, 2005c; Iovanni and Pringle, 2005a, 2005b, 2005c). A new Children Bill is about to come into force in England, mainly aimed at creating multi-agency structures for dealing with child protection and care. Interestingly, the words 'child sexual abuse' have disappeared from the policy, to be replaced by a wider 'safeguarding' of children – perhaps paving the way for sexualised, and gendered, violence against children to become less obvious.

Where children's experience of living with domestic abuse is concerned, Women's Aid refuges in the UK have a long history of providing support to children. Other agencies, both statutory and (mainly) the voluntary sector, have in the past decade increasingly developed support for children living in such circumstances (Hester et al, 2000). The availability of such support, however, remains sparse, with few opportunities for children who need in-depth support. Some work with children in schools, aimed at challenging violent behaviour, is developing and is showing some success (Hester and Westmarland, 2005). However, the general dearth of direct work with children experiencing men's violence in families may be seen as an indicator of the low priority afforded to children in the UK context.

All of the chapters in this book talk in some way about the invisibilisation of children's experiences of, and perspectives on, men's violence in families in the Nordic countries – whether in policies, by professionals working with families, or by parents themselves (see also Chapter One). Keith Pringle, for example, argues in Chapter Ten that welfare professionals and policy makers in Sweden construe practices and policies in a way that can be seen as 'ageist' in that they systematically omit or do not listen to children's voices, because they do not consider them relevant/important or because they do not have the skills to do so.

Hannele Forsberg and Katarina Weinehall (Chapters Four and Nine, respectively) both provide detailed expositions of what children actually say about their experiences and perceptions when asked. In Chapter Four, Hannele Forsberg's focus on children's emotions about their violent fathers shows the complex, and at times contradictory and thoughtful, contributions children themselves are able to provide. She argues for a move away from problem-centred approaches to children experiencing men's violence in families, as these tend to present the children in some way as 'deviant' or different. Instead, she indicates that a child-centred approach involving an openness towards the children's own interpretations of violence and its meaning in their lives provides a positive means of helping children to recover. The children's accounts in both chapters indicate the normality for these children of living with men's violence as well as the unpredictability, and the vigilance required by the children concerned. The children's own narratives in Chapter Four also make it clear that their view of the violence as normal behaviour is only really challenged when critical outsiders intervene – for example, the police, refuges, and so on. The *type* of alternative accounts they come across appear, however, to be crucial. This is apparent from the accounts of the young people in Katarina Weinehall's longitudinal study (Chapter Nine). Most had been in contact with various agencies, but had not obtained information that helped them to understand why their fathers or other adults behaved violently towards them. The violent behaviour as such did not appear to have been challenged by others. The young people thus linked the violence to 'being sick', or to alcohol, and found it difficult to see when they themselves were being abusive or abused in relationships.

The research by the authors in this book reiterates the aspects that have also been found by others to enhance, rather than damage, the welfare of children and to create a positive environment for contact with non-residential parents. Particularly important are:

- the elimination of violence to the mother and/or child;
- supporting the mother to be a well-functioning residential parent; and
- support for the child concerned, recovery work, treatment, or 'talking to someone' (Hester, 2003).

Both Forsberg and Weinehall's accounts from children and young people show the crucial importance of asking children about their experiences, listening to what they say, and providing alternative accounts of men's violence in families that they can relate to. They also indicate the complexities of taking children's own experiences and emotions into account, and that merely accepting that a child may see their violent father as in some ways positive should not be seen as a basis for agreeing to potentially unsafe contact between them.

Conclusion

This book provides a critical perspective on welfare systems and the societies that contextualise them, focusing on the countries that have a reputation internationally as progressive (see Chapter One). The authors show that when tackling men's violence in families is taken into account, the Nordic welfare systems no longer appear so progressive. There are also important differences between the Nordic countries, with different traditions of professional practice and some differing legislation, which also needs to be taken into account.

However, with regard to tackling men's violence in families, there are some persistent, and similar, problems across the Nordic countries, which are also paralleled in the English context. These relate to the permeation of policy and practices by discriminatory power relations associated with ageism, racism and sexism (Chapter Ten), and to the separating out of policies and practices related to the three areas of dealing with domestic violence (criminalising perpetrators and supporting victims), child protection and custody/parental responsibility and contact. As I have argued elsewhere (Hester, 2004), a major challenge in tackling men's violence in families, and in ensuring women's and children's safety and wellbeing, is to overcome this fragmentation of responses and the contradictions between these three areas.

Notes

[1] The focus is on England rather than the UK more widely, as England, Wales, Scotland and Northern Ireland now have separate parliaments and family policy is specific to each country.

[2] It should be noted that England is somewhat behind other regions of the UK in this respect, with the Scottish Parliament having developed such a strategy.

References

Aasted Halse, J. (2000) 'Børn og samvær' ['Children and contact: when contact is problematic or directly harmful to the child'], *Documentation* 7, Børns Vilkår [Children's Circumstances].

Acker, J. (2000) 'Revisiting class: thinking from gender, race, and organizations', *Social Politics*, vol 7, no 2, pp 192-214.

Alanen, L. (1992) *Modern childhood? Exploring the 'child question' in sociology*, Research Reports 50, Jyväskylä: Institute for Educational Research.

Amato, P.R. (1993) 'Contact with non-custodial fathers and children's well being', *Family Matters*, no 36, pp 32-4.

Amato, P.R. and Keith, B. (1991) 'Parental divorce and the well being of children. A meta-analysis', *Psychological Bulletin*, no 110, pp 26-46.

Andersson, R. (1998) 'Socio-spatial dynamics: ethnic divisions of labour and housing in post-Palme Sweden', *Urban Studies*, no 35, pp 397-428.

Antikainen, J. (1999) 'Perheväkivallan perhekeskeinen hoito' ['Family-centred treatment for family violence'], in J. Aaltonen and R. Rinne (eds) *Perhe terapiassa* [*Family in therapy*], Helsinki: Suomen Mielenterveysseura, pp 194-217.

Anttonen, A. (1997) *Feminismi ja sosiaalipolitiikka* [*Feminism and social policy: How gender was made into a key concept in social science and in social policy*], Tampere: Tampere University Press.

Anttonen, A. and Sipila, J. (1996) 'European social care services: is it possible to identify models?', *Journal of European Social Policy*, vol 6, pp 87-100.

Arnell, A. and Ekbom, I. (1999) *"...och han sparkade mamma"* [*"...and he kicked Mummy". Encounters with children who witness violence in their families*], Stockholm: Rädda Barnen.

Arts, W. and Gelissen, J. (2002) 'Three worlds of welfare capitalism or more? A state of the art report', *Journal of European Social Policy*, vol 12, no 2, pp 137-58.

Ashe, F., Finlayson, A., Lloyd, M., MacKenzie, I., Martinand, J. and O'Neill, S. (eds) (1999) *Contemporary social and political theory*, Buckingham: Open University Press.

Auvinen, M. (2002) 'Huoltoriita ja sosiaalitoimi' ['A custody fight and social service'], in M. Litmala (ed) *Lapsen asema erossa* [*The position of a child in divorce*], Helsinki: WSOY Lakitieto, pp 113-65.

Badinter, E. (1981) *Den kärleksfulla modern, om moderkärlekens historia* [The loving mother, on the history of mother's love], Stockholm: Gidlunds [*L'Un et l'autre*, Odile Jacob, 1986].

Bailey-Harris, R., Barron, J. and Brown, J.P. (1999) 'From utility to rights? The presumption of contact in practice', *International Journal of Law, Policy and the Family*, no 13, pp 111-31.

Balkmar, D. (2005a) 'A review of academic studies relating to men's practices in Sweden', Critical Research on Men in Europe (www.cromenet.org).

Balkmar, D. (2005b) 'A review of official statistical data relating to men's practices in Sweden', Critical Research on Men in Europe (www.cromenet.org).

Balkmar, D. (2005c) 'A review of governmental and policy documentation relating to men's practices in Sweden', Critical Research on Men in Europe (www.cromenet.org).

Barne- og familiedepartementet [Ministry of children and families] (2002) *Stortingsproposisjon* [*Proposition to the parliament*] no 1 2002-2003, Oslo: Barne- og familiedepartementet.

Beck, U. and Beck-Gernsheim, E. (1995) *The normal chaos of love*, Cambridge: Polity Press.

Bekkengen, L. (2002) *Man får välja* [*Man/one may choose: parenthood and parental leave at work and in family life*], Malmö: Liber.

Bergman, H. and Hobson, B. (2002) 'Compulsory fatherhood: the coding of fatherhood in the Swedish welfare state', in B. Hobson (ed) *Making men into fathers: Men, masculinities and the social politics of fatherhood*, Cambridge: Cambridge University Press, pp 92-124.

Björnberg, U. (2002) 'Ideology and choice between work and care: Swedish family policy for working parents', *Critical Social Policy*, vol 22, no 1, pp 33-52.

Boqvist, A.-K. and central government Children's ombudsman (2002) *Olämplig vårdnadshavare?* [*Unfit custodian? A study of legal practice concerning violence and custody*], Stockholm: Barnombudsmannen.

Børns Vilkår (2000) 'Børn og samvær' ['Children and contact: when contact is problematic or directly harmful to the child'], *Documentation* 7, Børns Vilkår [Children's Circumstances].

Boserup, B. and Rabøl Hansen, H. (2003) *Samvaers Klemmen* [Caught in the access peg. Failing the child of divorced parents during contact], Copenhagen: Gyldendal.

BRÅ [National Council for Crime Prevention] (2000) *Barnmisshandel* [*Child abuse*], Report 2000:15, Stockholm: Brottsförebyggande rådet.

BRÅ (2001) *Dödligt våld mot kvinnor in nära relationer* [*Lethal violence against women in close relationships*], Report 2001:11, Stockholm: Brottsförebyggande rådet.

Brah, A. (2001) 'Re-framing Europe: gendered racisms, ethnicities and nationalisms in contemporary Western Europe', in J. Fink, G. Lewis and J. Clarke (eds) *Rethinking European welfare: Transformations of Europe and social policy*, London: Sage Publications, pp 207-30.

Brown, T., Frederico, M., Hewitt, L. and Sheehan, R. (2001) 'Child abuse and the divorce myth', *Child Abuse Review*, vol 10, no 2, pp 113-24.

Burgess, A. (1997) *Fatherhood reclaimed*, London: Vermillion.

Busch, R. (1998) *Domestic violence, custody and access in New Zealand*, Paper presented to 4th International Conference on Children Exposed to Family Violence, London, Ontario, Canada.

Butler, I. and Williamson, H. (1994) *Children speak: Children, trauma and social work*, Harlow: Longman.

Chambers, D. (2001) *Representing the family*, London: Sage Publications.

Children Act Sub-Committee (1999) *Contact between children and violent parents: the question of parental contact in cases where there is domestic violence*, London: Lord Chancellor's Department.

Children Act Sub-Committee (2000) *A Report to the Lord Chancellor on the question of parental contact in cases where there is domestic violence*, London: Lord Chancellor's Department.

Children 5 to 16 programme (2001) *Children's needs, coping strategies and understanding of woman abuse. An ESRC research programme: Growing up into the 21st century* (www.hull.ac.uk/children5to16programme/details/mullende.htm).

Christensen, E. (1988) *Når mor får bank* [*When mummy is beaten*], Copenhagen: SUS.

Christensen, E. (1990) *Børnekår* [*Children's living conditions. An investigation into disregard of care in relation to children and teenagers in families of wife mal-treatment*], Nordisk Psykologis monografiserie no 31, Copenhagen: Akademisk Forlag.

Christensen, E. (2002) 'En oppvaekst hvor mor bliver mishandlet – fra barnets synsvinkel' ['Growing up when mother is being abused – from the perspective of the child'], in M. Eriksson, A. Nenola and M.M. Nilsen (eds) *Gender and violence in the Nordic countries*, TemaNord 2002: 545, Copenhagen: Nordic Council of Ministers, pp 245-60.

Christensen, E. and Koch-Nilsen, I. (1992) Vold ude og hjemme [*Violence outside and in the home: A survey of physical violence against women from men*], Report 92:4, Copenhagen: Socialforskningsionstitutet.

Civilretsdirektoratet [Directorate on civil law] (1999a) *Vejledning til samvær og børnesagkyndig rådgivning* [*Guidance for contact and child expert counselling*], Copenhagen: Civilretsdirektoratet.

Civilretsdirektoratet (1999b) *Samvær og børnesagkyndig rådgivning: Statistik 1998* [*Contact and child expert counselling: Statistics 1998*], Copenhagen: Civilretsdirektoratet.

Civilretsdirektoratet (2000) *Samvær og børnesagkyndig rådgivning: Statistik 1999* [*Contact and child expert counselling: Statistics 1999*], Copenhagen: Civilretsdirektoratet.

Civilretsdirektoratet (2003) *Samvær og børnesagkyndig rådgivning: Statistik 2002* [*Contact and child expert counselling: Statistics 2002*], Copenhagen: Civilretsdirektoratet.

Crenshaw, K. (1991) 'Mapping the margins: intersectionality, identity politics, and violence against women of color', *Stanford Law Review*, vol 403, pp 1241, 1244-5.

Crown Prosecution Service (2001) *Guidance on prosecuting cases of domestic violence*, London: Crown Prosecution Service.

Dahlberg, A., Nordborg, G. and Wicklund, E. (1990) *Kvinnors rätt* [*Women's law*], Stockholm: Tiden/Folksam.

Danielsen, S. (1997) *Lov om forældremyndighed og samvær, med kommentarer af Sven Danielsen* [*Law on custody and contact with comments by Sven Danielsen*], Copenhagen: Jurist- og økonomforbundets forlag.

Denzin, N. and Lincoln, Y.S. (eds) (1998) *Collecting and interpreting qualitative materials*, London: Sage Publications.

Diesen, C. (ed) (2001) *Sexuella övergrepp mot barn* [*Sexual assaults on children*], Stockholm: Norstedts Juridik.

Dingwall, R. (1988) 'Empowerment or enforcement? Some questions about power and control in divorce mediation', in R. Dingwall and J. Eekelaar (eds) *Divorce mediation and the legal process*, Oxford: Clarendon Press.

Dingwall, R. (1989) 'Some problems about predicting child abuse and neglect', in O. Stevenson (ed) *Child abuse: Professional practice and public policy*, Hemel Hempstead: Harvester Wheatsheaf, pp 28-53.

Dobash, R.E. and Dobash, R.P. (1992) *Women, violence and social change*, London: Routledge.

Dobash, R.P. and Dobash, R.E. (2004) 'Women's violence to men in intimate relationships: working on a puzzle', *British Journal of Criminology*, vol 44, no 3, pp 324-49.

Dominelli, L. (1998) 'Multiculturalism, anti-racism and social work', in C. Williams, H. Soydan and M.R.D. Johnson (eds) *Social work and minorities: European perspectives*, London: Routledge, pp 36-57.

Dufva, V. (2001) *Mikä lapsella hätänä? Perheväkivalta* [*What's troubling the child? Domestic violence from the perspective of school staff*], Helsinki: Ensi- ja turvakotien liitto.

Edleson, J. (1999) 'Children's witnessing of adult domestic violence', *Journal of Interpersonal Violence*, vol 8, no 14, pp 839-71.

Eduards, M. (1997a) 'The women's shelter movement', in G. Gustafsson, M. Eduards and M. Rönnblom (eds) *Towards a new democratic order? Women's organizing in Sweden in 1990s*, Stockholm: Publica, pp 120-68.

Eduards, M. (1997b) 'Interpreting women's organizing', in G. Gustafsson, M. Eduards and M. Rönnblom (eds) *Towards a new democratic order? Women's organizing in Sweden in 1990s*. Stockholm: Publica, pp 11-25.

Eduards, M. (2002) *Förbjuden handling* [*Forbidden action*], Malmö: Liber.

Eisenstein, Z.R. (1988) *The female body and the law*, Berkeley, CA: University of California Press.

Eriksson, M. (2001) 'Om vårdnad, boende och umgänge' ['Custody, residence and contact'], in B. Metell (ed) *Barn som ser pappa slå* [*Children who see daddy hit*], Stockholm: Förslagshuset Gothia, pp 104-37.

Eriksson, M. (2002) 'Men's violence, men's parenting and gender politics in Sweden', *NORA: Nordic Journal of Women's Studies*, vol 10, no 1, pp 6-15.

Eriksson, M. (2003) *I skuggan av Pappa* [*In the shadow of Daddy: The family law and the handling of fathers' violence*], Stehag: Förlags AB Gondolin.

Eriksson, M. and Hester, M. (2001) 'Violent men as good-enough fathers? A look at England and Sweden', *Violence Against Women*, vol 7, no 7, pp 779-98.

Eriksson, M., Nenola, A. and M.M. Nilsen (eds) (2002) *Gender and violence in the Nordic Countries*, TemaNord 2002: 545, Copenhagen: Nordic Council of Ministers.

Eskonen, I. (2001) 'Miten lapset kertovat läheisiin suhteisiin liittyvästä väkivallasta?' ['How children speak about violence in close relations? Analysing narration of children in therapy groups'], *Janus*, vol 1, no 9, pp 22-39.

Esping-Andersen, G. (1990) *The three worlds of welfare capitalism*, Cambridge: Polity Press.

Esping-Andersen, G. (ed) (1996) *Welfare states in transition*, London: Sage Publications.

Esping-Andersen, G. (2003) *Why we need a new welfare state*, Oxford: Oxford University Press.

Fairclough, N. (2001) *Language and power*, (2nd edn), Harlow: Longman.

Finkelhor, D. (1991) 'The scope of the problem', in K. Murray and D.A. Gough (eds) *Intervening in child sexual abuse*, Edinburgh: Scottish Academic Press, pp 9-17.

Flendt, H. (1999) *Fælles forældremyndighed i praksis [Joint custody in practice]*, Copenhagen: Jurist- og økonomforbundets forlag.

Fleury, R.E., Sullivan, C.M. and Bybee, D.I. (2000) 'Domestic abuse by ex-partners: when ending the relationship does not end the violence. Women's experiences of violence by former partners', *Violence Against Women*, vol 6, no. 12, pp 63-81.

Foley, M. (1994) 'Professionalising the response to rape', in C. Lupton and T. Gillespie (eds) *Working with violence*, Basingstoke and London: Macmillan.

Forsberg, H. (1995) 'Sosiaalitoimiston Tsä: kaivattu, toivottu, ja uhkaara' ['The father in the social services office: expected, wished for and threatening'], in L. Eräsaari, R. Julkunen and H. Silius (eds) *Naiset yksityisen ja julkisen rajalla [Women at the border of private and public]*, Tampere: Vastapaino.

Forsberg, H. (2002) *Lasten asiakkuudet ja asiakkuuskokemukset turvakodeissa. Arviointitutkimus lapsen aika – projektista [The clienthoods and experiences of children in the shelters of battered women. An evaluation study of the child's time – project]*, Ensi- ja turvakotien liiton julkaisuja 31, Helsinki: Ensi- ja turvakotien liitto.

Forsberg, H., Kuronen, M., Pösö, T. and Ritala-Koskinen, A. (1994) 'Perheongelmat ja asiantuntijakäytännöt' ['Family problems and professional practices'], in P. Linna (ed) *Perhe [The family]*, Sosiaalipolitiikan laitos C-sarja 6/1994, Tampere: University of Tampere, pp 172-87.

Forsberg, H. and Pösö, T. (2002) 'Social work evaluation – do the words matter?', Invited plenary speech at the 4th International Conference on Evaluation for Practice, July 4-6, Tampere, Finland (www.uta.fi/laitokset/sospol/eval2002/ForsbergandPoso.PDF).

Giddens, A. (1992) *The transformation of intimacy. Sexuality, love and eroticism in modern societies*, Cambridge: Polity Press.

Giddens, A. (1999) *Runaway world. How globalisation is reshaping our lives*, London: Profile Books.

Grillo, T. (1991) 'The mediation alternative: process dangers for women', *The Yale Law Journal*, no 100, pp 1545-610.

Haaland, T. (1997) *Hjelp til voldsofre i Oslo. En brukerrettet evaluering [Help to victims of violence in Olso]*, Prosjektrapport 1997: 29, Oslo: NIBR.

Haapasalo, J. (2000) 'Vankien kaltoinkohtelu, käytösongelmat ja aikuisiän psyykkiset häiriöt' ['Abuse, behavioral problems and mental disturbances of prisoners'], *Psykologia*, no 1, pp 45-57.

Hague, G., Mullender, A., Kelly, L. and Malos, E. (2000) 'Unsung innovation: the history of work with children in UK domestic violence refuges', in J. Hanmer and C. Itzin (eds) *Home truths about domestic violence. Feminist influences on policy and practice*, London and New York, NY: Routledge, pp 113-30.

Hantrais, L. and Letablier, M.-T. (1996) *Families and family policies in Europe*, Harlow: Longman.

Hart, B. (1990) 'The further endangerment of battered women and children in custody mediation', *Mediation Quarterly*, vol 7, no 3, pp 278-91.

Hearn, J. (1998) *The violences of men*, London: Sage Publications.

Hearn, J. (2001) 'Nation, state and welfare: the cases of Finland and the UK', in B. Pease and K. Pringle (eds) *A man's world? Changing men's practices in a globalised world*, London: Zed Books, pp 85-102.

Hearn, J. and Lattu, E. (2002) 'The recent development of Finnish studies on men: a selective review and a critique of a neglected field', *Nordic Journal of Women's Studies/NORA*, vol 10, no 1, pp 49-60.

Hearn, J. and Pringle, K. (forthcoming) *European perspectives on men and masculinities*, London: Palgrave.

Hearn, J., Pringle, K., Müller, U., Oleksy, E., Lattu, E., Chernova, J., Ferguson, H., Holter, Ø.G., Kolga, V., Novikova, I., Ventimiglia, C., Olsvik, E. and Tallberg, T. (2002) 'Critical studies on men in ten European countries: (1) the state of academic research', *Men and Masculinities*, vol 4, no 4, pp 380-408.

Heinänen, A. (1992) *Lapsen tasa-arvoa avoittamassa* [*Pursuing the equality of a child: The history of the Federation of Mother and Child Homes and Shelters 1945-1990*], Helsinki: Ensi- ja turvakotien liiton julkaisu no 13.

Heiskanen, M. and Piispa, M. (1998). *Faith, hope and battering: A survey of men's violence against women*, Helsinki: Statistics Finland.

Hester, M. (2000) 'Child protection and domestic violence: findings from a Rowntree/NSPCC study', in J. Hanmer and C. Itzin (eds) *Home truths about domestic violence: Feminist influences on policy and practice*. London and New York: Routledge, pp 96-112.

Hester, M. (2002) 'One step forward and three steps back? Children, abuse and parental contact in Denmark', *Child and Family Law Quarterly*, vol 14, no 3, pp 267-79.

Hester, M. (2003) 'Effective intervention with children experiencing domestic violence', in Proceedings from Diakonie Conference on Children and Domestic Violence, Kiel, Germany, September.

Hester, M. (2004) 'Future trends and developments: violence against women in Europe and East Asia', *Violence Against Women*, vol 10, no 12, pp 1431-48.

Hester, M. and Harne, L. (1999) 'Fatherhood, children and violence: placing the UK in an international context', in S. Watson and L. Doyal (eds) *Engendering social policy*, Buckingham: Open University Press, pp 148-64.

Hester, M. and Pearson, C. (1993) 'Domestic violence, mediation and child contact arrangements: issues from current research', *Family Mediation*, vol 3, no 2, pp 3-6.

Hester, M. and Pearson, C. (1997) 'Domestic violence and parental contact: children's right to safety', in M. John (ed) *A charge against society: The child's right to protection*, London: Jessica Kingsley, pp 281-90.

Hester, M. and Radford, L. (1992) 'Domestic violence and access arrangements for children in Denmark and Britain', *Journal of Social Welfare and Family Law*, no 1, pp 57-70.

Hester, M. and Radford, L. (1996) *Domestic violence and child contact arrangements in England and Denmark*, Bristol: The Policy Press.

Hester, M. and Westmarland, N. (2005) *Tackling domestic violence: Effective interventions and approaches*, Home Office Research Study 290, London: Home Office.

Hester, M., Pearson, C. and Harwin, N. (2000) *Making an impact: Children and domestic violence. A reader*, London: Jessica Kingsley Publishing.

Hester, M., Pearson, C. and Radford, L. (1997) *Domestic violence: A national survey of court welfare and voluntary sector mediation practice*, Bristol: The Policy Press.

Hester, M., Humphries, J., Pearson, C., Qaiser, K., Radford, L. and Woodfield, K. (1994) 'Domestic violence and child contact', in A. Mullender and R. Morley (eds) *Children living with domestic violence*, London: Whiting and Birch, pp 1-26.

Hjemdal, O.K. and Stefansen, K. (2003) *Hjelpeapparatets rutiner for avdekking og registrering av vold* [*The routines of help agencies for discovering and registering violence. Report from a project under the action plan on violence against women*], Oslo: Høgskolen i Oslo, Kompetansesenter for voldsofferarbeid.

Hochschild, A.R. (1983) *The managed heart. Commercialization of human feeling*, Berkeley, CA and London: University of California Press.

Højgaard, L. (1997) 'Working fathers – caught in the web of the symbolic order of gender', *Acta Sociologica*, vol 40, no 3, pp 245-62.

Højlund, (2000) 'Børn og samvær' ['Children and contact: when contact is problematic or directly harmful to the child'], Documentation no 7, Børns Vilkår [Children's Circumstances].

Holden, G.W. (1998) 'Introduction: the development of research into another consequence of family violence', in G.W. Holden, R. Geffner and E.N. Jouriles (eds) *Children exposed to marital violence. Theory, research and applied issues*, Washington, DC: American Psychological Association, pp 1-18.

Holm, U.M. (1993) *Modrande & praxis* [*Mothering and practice: A feminist philosophical investigation*], Göteborg: Diadalos.

Hooper, C.-A. (1994) 'Do families need fathers? The impact of divorce on children', in A. Mullender and R. Morley (eds) *Children living with domestic violence*, London: Whiting and Birch.

Hooper, C.-A. (1997) 'Child sexual abuse and the regulation of women. Variations on a theme', in L. O'Toole and J. Schiffman (eds) *Gender violence. Interdisciplinary perspectives*, London and New York, NY: New York University Press (originally published 1992).

Hughes, C. and Dunn, J. (2002) '"When I say a naughty word". A longitudinal study of young children's accounts of anger and sadness in themselves and close others', *British Journal of Developmental Psychology*, vol 20, no 4, pp 515-35.

Humphreys, C., Hester, M., Hague, G., Mullender, A., Abrahams, H. and Lowe, P. (2000) *From good intentions to good practice: Mapping services working with families where there is domestic violence*, Bristol: The Policy Press.

Husso, M. (2003) *Parisuhdeväkivalta. Lyötyjen aika ja tila* [*Violence in intimate relationships. Time and space of the beaten*], Tampere: Vastapaino.

Huttunen, J. (1999) 'Muuttunut ja muuttuva isyys' ['The changed and changing fatherhood'], in A. Jokinen (ed) *Mies ja muutos. Kriittisen miestutkimuksen teemoja* [*Man and change. Themes of the critical studies on men*], Tampere: Tampere University Press, pp 169-93.

Huttunen, J. (2001) *Isänä olemisen uudet suunnat* [*New directions in being a father*], Jyväskylä: Ps-kustannus.

Interdepartmental arbeidsgruppe (1983) *Tiltak mot Kvinnemishandling* [*Relief measures against wife battering: A plan of action*], Oslo: Sostaldepartementet, Justizdepartementet og Forbruker og administrasjonsdepartementet.

Iovanni, L. and Pringle, K. (2005a) 'A review of academic studies relating to men's practices in Denmark', Critical Research on Men in Europe, www.cromenet.org.

Iovanni, L. and Pringle, K. (2005b) 'A review of official statistical data relating to men's practices in Denmark', Critical Research on Men in Europe, www.cromenet.org.

Iovanni, L. and Pringle, K. (2005c) 'A review of governmental and policy documentation relating to men's practices in Denmark', Critical Research on Men in Europe, www.cromenet.org.

Itzin, C. (ed) (2000a) *Home truths about child sexual abuse: Influencing policy and practice. A reader*, London: Routledge.

Itzin, C. (2000b) 'Gendering domestic violence: the influence of feminism on policy and practice', in J. Hanmer and C. Itzin (eds) *Home truths about domestic violence. Feminist influences on policy and practice*, London and New York: Routledge, ch 3, pp 356-80.

Jaffe, P.G., Wolfe, D. and Wilson, S. (1990) 'Children of battered women', *Developmental Clinical Psychology and Psychiatry*, vol 21, Newbury Park: Sage Publications.

Jaffe, P.G., Lemon, N.K.D. and Poisson, S.E. (2003) *Child custody and domestic violence: A call for safety and accountability*, Thousand Oaks, CA, London, New Delhi: Sage Publications.

Jallinoja, R. (2000) *Perheen aika* [*Time of family*], Helsinki: Otava.

James, A. and James, A. (2004) *Constructing childhood: Theory, policy, and social practice*, Basingstoke: Palgrave Macmillan.

James, A. and Prout, A. (1990) (eds) *Constructing and reconstructing Childhood*, Basingstoke: Falmer Press.

Jeffner, S. (1994) *Kvinnojourskunskap* [*The knowledge of the women's shelters*], Report 1994: 10, Stockholm: Folkhälsoinstitutet.

Johnson, H. (1998) 'Rethinking survey research on violence against women', in R.E. Dobash and R.P. Dobash (eds) *Rethinking violence against women*, Thousand Oaks, CA, London, New Delhi: Sage Publications, pp 23-51.

Jokinen, A. (ed) (1999) *Mies ja muutos. Kriittisen* [*Man and change. Themes of the critical studies on men*], Tampere: Tampere University Press.

Jokinen, E. (1996) *Väsynyt äiti. Äitiyden* [*The tired mother. Autobiographical presentations of motherhood*], Helsinki: Gaudeamus.

Jonassen, W. (1987) *Vennetjeneste eller offentlig tiltak?* [*A favour or a public service? An analysis of the organisation and running of crisis centres*], Report 1987: 10, Oslo: NIBR.

Jonassen, W. (2001) *Fra kompetanse til handling* [*From competence to action*], Project Report 2001: 13, Oslo: NIBR.

Jonassen, W. (2004) *Krisesentrene 2003 – en kommentert statistikk* [*The refuges/shelters 2003 – statistics with comments*], Report no 1/2004, Oslo: Nasjonalt kunnskapssenter om vold og traumatisk stress.

Jonassen, W. and Eidheim, F. (2001) *Den gode vilje* [*Good intentions: Battered women's experiences of the welfare system*], PLUSS-SERIE 1 – 2001, Oslo: NIBR.

Jonassen, W. and Stefansen, K. (2003) *Ideologi eller profesjonstenkning?* [*Ideology or professionalism? A state of affairs report about the crisis centres*], Oslo: Høgskolen i Oslo, Kompetansesenter for voldsofferarbeid.

Justis- og politidepartementet [Ministry of law and police] (2003) *Retten til et liv uten vold* [*The right to a life without violence: Men's violence against women in intimate relations*], Nov 2003:31 [Norwegian public investigations] Oslo: Justis- og politidepartementet.

Justis- og politidepartementet [Ministry of Law and Police] et al (2000) *Regjeringens handlingsplan 'Vold mot kvinner'* [*The goverment's plan of action 'Violence against women'*], Oslo, Justis- og politidepartementet, Barne- og familiedepartementet, Sosial- og helsedepartementet [Ministry of Children and Families, Ministry of Social Affairs and Health].

Justitsministeriets Forældremyndighedsudvalg [The Department of Law's Committee on Custody] (1994) *Fælles forældremyndighed, samværsvanskeligheder, børnesagkyndig rådgivning, Betænkning nr 1279* [*Joint custody, contact problems, child expert counselling, Report no 1279*], Copenhagen: Statens Information.

Kaganas, F. (2000) 'Re: L (Contact: Domestic Violence); Re: V (Contact: Domestic Violence); Re: M (Contact: Domestic Violence): Contact and domestic violence', *Child and Family Law Quarterley*, vol 12, no 3, pp 312-24.

Kamali, M. (1997) *Distorted integration: Clientization of immigrants in Sweden*, Uppsala: Uppsala Multiethnic Papers.

Kautto, M., Heikkila, M., Hvinden, B., Marklund, S. and Ploug, N. (eds) *Nordic social policy: Changing welfare states*, London: Routledge.

Keeler, L. (ed) (2001) *Recommendations of the EU expert meeting on violence against women*, Report 2000: 13, Helsinki: Ministry of Social Affairs and Health.

Kelly, L. (2002) *Fornyelse av våre visjoner* [*Renewal of our visions: The service of the crisis centres in the 21st century. Collection from consultation conference arranged by the committee on violence against women*], Oslo: Justis- og politidepartementet.

Kelly, L., Regan, L. and Burton, S. (1991) *An exploratory study of the prevalence of sexual abuse in a sample of 16-21 year olds*, London: Polytechnic of North London.

Keskinen, S. (2002) 'The threat of violence and the strength of motherhood?', in M. Eriksson, A. Nenola and M.M. Nielsen (eds) *Gender and violence in the Nordic countries*, TemaNord 2002: 545, Copenhagen: The Nordic Council of Ministers, pp 219-32.

Kirmanen, T. (1999) 'Pelko lapsen maailmassa' ['Fear in the child's world'], in J. Eskola (ed) *Hegelistä Harreen, narratiivista Nudistiin [From Hegel to Harre, from narrative to Nudist]*, Kuopio: University of Kuopio.

Kiviaho, P. (ed) (1998) *Puheenvuoroja naisiin kohdistuvasta väkivallasta [Discussions on violence against women]*, Helsinki: Sosiaali- ja terveysministeriö.

Klinth, R. (2002) *Göra pappa med barn [Making daddy with child: The Swedish daddy politics 1960-95]*, Umeå: Boréa.

Komiteanmietintö [Report of the Father Committee] (1999) *Isätoimikunnan mietintö [The report of the father committee]*, Komiteanmietintö 1999: 1, Helsinki: Sosiaali- ja terveys-ministeriö [Ministry of Social Affairs and Health].

Korhonen, M. (1999) *Isyyden muutos [The change of fatherhood: Childhood experiences of middle-age men and their own parenting]*, Joensuu: University of Joensuu.

Kosonen, P. (2001) 'Globalization and the Nordic welfare states', in R. Sykes, B. Palier and P. Prior (eds) *Globalization and European welfare states: Challenges and change*, London: Palgrave.

Kraft, K. (2000) *Det är förbjudet! [It is forbidden!]*, Uppsala: Ståpäls AB.

Kurki-Suonio, K. (1995) 'Gemensam vårdnad' ['Shared custody: what is concealed by the best interest of the child'], in G. Nordborg (ed) *13 kvinnoperspektiv på rätten [13 Women's perspectives on the law]*, Uppsala: Iustus, pp 169-95.

Kurki-Suonio, K. (1999) *Äidin hoivasta yhteishuoltoon [From mother's care to joint custody: The changing legal interpretations of the welfare of the child]*, Helsinki: Suomalainen lakimiesyhdistys.

Kurki-Suonio, K. (2000) 'Joint custody as an interpretation of the best interests of the child in critical and comparative perspective', *International Journal of Law, Policy and the Family*, vol 14, no 3, pp 183-205.

Kuronen, M. (1995) 'Naiset kohtaavat neuvolassa' ['Female encounters in child health centres'], in L. Eräsaari, R. Julkunen and H. Silius (eds) *Naiset yksityisen ja julkisen rajalla [Women at the border of private and public]*, Tampere: Vastapaino.

Kuronen, M. (2003) 'Eronnut perhe?' ['The divorced family?'], in H. Forsberg and R. Nätkin (eds) *Perhe murroksessa [Family in transition: Tracing the critical studies on the family]*, Helsinki: Gaudeamus.

Kvinnevoldsutvalget [Committee on violence against women] (2002) *Delrapport om krisesentrene i tilknytning til omlegging av tilskuddsordningen* [*Report about the crisis centres in relation to the reorganisation about funding*], Oslo: Justis- og politidepartementet.

Kvist, J. (1999) 'Welfare reform in the Nordic countries in the 1990s: using fuzzy-set theory to assess conformity to ideal types', *Journal of European Social Policy*, vol 9, no 3, pp 231-52.

Laaksamo, E.-M. (2001) 'Kuuleeko äiti, näkyykö isä?' ['Does mother hear, is father visible? Parenthood and violence in a family'], in M. Oranen (ed) *Perheväkivallan varjossa* [*In the shadows of family violence: Report on developing child-centred work*], Helsinki: Ensi- ja turvakotien liitto, pp 98-122.

Labour Party (1997) *Supporting women*, London: Labour Party.

Laclau, E. (ed) (1990) *New reflections on the revolution of our time*, London: Verso.

Lagutskottet 1992/93 LU22 [Report from the Committee on Civil Law] *Olovligt bortförande av barn samt vårdnad och umgänge m.m* [*Abduction of children, custody and contact, etc*], Sweden, Stockholm: Fritzes, ch 7.

Lagutskottet 1997/98 LU12 [Report from the Committee on Civil Law] *Vårdnad, boende, umgänge* [*Custody, residence, contact*], Sweden, Stockholm: Fritzes, ch 7.

Lehtonen, A. and Perttu, S. (1999) *Naisiin kohdistuva väkivalta* [*Violence against women*], Helsinki: Kirjayhtymä Oy.

Leira, H. (2002) 'From tabooed trauma to affirmation and recognition. An explanatory model to understand and work with children who have experienced violence in the family', in M. Eriksson, A. Nenola and M.M. Nilsen (eds) *Gender and violence in the Nordic countries*, TemaNord 2002: 545, Copenhagen: Nordic Council of Ministers, pp 285-96.

Leskinen, R. (1982) *"Kuka kuulisi minua?"* [*"Who would listen to me?":* *Family violence in the eyes of the child*], Helsinki: Ensi- ja turvakotien liitto.

Lewis, C. and O'Brien, M. (1987) 'Constraints on fathers: research, theory and clinical practice', in C. Lewis, and M. O'Brien (eds) *Reassessing fatherhood*, London: Sage Publications.

Lewis, J. (ed) (1993) *Women and social policies in Europe: Work, family and the state*, Aldershot: Edward Elgar Publishing.

Lindberg, S. (1999-2000) 'Föräldrakonflikter och vårdnadstvister' ['Parents' conflicts and custody disputes'], *Juridisk tidskrift* [*Journal of Law*] 1999-2000, pp 740-4.

Lundgren, E., Heimer, G., Westerstrand, J. and Kalliokoski, A.-M. (2001) *Slagen dam* [*Captured queen: Men's violence against women in 'equal' Sweden – a national survey*], Stockholm and Umeå: Fritzes and Brottsoffermyndigheten

Lundström, A., Nordenfors, G., Christenson, G. and Wikström, M. (2001) *Tystnaden är bruten. Ta ansvar!* [*The silence is broken: Take responsibility!*], Stockholm: ROKS/The National Organisation for Women's Refuges in Sweden.

Lupton, C. (1994) 'The British refuge movement. The survival of an ideal?', in C. Lupton and T. Gillespie (eds) *Working with violence*, Basingstoke and London: Macmillan.

Malterud, K. (1981) *Kvinnemishandling- et helseproblem* [*Violence against women as a health problem: An investigation into the welfare system responsibility and function in Oslo*], Oslo: Oslo Helseråd, Avdeling for morog barn.

Månsson, S.-A. (2001) 'Men's practices in prostitution: the case of Sweden', in B. Pease and K. Pringle (eds) *A man's world? Changing men's practices in a globalised world*, London: Zed Books, pp 85-102.

Marecek, J. (1999) 'Trauma talk in feminist clinical practice', in S. Lamb (ed) *New versions of victims: Feminists struggle with the concept*, New York, NY: New York University Press, pp 158-82.

Marsiglio, W. (1995) *Fatherhood: Contemporary theory, research and social policy*, London and California: Sage Publications.

Mason, J. and Falloon, J. (2001) 'Some Sydney children define abuse: implications for agency in childhood', in L. Alanen and B. Mayall (eds) *Conceptualizing chid–adult relations*, London and New York: Routledge and Falmer.

McGee, C. (2000) *Childhood experiences of domestic violence*, London: Jessica Kingsley.

McKee, L. and O'Brien, M. (1982) *The Father figure*, London, Tavistock Publications.

McKie, L. (2002) 'Theorising families, violences and social change', Paper presented at a seminar at Glasgow Caledonian University, November.

McMahon, M. and Pence, E. (1995) 'Doing more harm than good? Some cautions on visitation centres', in E. Peled, P.G. Jaffe and J.L. Edleson (eds) *Ending the cycle of violence: Community responses to children of battered women*, California: Sage Publications, pp 186-206.

McMillan, L. (2002) 'Women's anti-violence organisations in Sweden and the UK', in M. Eriksson, A. Nenola and M.M. Nilsen (eds) *Gender and violence in the Nordic countries*, TemaNord 2002: 545, Copenhagen: The Nordic Council of Ministers, pp 165-80.

Mellberg, N. (1997) 'Sexuella övergrepp mot barn ur ett feministiskt sociologiskt perspektiv' ['Sexual abuse of children from a feminist sociological perspective'], in G. Nordborg (ed) *Makt & kön* [*Power and gender: Thirteen contributions to feminist knowledge*], Stockholm/ Stehag: Symposion, pp 199-225.

Mellberg, N. (2002) *När det overkliga blir verklighet* [*When the unreal becomes a reality: Mothers' situation when their children are sexually abused by fathers*], Umeå: Boréa.

Metell, B. (ed) (2001) *Barn som ser pappa slå* [*Children who see Daddy hit*], Stockholm: Förlagshuset Gothia.

Micklewright, J. and Stewart, K. (2000) *The welfare of Europe's children: Are EU member states converging?*, Bristol: The Policy Press.

Miller, A. (1986) *Du skall icke märka. Variationer över paradistemat* [*You shall not notice: Variations on the Paradise-theme*], Stockholm: Wahlström and Widstrand.

Milner, J. (1996) 'Men's resistance to social workers', in B. Fawcett, B. Featherstone, J. Hearn and C. Toft (eds) *Violence and gender relations. Theories and interventions*, London: Sage Publications, pp 115-29.

Mirrlees-Black, C. (1999) *Domestic violence: Findings from a new British Crime Survey self-completion questionnaire*, Home Office Research Study 191, London: Home Office.

Molina, I. (1997) *Stadens rasifering* [*The racialisation of the city: Ethnic housing segregation in the 'people's home'*], Uppsala: Geografiska Regionstudier, 32.

Morley, R. and Mullender, A. (1994) 'Domestic violence and children: what do we know from research?', in A. Mullender and R. Morley (eds) *Children living with domestic violence. Putting men's abuse of women on the childcare agenda*, London: Whiting and Birch, pp 24-42.

Mott, F.L. (1993) *Absent fathers and child development: Emotional and cognitive effects at ages five to nine*, Columbus, OH: Ohio State University, Centre for Human Resource Research.

Mullender, A., Hague, G., Imam, U.F., Kelly, L., Malos, E. and Regan, L. (2002) *Children's perspectives on domestic violence*, London: Sage Publications.

Näre, S. (2000) 'Nuorten tyttöjen kohtaama seksuaalinen väkivalta ja loukattu luottamus tunnetaloudessa' ['Sexual abuse and hurt trust experienced by young girls in emotion economy'], in P. Honkatukia, J. Niemi-Kiesiläinen and S. Näre (eds) *Lähentelystä raiskauksiin. Tyttöjen kokemuksia seksuaalisesta väkivallasta* [*From advance to rape. Girls' experiences of sexual abuse*], Helsinki: Nuorisotutkimusverkosto.

Nätkin, R. (1997) *Kamppailu suomalaisesta äitiydestä* [*The struggle on Finnish motherhood. Maternalism, population policy and women's narratives*], Helsinki: Gaudeamus.

Nesvold, H. (1997) *Helsetjeneste for seksualvoldsutsatte* [*Health services for victims of sexual violence: Report from a jubilee seminar*], Oslo: Ullevål sykehus.

Nilsen, S. and Prøis, L.O. (2002) *Fra krisesenter til eget lokalmiljø* [*From crisis centres to a local context of one's own: What has to happen for women from ethnic minorities to re-establish themselves after leaving an abusive relationship?*], Oslo: Oslo Krisesenter.

Nisja, R. and Aslaksen, I. (1980) *Krisesenteret for voldtatte og mishandlete kvinner* [*Crisis centres for women subjected to rape and battering: An analysis of functions and needs*], Oslo: INAS Rapport 80:2.

Nordborg, G. (1995) 'Konstruktioner av moderskap och faderskap' [*Constructions of motherhood and fatherhood: by reproduction technology and in the law*], in G. Nordborg (ed) *13 kvinnoperspektiv på rätten* [*13 women's perspectives on the law*], Uppsala: Iustus, pp 135-67.

Nordborg, G. (1997) 'Om juridikens kön' ['On the gender of law'], in G. Nordborg (ed) *Makt & kön* [*Gender and power: Thirteen contributions to feminist knowledge*], Stockholm/Stehag: Symposion, pp 171-98.

Nordborg, G. (1999) 'Kärlek och ekonomi – juridiskt undantagstillstånd?' ['Love and economy – a legal state of emergency?'], *Kvinnovetenskaplig tidskrift* [*Journal of Women's Studies*] no 1, pp 49-63.

Nordborg, G. (2001) *Kvinnofrid* [*Woman's peace: Understanding the background to men's violence against women and its effects*], Umeå: Brotts-offermyndigheten.

Nordborg, G. and Niemi-Kiesiläinen, J. (2001) 'Women's peace: a criminal Law reform in Sweden', in K. Nousiainen, Å. Gunnarsson, K. Lundström and J. Niemi-Kiesiläinen (eds) *Responsible selves. Women in the Nordic legal culture*, Aldershot: Ashgate, pp 353-73.

Nordenfors, G. (1996) *Fadersrätt, kvinnofrid och barns säkerhet* [*The right of the father, women's peace and the safety of children*], Stockholm: ROKS/ The National Organisation for Women's Refuges in Sweden.

Notko, M. (2000) *Väkivalta parisuhteessa ja perheessä* [*Violence in intimate relationships and in a family*], Jyväskylä: University of Jyväskylä.

Nousiainen, K. (2001a) 'Yksityinen ja julkinen – perhe ja markkinat' ['Private and public – family and market'], *Naistutkimus*, vol 14, no 4, pp 6-21.

Nousiainen, K. (2001b) 'Introductory remarks on Nordic law and gender identities', in K. Nousiainen, Å. Gunnarsson, K. Lundström and J. Niemi-Kiesiläinen (eds) *Responsible selves: Women in the Nordic legal culture*, Aldershot: Ashgate, pp 1-22.

Nummelin, R. (1997) *Seksuaalikasvatusmateriaalit [Sex education materials: What kind of sexuality to young people?]*, Raportteja 206, Helsinki: Stakes.

Nyqvist, L. (2001) *Väkivaltainen parisuhde, asiakkuus ja muutos [A violent relationship, clienthood and change]*, Helsinki: Ensi- ja turvakotien liitto.

Olsen, M. (1998) *Der vi bor der gråter alle damene [Where we live all the women are crying]*. A report about services to children at the crisis centre in Oslo, Oslo: Barne- og familiedepartementet.

Oranen, M. (2001a) 'Juuret, raamit ja numerot' ['Roots, frames and numbers: Child's Time project'], in M. Oranen (ed) *Perheväkivallan varjossa [In the shadows of family violence: Report on developing child-centred work]*, Helsinki: Ensi- ja turvakotien liitto, pp 13-40.

Oranen, M. (2001b) 'Taistelut ja tulokset' ['Battles and results. Sharing the experiences of a child'], in M. Oranen (ed) *Perheväkivallan varjossa [In the shadows of family violence: Report on developing child-centred work]*, Helsinki: Ensi- ja turvakotien liitto, pp 66-97.

Oslo Krisesenter [Oslo crisis centre] (2004) *Årsberetning 2003 [Annual report 2003]*, Oslo: Oslo Krisesenter.

Pape, H. and Stefansen, K. (eds) (2004) *Den skjulte volden? [Hidden violence? A survey of threats, violence and sexual abuse in the population of Oslo]*, Report no 1/2004, Oslo: Nasjonalt kunnskapssenter om vold og traumatisk stress and NOVA.

Partanen, T. and Holma, J. (2002) 'Vaihtoehto väkivallalle. Toimijuutta kaikille perheenjäsenille' ['Alternative to violence. Agency for all family members'], in A. Rönkä and U. Kinnunen (eds) *Perhe ja vanhemmuus. Suomalainen perhe-elämä ja sen tukeminen [Family and parenthood. Finnish family life and supporting it]*, Jyväskylä: PS-kustannus, pp 188-205.

Parton, N. (ed) (1997) *Child protection and family support*, London: Routledge.

Paul, R.E. (1998) *Shelters for battered women and the needs of immigrant women*, Copenhagen: Nordic Council of Ministers.

Pease, B. and Pringle, K. (eds) (2001) *A man's world? Changing men's practices in a globalised world*, London: Zed Books.

Peled, E. (1998) 'The experience of living with violence for preadolescent children of battered women', *Youth and Society*, vol 29, no 4, pp 395-431.

Peled, E. (2000) 'Parenting by men who abuse women: issues and dilemmas', *British Journal of Social Work*, vol. 30, no 1, pp 25-36.

Peltoniemi, T. (1984) *Perheväkivalta [Family violence]*, Helsinki: Otava.

Perttu, S. and Söderholm, A.-L. (1998) *Väkivaltaa kokeneiden auttaminen [Helping persons who have experienced violence: A guide for professionals]*, Helsinki: Sosiaali- ja terveysministeriö.

Perttu, S., Mononen-Mikkilä, P., Rauhala, R. and Särkkälä, P. (1999) *Päänavaus selviytymiseen* [*Starting to survive: Handbook for the women who have experienced violence*], Jyväskylä: Gummerus.

Pettilä, U. and Yli-Marttila, L. (1999) *Eron vaiheet. Kirja eroaville ja eroavien auttajille* [*The stages of divorce. Book for the divorcing people and their helpers*], Helsinki: Tietosanoma.

Pitkäkangas-Laitila, S. and Räisälä, R. (1999) *Pippurimuorikerho* [*Peppermum Club. A group of children exposed to family violence in the shelter context*], Jyväskylä: University of Jyväskylä.

Pred, A. (2000) *Even in Sweden: Racisms, racialized spaces and the popular geographical imagination*, Berkeley and Los Angeles, CA: University of California Press.

Pringle, K. (1995) *Men, masculinities and social welfare*, London: UCL Press.

Pringle, K. (1998) *Children and social welfare in Europe*, Buckingham: Open University Press.

Pringle, K. (2001a) 'A review of academic studies relating to men's practices in the United Kingdom', Critical Research on Men in Europe (www.cromenet.org).

Pringle, K. (2001b) 'A review of governmental and policy document-ation relating to men's practices in the United Kingdom', Critical Research on Men in Europe (www.cromenet.org).

Pringle, K. (2002) 'Final report to the ESRC on project R000223551' (www.regard.ac.uk/cgi-bin/regardng/showReports.pl?ref= R000223551).

Pringle, K. and Harder, M. (1999) *Through two pairs of eyes: A comparative study of Danish social policy and child welfare*, Aalborg: Aalborg Univer-sitetsforlag.

Pringle, K., Raynor, A. and Millett, J. (2001) 'A review of official statistical data relating to men's practices in the United Kingdom', Critical Research on Men in Europe, www.cromenet.org.

Pringle, K., Hearn, J., Ferguson, H., Kambouvov, D., Kolga, V., Lattu, E., Müller, U., Nordberg, M., Novikova, I., Oleksy, E., Rydzewska, J. Smidova, I., Tallberg, T., Niemi, H. (forthcoming) *Men and masculinities in Europe*, London: Whiting and Birch.

Profitt, N.J. (2000) *Women survivors, psychological trauma and the politics of Resistance*, New York, NY, London and Oxford: The Haworth Press.

Proposition (Prop) 1997/98: 7 [Government's proposition] *Vårdnad, boende, umgänge* [*Custody, living, contact*], Stockholm: Fritzes.

Prop 1997/98: 55 *Kvinnofrid* [*Woman's peace/Gross violation of women's integrity*], Stockholm: Fritzes.

Prop 2001/02: 123 *Partnerskap och adoption* [*Partnership and adoption*], Stockholm: Fritzes.

Prop 2002/03: 53 *Stärkt skydd för barn i utsatta situationer* [*Strengthened protection for children in exposed positions*], Stockholm: Fritzes.

Radford, L., Sayer, S. and AMICA (1999) *Unreasonable fears: Child contact in the context of domestic violence. A survey of mothers' perceptions of harm*, Bristol: Women's Aid Federation (England).

Råkil, M. (ed) (2002) *Menns vold mot kvinner* [*Men's violence against women: experiences from treatment and the state of knowledge*], Oslo, Univer-sitetsforlaget.

Rasmussen, N. (2000) *Familieret* [*Family law*] (6th edn), Copenhagen: Greens Jura.

Rautava, M. and Perttu, S. (2002) *Naisin Kohdistuva pari- ja lähisuhdeväkivalta* [*Violence against women in intimate relationships*], Helsinki: Stakes/Naisiin Kohdistuvan väkivaltan ehkäisy- projelcti.

Rautava, M. and Perttu, S. (2001) Tavoitteena uhrin turvallisuus [Safety of the victim as a goal – perspectives to preventing violence against women], Helsinki: Stakes/Naisiin Kohdistuvan väkivaltan ehkäisy- projelcti.

Rejmer, A. (2003) *Vårdnadstvister* [*Custody disputes. A study in the sociology of law of the courts' function at custody disputes with the best interests of the child as the point of departure*], Lund: University of Lund.

Richards, M. (1997) *The needs of children at divorce*, Dartmouth: Aldershot.

Richards, M.P.M and Dyson, M. (1982) *Separation, divorce and the development of children*, London, DHSS.

Roberts, M. (1988) *Mediation in family disputes*, Aldershot: Wildewood House.

Rodgers, B. and Pryor, J. (1998) *Divorce and separation: The outcomes for children*, York: Joseph Rowntree Foundation.

Ronkainen, S. (1994) 'Seksuaalisuus ja sukupuoli-identiteetti' ['Sexuality and sexual identity'], in S. Ronkainen, P. Pohjolainen and J.-E. Ruth (eds) *Erotiikka ja elämänkulku* [*Erotics and life course*], Porvoo: WSOY, pp 124-42.

Ronkainen, S. (1998) *Sukupuolistunut väkivalta ja sen tutkimus Suomessa* [*Sexualized violence and research on it in Finland*], Helsinki: Sosiaali- ja terveysministeriö.

Ronkainen, S. (1999) 'Subjektius, häpeä ja syyllisyys parisuhdeväkivallan elementteinä' ['Subjectivity, shame and guilt as elements of intimate violence'], in S. Näre (ed) *Tunteiden sosiologiaa II* [*Sociology of emotions II: History and regulating*], Helsinki: SKS.

Ronkainen, S. (2001a) 'Sukupuolistunut väkivalta ja uhriutumisen paradoksit Suomessa' ['Sexualized violence and the paradoxes of victimisation in Finland'], *Sosiaalilääketieteellinen aikakauslehti*, vol 38, no 2, pp 139-51.

Ronkainen, S. (2001b) 'Gendered violence and genderless gender', *Kvinder, Kön and Forskning* [*Women, Gender and Research*], vol 10, no 2, pp 45-57.

Roy, M. (1988) *Children in the cross fire*, Deerfield Beach, Florida: Health Communications Inc.

Ruxton, S. (1997) 'Children in Europe – policies and prospects', *Social Work in Europe*, vol 4, no 1, pp 17-23.

Säävälä, H. (2000) 'Aktiivinen isyys on tullut jäädäkseen' ['The active fatherhood is here to stay'], *Esikko*, no 2, pp 15-17.

Sainsbury, D. (ed) (1999) *Gender and welfare sate regimes*, Oxford: Oxford University Press.

Saksa, E. (1993) *Ja eron julma terä leikkasi* [*And the cruel blade of divorce cut: Report on custody fights*], Lempäälä: Erkki Saksa.

Saradjian, J. (1996) *Women who sexually abuse children: From research to clinical practice*, London: Wiley.

Saunders, A. (1995) 'The perspective of abused', in A. Saunders et al (eds) *"It hurts me too". Children's experiences of domestic violence and refuge life*, London: WAFE, NISW, ChildLine, pp 5-16.

SCB [Statistics Sweden] (1989) *Vårdnad och underhåll* [*Custody and child maintenance*], Stockholm and Yrelsvo: Statistiska Centralbyrån.

SCB (1992) *Vårdnad och underhåll* [*Custody and child maintenance*], Stockholm and Yrelsvo: Statistiska Centralbyrån.

SCB (2003) *Barn och deras familjer 2001* [*Children and their families 2001*], Demographical Reports 2003: 1, Stockholm and Yrelsvo: Statistiska Centralbyrån.

SCB (2004) Statistiska Centralbyrån (www.scb.se).

Schiratzki, J. (1997) *Vårdnad och vårdnadstvister* [*Custody and custody disputes*], Stockholm: Nordstedts.

SFS 1999:845 [Swedish collection of law].

SFS 2001:453 [Swedish collection of law], Socialtjänstlag [Law on Social Services].

Singer, A. (2000) *Föräldraskap i rättslig belysning* [*Legal perspectives on parenthood*], Uppsala: Iustus förlag.

Sinkkonen, J. (1998) *Yhdessä isän kanssa* [*Together with a father*], Porvoo: WSOY.

Skinner, T., Hester, M. and Malos, E. (2005) 'Methodology, feminism and gender violence', in T. Skinner, M. Hester and E. Malos (eds) *Researching gender violence: Feminist methodology in action*, Cullompton: Willan, pp 1-22.

Skjørten, K. (2004) 'Førståelser av overgrep i barnefordelningssaker' ['Perceptions of abuse in custody cases'], *Tidsskrift for Familierett, Arverett og Barnevernrettslige Spørsmål [Journal for Family Law, Inheritance Law and Issues in Child Protection Law]*, 2, pp 3-4.

Smaadahl, T., Hernes, H. and Langberg, L. (2002) *Drømmen om det gode liv [The dream about the good life: A report on foreign women, married to Norwegian men, who had to seek refuge at the crisis centres in 2001]*, Oslo: Krisesentersekretariatet.

Smart, C. (1997) 'Wishful thinking and harmful tinkering? Sociological reflections on family policy', *Journal of Critical Social Policy*, vol 26, no 3, pp 301-21.

Smart, C. (1999) 'The "new" parenthood: fathers and mothers after divorce', in E. Silva and C. Smart (eds) *The NEW family?* London: Sage Publications, pp 106-114.

Smart, C., Neale, B. and Wade, A. (2001) *The changing experience of childhood. Families and divorce*, Cambridge: Polity Press.

Socialstyrelsen [National Board of Health and Welfare] (2001) *Sexual abuse of children: A survey of current knowledge*, Stockholm: Social-styrelsen.

SOU 1995:60 [Swedish public investigations] *Kvinnofrid [Woman's peace/Gross violation of women's integrity]*, Final report from the Parliamentary Committee on Violence against Women, Stockholm: Fritzes.

SOU 1995:79 *Vårdnad, boende, umgänge [Custody, residence, contact]*, Final report from the Parliamentary Committee on Custody Conflicts, Stockholm: Fritzes.

SOU 2001:14 *Sexualbrotten [Sexual crimes. An increased protection of sexual integrity and connected issues]*, Final report from the 1998 Parliamentary Committee on Sexual Crimes, Stockholm: Fritzes.

SOU 2001:18 *Barn och misshandel [Children and abuse]*, Report from the Parliamentary Committee against Child Abuse, Stockholm: Fritzes.

SOU 2001:72 *Barnmisshandel. Att förebygga och åtgärda [Child abuse. Prevention and protection]*, Final report from the Parliamentary Committee against Child Abuse, Stockholm: Fritzes.

Stetson, D.M. and Mazur, A. (1995) 'Introduction', in D.M. Stetson and A. Mazur (eds) *Comparative state feminism*, Thousand Oaks, CA, London and New Delhi: Sage Publications.

Stone, L. (ed) (2001) *New directions in anthropological kinship*, Lanhamn and Oxford: Rowman and Littlefield Publishers Inc.

Suomen ev.lut. kirkon kirkkohallituksen julkaisuja [*Women, men and violence. Perspectives on violence from the Evangelical Lutheran Church of Finland*] (2000) *Naiset, miehet ja väkivalta*, 2000:1, Helsinki: Suomen ev.lut. kirkon kirkkohallituksen julkai.

Sutorius, H. (1999–2000) 'Sexuella övergrepp mot barn', ['Sexual abuse against children'] *Juridisu tidskrift* [*Journal of Law*], 1999–2000, pp 117–139.

Taipale, V. (1971) 'Pahoinpidellyn lapsen kokemuksista' ['On the experiences of abused children'], *Suomen Lääkärilehti*, vol 23, no 26, pp 2180-4.

Taskinen, S. (2001) *Lapsen etu erotilanteissa* [*The welfare of the child in divorce cases: Guide for social services*], Helsinki: Stakes, oppaita 46.

Taylor-Browne, J. (2001) *What works in reducing domestic violence?*, London: Whiting and Birch.

Thorpe, D. (1994) *Evaluating child protection*, Buckingham: Open University Press.

Tigerstedt, C. (1996) 'Isyys' ['Fatherhood'], in T. Hoikkala (ed) *Miehenkuvia* [*Images of men*], Helsinki: Gaudeamus, pp 262-9.

Työryhmämuistio (2003) *Raportti viranomaisyhteistyöstä lasten huoltoon ja tapaamisoikeuteen liittyvissä kiistatilanteissa* [*Report on cooperation of the authorities concerning disputed cases of child custody and contact*], Työryhmämuistioita 2003:2, Helsinki: Sosiaali- ja terveysministeriöy.

Utting, W. (1997) *People like us: The report of the review of the safeguards for children living away from home*, London: The Stationery Office.

Vuori, J. (2001) *Äidit, isät ja ammattilaiset* [*Mothers, fathers and professionals*], Tampere: Tampere University Press.

Walby, S. and Allen, J. (2004) *Domestic violence, sexual assault and stalking: Findings from the British Crime Survey*, London: Home Office.

Wallerstein, J.S. and Kelly, J.B. (1980) *Surviving the breakup: How children and parents cope with divorce*, Grant McIntyre.

Weinehall, K. (1997) *Att växa upp i våldets närhet* [*Growing up in the proximity of violence: Young people's narratives about violence in the home*], Umeå: Umeå University.

Weinehall, K. (1999) *Gymnasieelevers möten med våld* [*High school students' encounters with violence: In the home, in school and in their leisure time*], Report no 59, Umeå: Department of Education, Umeå University.

Weinehall, K. (2002a) 'Våld i barndomshemmet ökar risken för ytterligare erfarenheter av våld' ['Violence in the childhood home increases the risk for further experiences of violence'], in M. Eriksson, A. Nenola and M.M. Nilsen (eds) *Gender and violence in the Nordic countries*, TemaNord 2002: 545, Copenhagen: Nordic Council of Ministers, pp 273-84.

Weinehall, K. (2002b) 'Våld mot kvinnor och barn' ['Violence against women and children – research and experiences'], in *Se till mig som liten är* [*When dad hits mum*], Stockholm: National Council for Women's Peace, pp 6-20.

Wendt-Höjer, M. (2002) *Rädslans politik* [*The politics of fear: Violence and sexuality in the Swedish democracy*], Malmö: Liber.

West, C. and Fenstermaker, S. (1995) 'Doing difference', *Gender and Society*, vol 9, no 1, pp 8-37.

West, C. and Zimmerman, D. (1987) 'Doing gender', *Gender and Society*, vol 1, no 2, pp 125-51.

Westh, B. (1995), *Lov om forældremyndighed og samvær* [*Law on custody and contact*], Lovforslag nr. L 176 [Suggestion to the law no L176], presented to the Danish Parliament 22 February.

Wilkinson, S. and Kitzinger, C. (1995) *Feminism and discourse*, London: Sage Publications.

Women's Unit (1999) *Freedom from fear*, London: Women's Unit.

Court cases

The Swedish Supreme Court: NJA 1989 p 335 and *NJA 2000* p 345.

The Swedish Courts of Appeal: RH 1991: 92, *RH 1999*: 74 and Svea Court of Appeal verdict *DT 27, 1996-05-29*, in case *T 1748/95*.

Crown Court transcript (2000) *Re: L, Re: V, Re: M & Re: H*, June.

Index

References to figures and tables are in *italics*

A

Aasted Halse, J. 24–5
Academy of Finland (2001–03) 2
Acker, J. 5, 157
ageism, in relation to children 157–61
Alanen, L. 132
alcohol abuse, and parental violence 139–40
Amato, P.R. 20
Amato, P.R. and Keith, B. 27
Andersson, R. 4
Antikainen, J. 68
Anttonen, A. 72
Anttonen, A. and Sipila, J. 155
Arnell, A. and Ekbom, I. 108, 138, 159
Arts, W. and Gelissen, J. 4, 169
Ashe, F. et al 156–7
attachment issues, child-father 58–60
Auvinen, M. 78

B

Badinter, E. 72
Balkmar, D. 169, 179
Barne- og familiedepartementet (2002) 93
Beck, U. and Beck-Gernsheim, E. 50–1
Bekkengen, L. 4, 7
Bergman, H. and Hobson, B. 4, 7
Björnberg, U. 4
Boqvist and central government Children's ombudsman 121
Børns Vilkår 24–5
Boserup, B. and Rabøl Hansen, H. 14, 24–5
BRÅ [National Council for Crime Prevention] 104, 165, 167
Brah, A. 5
Brown, T. et al 22
bullying 152–3
Busch, R. 26

C

Chambers, D. 51
child abuse *see* child experiences of violence; fatherhood and violence; sexual abuse of children

child and adolescent psychiatry services, supporting children 150–1
child experiences of violence 37, 49–53, 137–54, 179–81
  coping strategies 141–2, 144–6
  and 'cycles of abuse' 51–2, 144–5
  experience of staying in shelters 89–90
  gender differences 51–2
  incidence studies 108–9, 137–8
  legal considerations 108–10
  macro-sociological perspectives 52–3, 60–4
  narrative accounts
    'trapped feelings' 56–7
    'ambivalent awakenings' 57–8
    father hatred 143
    'change and new directions' 59–60
    seeking help from agencies 146–51
    self-blame 141
  as objects of adult emotion 50–1
  parental use of alcohol/drugs 139–40
  pathologising the child 50, 51–2
  professional agencies refusal to acknowledge 146–51, 153–4
  and ageism 157–61
  ethnicity issues 165–7
  gender issues 161–5
  voluntary sector support 179–80
  Finland 49, 53–64
    background 49, 50–3
    design of study 53–6
    further research studies 70–1
  Sweden 102–5, 108–10, 137–54
    design of study 138–40
    findings 140–51
    legal considerations 108–10
  see also children's rights
child welfare studies 27
Children Act Sub-Committee 26
children's rights
  Sweden 111–16
    professional agency perspectives and 'symmetrical family models' 132–4, *133*
    in violent contexts 115–16, 132–4, *133*
Child's Time project (Federation of Mother and Child Homes and Shelters) 71

Christensen, E. 6, 26, 108, 127, 138
Christensen, E. and Koch-Nielsen, I. 6
Civilretsdirektoratet 22, 24, 27
contact arrangements *see* custody and
    contact arrangements
'contact sabotage' 21-3, 112-14
    professional agency perspectives 123,
    127
Copenhagen conference on child safety/
    parental contact (2000) 25
corporal punishment of children 3, 9, 160
    Sweden 102, 103-4, 160
Crenshaw, K. 5
critical analysis of welfare policies *see*
    welfare systems overview
Crown Prosecution Service (2001) 174
cultural values
    and ethnicity 4-5, 94, 165-7
    and male violence 70-1, 107
    see also fatherhood; motherhood
custody and contact arrangements
    Denmark 13-29, 176, 178
        background 13-14
        decision-making processes 16, *17*
        pre-1995 16-19
            1995 legislation 19-21
    post-1995 impact 21-3, 23-5
        issues of 'contact sabotage' 21-3
        transfer of custody criteria 21-3
    Finland 41-8, 76-80
        restraining orders and joint custody
        retention 62, 78-9
        recent child-parent contact tragedies
        79
        supervised contact orders 79
        unmarried parents 77
    Sweden 111-16, 120-2, 164-5, 178
        contact sabotage 112-14, 123, 127
        legal cases 112-14, 115-16
    UK policy 174-5, 176-8
    see also children's rights
'cycles of abuse' 51-2, 144-5

D

Dahlberg, A. et al 110, 113
Danielsen, S. 17
day-care provision 3
Denmark
    custody and contact negotiations 13-29,
    176, 178
        background 13-14

decision-making processes 16, *17*
design of research study 14-15
    pre-1995 findings 16-19
    1995 legislation 19-21
    post-1995 impact 21-3, 23-5
    principles of agreement and contact
    presumption 23-7
    issues of 'contact sabotage' 21-3
    safety-orientated 'pragmatic' approach
    13-14, 17-19
    'sole custody' principles 18, 21
    transfer of custody criteria 21-3
mediation services 27-9
    effectiveness in domestic violence
    circumstances 28-9
Denzin, N. and Lincoln, Y.S. 156
Diesen, C. 104-5
Dingwall, R. 23, 121
disclosure and validation issues
    professional reluctance to initiate
    investigation 123-4, 125-6, 153-4, 164
    children's accounts 146-51
divorce and continuing violence 1, 6
    see also shared parenting policies
Dobash, R.E. and Dobash, R.P. 32
Domestic Violence, crime and Victims
    Act (2004) 174-5
Dominelli, L. 169
Dufva, V. 71

E

Edleson, J. 52
Eduards, M. 33, 69
Eisenstein, Z.R. 102-3
English welfare systems *see* UK welfare
    policies
Eriksson, M. 5-6, 39, 119-22, 157, 163-7,
    178-9
Eriksson, M. and Hester, M. 6-7, 13, 22-3,
    42, 113, 116, 120-1, 131, 165, 176, 178
Eriksson, M. et al (2002) 2
Esping-Andersen, G. 4, 8, 155, 168
ethic of rules vs. morals of love 62-5
ethnicity
    as focus for child abuse investigations
    165-7
    and social policy development 4-5
    Norway 94
Evangelical Lutheran Church of Finland
    73-4

F

Fairclough, N. 156
family counselling agency research 31–48,
    87
  background to need 31–2
  design of study 33–4
  general service aims 34–5
  influence of trauma theory 37–9
  perceptions of fatherhood 41–7
  perceptions of motherhood 37–41
  profession-led contact arrangements
    44–7
  see also family law secretaries (Sweden)
family law secretaries (Sweden)
  key roles 119
  non-specific working models 122
  perspectives on children and
    'symmetrical family models' 132–4,
    133
  perspectives on parents and mother-
    centred family model approaches
    128–31, *131*
  research studies 119–20
family support policies 1–2, 8, 9–10
  see also shared parenting policies
'father deprivation'
  evidence studies 14, 27
  psychoanalytic theories 45–6
  see also 'new' fatherhood
fatherhood
  attachment issues 58–60, 63, 124–5
  deprivation studies
  evidence 14, 27
  psychoanalytic theories 45–6
  as motherhood's responsibility 71–4,
    130–1
  'new' fatherhood 44, 75–6, 179
  professional agency perceptions 41–7,
    76–80
fatherhood and violence 6, 37, 41–7,
    51–2, 67–80, 120–34
  child custody arrangements 76–80,
    124–5
  presumption of need 124–5
  see also custody and contact
  arrangements
  conceptual frameworks
  family-/relationship-centred constructs
    68–9
  masculinity constructs 70
  motherhood as 'responsible for
    fatherhood' 71–4, 130–1
  'cycles of abuse' 51–2, 144–5
  professional agency approaches 36,
    41–7, 76–80, 122–34, 137–54, 155–70
  reluctance to initiate investigation
    123–4, 125–6, 146–51, 153–4
  studies from Denmark 18–19
  studies from Finland 57–8
  studies from Sweden 119–34, 138–40,
    140–54
  see also 'father deprivation'; joint
  custody; shared parenting policies
fathers pressure groups, influence on
  government policies 22
Finland
  child experiences of violence studies 49,
    53–64
  background 49, 50–3
  design of study 53–6
  findings56–60
  macro-sociological perspectives 52–3,
    60–4
family counselling service research 31–48
  background to need 31–2
  design of study 33–4
  findings 34–48
  fatherhood and violence studies 67–80
  recent child-parent contact tragedies
    79
Flendt, H. 20, 22, 24
Fleury, R.E. et al 6
Foley, M. 33, 48
Föräldrabalken 125
Forsberg, H. 43–4, 56, 178, 180–1
Forsberg, H. and Pösö, T. 54–5
Forsberg, H. et al 72–3
Freedom from fear (Women's Unit) 175

G

gender equality parenting policies *see*
  shared parenting policies
gender and violence, and child sexual
  abuse 161–5
*Gender and Violence – a Nordic research
  programme* (Nordic Council of
  Ministers 2000–04) 2
Gender and Violence (2000) 1–2
Gender, power and violence (Academy of
  Finland 2001–03) 2
Giddens, A. 50–1, 62
Grillo, T. 28

H

Haaland, T. 95
Haapasalo, J. 52
Hague, G. et al 40, 174
Hantrais, L. and Letablier, M.-T. 3
Hart, B. 28
healthcare services, and victim support 86-7, 96-7
Hearn, J. 7, 68, 179
Hearn, J. and Pringle, K. 168
Hearn, J. et al 2
Heinänen, A. 69
Heiskanen, M. and Piispa, M. 1, 70-1
Hester, M. 39, 176, 180
Hester, M. and Harne, L. 26-7, 75
Hester, M. and Pearson, C. 20, 28-9
Hester, M. and Radford, L. 6, 13-28, 40, 115, 127-8
Hester, M. and Westmarland, N. 180
Hester, M. et al 6, 26, 28-9, 138, 164, 179-80
Hjemdal, O.K. and Stefansen, K. 88
Hochschild, A.R. 49
Højgaard, L. 7
Højlund 25
Holden, G.W. 70
Holm, U.M. 72
homelessness, and male divorcees 77
homosexual relationships 105-6
Hooper, C.-A. 27, 39
housing needs 88-9
Hughes, C. and Dunn, J. 50, 52
Humphreys, C. et al 29
Husso, M. 69, 73
Huttunen, J. 43, 74-5

I

incidence of male violence
  cohabiting relationships 1
  post-separation 1, 6
  sexual abuse 161-2
Interdepartemental arbeidsgruppe (1983) 84
Iovanni, L. and Pringle, K. 169, 179
Itzin, C. 34, 163

J

Jaffe, P.G. et al 6, 13, 19, 26, 121, 138, 165, 178
Jallinoja, R. 50, 62-3
James, A. and Prout, A. 53, 124, 132

Jeffner, S. 32
joint custody
  Denmark 13
  and contact sabotage 21-3
  principles of agreement and contact presumption 23-5
  safety-orientated 'pragmatic' approach 13-14, 17-19
  Finland 76-80
  and violent partners 79-80
  Sweden 111, 120-2, 164-5
  UK 176-8
  see also custody and contact arrangements; shared parenting policies
Jokinen, A. 70, 73, 94
Jonassen, W. 83, 86-7, 97, 175
Jonassen, W. and Eidheim, F. 94, 96-7
Jonassen, W. and Stefansen, K. 83, 85, 88-9, 92
Justis- og politidepartementet et al (2000) 84
Justis- og politidepartementet et al (2003) 91
Justis- og politidepartementet et al (2004) 98
Justitsministeriets Foraeldremyndighedsudvalg (1994) 20-1, 23, 27

K

Kaganas, F. 13, 26
Kamali, M. 4, 167
Keeler, L. 34
Kelly, L. 94-5, 97
Keskinen, S. 41
Key, E. 103
Kirmanen, T. 52
Klinth, R. 7
Komiteanmietintö (Report of the Father Committee) 76
Korhonen, M. 75
Kraft, K. 101-2
Kurki-Suonio, K. 7, 77-9
Kuronen, M. 47, 77
Kvinnevoldsutvalget (2002) 91
Kvist, J. 3

L

Laaksamo, E.-M. 71
Labour government welfare policies 174-5

'third way' initiatives 8
Labour Party (1997) 175
Laclau, E. 156-7
Lagutskottet (1992/3) 112
Lagutskottet (1997/8) 113
law and power 102
Laxén, Marianne 99
legal aid 90
legal system
  adult victim support measures 90, 95-6
  children's rights 104-6
legislation
  Denmark, custody and contact 15-16,
    18, 19-21
  regulation of prostitution 3
  Sweden 105-6
  UK 174, 176-8
  'women's peace' (Kvinnofrid) 3, 10-11,
    175
Lehtonen, A. and Perttu, S. 79
Leira, H. 142, 153
Lewis, C. and O'Brien, M. 26
Lewis, J. 4
Lindberg, S. 113
Lundgren, E. et al 1, 6, 107, 110, 137, 140,
  162, 165
Lundström, A. et al 113
Lupton, C. 32-3, 48

M

McGee, C. 19
McKee, L. and O'Brien, M. 27
McKie, L. 51
McMahon, M. and Pence, E. 19
McMillan, L. 96
mail-order brides 94
Malterud, K. 84
Månsson, S.-A. 3
Marsiglio, W. 27
masculinity and violence 70-1
Mason, J. and Falloon, J. 50-2, 61
mediation services
  Denmark 27-9
  effectiveness in domestic violence
    circumstances 28-9
  Sweden, role of family law secretaries
    119
Mellberg, N. 6, 39, 103, 107, 123, 131
Menns vold mot kvinner [*Men's violence
  against women*] (Råkil) 92
men's parenting *see* fatherhood;
  fatherhood and violence; shared
  parenting policies

men's violence surveys 1-2
  Finland 70-1
men's violence to women 6
  government perceptions, Finland 31-2
  incidence
    cohabiting relationships 1
    post-separation 1, 6
    and violence to children 164
men's violence and welfare practices 7
  conceptual frameworks 3, 120-34
  family-/relationship-centred constructs
    68-9
  mother-centred family models 128-31,
    131
  'new' fatherhood 44, 75-6
  symmetrical family models 133-4, *133*
  Finland 36-7, 41-7
  Sweden 120-34
Metell, B. 113, 127, 158
Micklewright, J. and Stewart, K. 8
Milner, J. 73
Mirlees-Black, C. 6
Molina, I. 4
mother-child dyad 39-41
motherhood
  conceptual frameworks 128-31
  as 'responsible for fatherhood' 71-4,
    130-1
  as 'strong and responsible' 71-4
  perceptions following abuse 37-9, 123-4
  distrust issues 123, 127, 164
mothers and contact sabotage 21-3,
  112-14
  professional agency perspectives 123,
    127
Mott, F.L. 27
Mullender, A. et al 19
Muslim families *see* ethnicity issues

N

Naiset, Miehet ja Vakivalta [*Men, women
  and violence*] (Evangelical Lutheran
  Church of Finland) 73-4
Näre, S. 64
Nätkin, R. 40, 72-3
Nesvold, H. 86
'new' fatherhood 44, 75-6, 179
  see also shared parenting policies
New Zealand, domestic violence and
  contact risk assessments 26, 109, 168
Nilsen, S and Prøis, L.O. 94
Nisja, R. and Aslaksen, I. 84, 89
Nordborg, G. 110-11, 115, 120, 175

Nordborg, G. and Niemi-Kiesiläinen, J. 105, 121
Nordenfors, G. 22, 113
Nordic welfare systems *see* men's violence and welfare practices; welfare systems overview
Norway
  provisions for women and children 83-99
    background 83-4
    children in shelters 89-90
    ethnicity considerations 94
    family counselling shortcomings 87
    future challenges 93-8
    government initiatives post-1983 84-90
    government initiatives post-2000 90-3
    housing provisions 88-9
    legal improvements 90
    monitoring and recording 87-8
    public agency support 86-7
    security measures 88, 97
    shelter funding 85
    shelters 84-6
    social awareness 95-6
    training staff 88
Notko, M. 68-9
Nousiainen, K. 62
Nummelin, R. 72
Nyqvist, L. 33

O

Oranen, M. 32, 71
Oslo Krisesenter (2004) 94

P

Pape, H. and Stefansen, K. 99
Parental Code [Föräldrabalken] 111-12
Partanen, T. and Holma, J. 68
Parton, N. 8, 160
Pease, B. and Pringle, K. 4, 164
Peled, E. 6, 55-6, 121
Peltoniemi, T. 68
Perheen aika [*Family time*] (Jallinoja) 50
personal alarms for women 97
Perttu, S. and Söderholm, A.-L. 36
Perttu, S. et al 79
Pettilä, U. and Yli-Marttila, L. 78
police
  and victim support 87, 88, 91
  children 149-50

power and control issues 26, 28, 32, 42, 47, 107, 117
Pred, A. 4
Pringle, K. 4, 8, 155-7, 159, 162-3, 168-9, 175-6, 179-80
Pringle, K. and Harder, M. 8, 160, 168
Pringle, K. et al 168-9
Profitt, N.J. 33
Prop (1997) 107, 115
Prop (2002) 109
prostitution, Swedish law 3, 105
psychoanalytic theories, fatherhood 45-6

R

racism 4-5
Radford, L. et al 22
Råkil, M. 92
Rasmussen, N. 22-3, 26
Rautava, M. and Perttu, S. 32, 36
Rejmer, A. 113, 121
restraining orders
  and custody 62
  Norway 90, 97
revenge feelings 143
Richards, M. 20, 27
Richards, M.P.M. and Dyson, M. 27
Roberts, M. 28
Rodgers, B. and Pryor, J. 27
Ronkainen, S. 32, 35, 58, 68, 70, 72-4
Roy, M. 6, 140
Ruxton, S. 8

S

Säävälä, H. 75
Sainsbury, D. 4, 155
Saradjian, J. 163
SCB (1989) 111
SCB (2003) 120
Schiratzki, J. 120, 126
schools
  and bullying 152-3
  and teacher support 148-9 57-8, 142
secrecy 61
  and silence 57-8, 142
self-blame, children's feelings 141
sexual abuse of children 19, 105, 111, 115-16, *139*, 140
  abusers obtaining custody 22, 115-16
  blaming the victim 104
  legal considerations 107, 176-8
  men who also abuse women 164
  percentage cases bought to trial 104

perpetrator gender issues 161-5
prevalence studies 161-2
professional reluctance to initiate
   investigation 123-4, 125-6
and sexualisation of children 103
sexualisation of children 103
SFS (1999) 106
shame, child experiences 57-8, 140-2
shared parenting policies 4, 7, 9
   in Denmark post-1995 19-25
      concerns and criticisms 24-5, 28-9
      evidence deficits 25-7
      Sweden 109, 112-13, 120-2, 124-5
shelters and refuges
   Norway 84-6
      children's provisions 89-90
      funding 85, 98
      physical security measures 92
      and political movements 96
      staff training 92-3
Singer, A. 120, 126
Sinkkonen, J. 75
Skinner, T. et al 174-5
Skjørten, K. 6
Slagen dam [*Captured queen*] 107
Smaadahl, T. et al 94
Smart, C. 51, 76, 130-1, 133
Smart, C. et al 124, 132
social services *see* family counselling
   agency research; family law secretaries
   (Sweden); men's violence and welfare
   practices; welfare systems overview
socialisation processes, and experiences of
   violence 51-2
Socialstyrelsen (2001) 162-3
Socialtjänstlagen (2001) 123
SOU (1995) 111
SOU (2001) 107-9, 137-8, 160, 165-6
state welfare *see* welfare systems overview
Stone, L. 120
Strauss, M. 68
substance abuse, and parental violence
   139-40
suicidal feelings, in children 56-7, 142,
   143
supervised contact orders, Finland 79
Sutorius, H. 105
Sweden
   child experiences of violence 103-5,
      137-54
      research studies 61, 138-40, 140-54
   child welfare research studies, profession
      responses to violence 137-54, 155-70

ethnicity policies 4-5
gender equality parenting policies 4
legal systems and power 102-3
welfare services, positive studies 155
'women's peace' initiatives (Kvinnofrid)
   3, 11, 105-6, 175

T

Taylor-Browne, J. 174
teachers, support for children seeking
   help 148-9
Thorpe, D. 160
Tigerstedt, C. 75
'toxic' parents (Giddens) 62
'trafficking' victims 94
training and education
   child abuse 159, 169
   professional agency workers 88, 159,
      169
   shelter workers 92-3
trauma theory, influence on family
   counselling services 37-9
Työryhmamuistio report (2003) 79

U

UK welfare policies 160, 168-9, 174-82
   domestic violence
      and custody risk assessments 26, 178
      mediation services 29
      and men's responsibilities 73
   Nordic welfare as role models 8-9,
      181-2
UN Convention on the Rights of the
   Child (article 9) 13, 112, 117, 120, 126
UN Women's Convention 117
UNICEF-commissioned child welfare
   report (2000) 8
unmarried parents
   custody arrangements
      Denmark 21
      Finland 77
Utting, W. 162

V

validation *see* disclosure and validation
   issues
violence
   'ethic of rules vs. morals of love' 62-5

see also fatherhood and violence; men's
violence to women; men's violence
and welfare practices
voluntary organisations
political influence 1-2
supporting children 179-80
see also shelters and refuges
Vuori, J. 39, 43, 45-7, 75-6, 131

W

Walby, S. and Allen, J. 6
Wallerstein, J.S. and Kelly, J.B. 27
Weinehall, K. 6, 55, 61, 108, 137-8, 180-1
welfare systems overview 3-5
critical analysis 3-5, 155
instruments for comparative analysis
168-9
limitations 5, 7, 155, 168-70
impact of shared parenting policies 4, 7,
9
professionalisation and violence work
feminist discourse and critiques 31-3,
155
impact of trauma theory 37-9
influence of 'new' fatherhood 43-7
as 'role model' 3, 8-9
criticisms 8-9
UK role models 168-9160
see also men's violence and welfare
practices
Wendt-Höjer, M. 120-1
West, C. and Fenstermaker, S. 5, 157
Westh, B. 28
Wilkinson, S. and Kitzinger, C. 34
'women's peace' (Kvinnofrid) 3, 11,
105-6, 175
Women's Unit 175
www.nordforsk.org 2